THE WILD TRIBES OF
THE SOUDAN

AN ACCOUNT OF

PERSONAL EXPERIENCES AND ADVENTURES

DURING THREE WINTERS SPENT IN THAT COUNTRY
CHIEFLY AMONG THE BASÉ TRIBE

BY

F. L. JAMES, M.A., F.R.G.S.

SECOND EDITION

WITH AN ACCOUNT OF THE ROUTES FROM WADY HALFAH
TO BERBER, BY THE AUTHOR; AND
A CHAPTER ON KHARTOUM AND THE SOUDAN
BY SIR SAMUEL BAKER

WITH MAP AND ILLUSTRATIONS

LONDON
JOHN MURRAY, ALBEMARLE STREET
1884

TO

The Memory of

THE HONOURABLE

JOHN CONSTABLE MAXWELL

OUR COMPANION IN A PREVIOUS JOURNEY IN THE SOUDAN

THIS RECORD OF OUR WANDERINGS IS

AFFECTIONATELY INSCRIBED.

R.I.P.

PREFACE TO THE SECOND EDITION.

THE favourable reception my book has met with has encouraged me to publish a new edition. I have curtailed some of the purely shooting incidents, and have added an account of the country between Wady Halfah and Berber, a country which I visited during the spring of 1878, and which is particularly interesting at the present time, when the thoughts of so many are turned to the expedition now taking place in that region.

I have endeavoured to describe the tedious desert journeys from Merowi to Berber, and from Wady Halfah to Dongola, and also that by river from Dongola to Merowi.

I trust that, should our troops return to Cairo by the Nile, they will not be as much retarded in their progress by contrary winds and the lowness of the Nile as we were, nor so much plagued by midges,—a plague that must be experienced to be understood!

My friend, Sir Samuel Baker, has very kindly written a prefatory chapter for me to the present Edition, on "the Political Aspect of the Soudan," and I am sure that whatever such a well-known authority on African travel has to say on a country in which he has spent so many years, will be read with great interest by all.

A considerable portion of my book is taken up with a description of the Basé country, the greater part of which had not been explored previous to our visit.

The Basé, or Kunama tribe, who inhabit this district, are far less civilised than any of the other tribes who dwell in that part of Africa ; they are of a totally different type, much blacker and more closely allied to the pure negro than any of their neighbours. To penetrate into the heart of their country had for some time been with me a cherished project ; and I had often discussed its feasibility with Egyptian officials and others in the Soudan during previous journeys made in the country, but had been invariably told that it was next to impossible to accomplish my desire.

On all hands we were informed that the Basé were most treacherous, and that although there was not much danger of their attacking so large a party as we were by day, they would not hesitate to take advantage of us during the darkness of night if an opportunity presented itself.

My narrative will show that a little tact and care on our part overcame these obstacles, and we became the best of friends with the Basé. Our chief difficulty was in first entering their country, and in setting their minds at rest as to our peaceable and non-political intentions towards them. On one occasion only, when our party was divided, we had good reason to believe that they meditated treachery, but on their discovering that we were apprised of their intentions they apparently gave up their project, and we never had cause to suspect them again.

The only travellers I could hear of who had ever ventured into this country were a Mr. and Mrs. Powell, who, together with their child, had been treacherously murdered by the Basé before they had advanced very far into their territory.

I would, in conclusion, ask the indulgence of the public for this effort of one who for the first time publishes a record of his daily life and experience, and especially for the additional matter contained in the present edition which, owing to my leaving England for some months on a fresh expedition, I have been unable personally to see through the press.　　　　　　　　　　　　　　F. L. J.

14 GREAT STANHOPE STREET, LONDON, W.
October 25, 1884.

CONTENTS.

PAGE

PREFATORY CHAPTER.

The Political Aspect of the Soudan   xix

CHAPTER I.

We leave Cairo for the Egyptian Soudan.—The Basé Country.
—Egyptian Officials.—Quarantine Regulations.—Our Party.
—Servants of the Party.—Ali the Cook.—Shereef the staid
and stately Waiter.—Mahoom.—The Agra's Passengers   .   1

CHAPTER II.

Arrival at Souakim.—The *Wakeel.*—Thieving Propensities of
Egyptian Officials.—Encouragement of Slavery.—Souakim.
—Caravan-routes from Souakim.—Ala-ed-Deen Pacha.—
The Governor's "Palace."—Bedouin Government Prisoners.
—Omnipresence of Greeks.—*Dhurra.*—"Hôtel du Soudan."
—Curious Manner of dressing the Hair.—An African Hurling-
ham. — Story of the Seven Virgins. — Departure from
Souakim   9

CHAPTER III.

The First Halt.—The Rainy Season.—The Camel-sheik comes
for *Baksheesh.*—Three Caravan-routes to Cassala.—Disputes
with the Camel-drivers.—Gazelles.—Management of Camels.
—Halt at Siterabb.—A Piteous Tale   21

CHAPTER IV.

PAGE

Journey continued.—Buck Gazelle shot.—More Trouble with the Camel-drivers.—A rose-breasted Shrike.—Sand-storm at Ellegua. — Jules taken ill. — Death in Camp. — Takroori Woman abandoned by her People.—We divide the Camp.— Mishaps of those left behind.—Christmas Day at Wandi.— " Molly " 27

CHAPTER V.

We divide the Camp.—Part start for Cassala.—The Rest remain at Wandi.—Continued Illness of Jules.—*Dhurra* runs short. —Departure from Wandi.—Khor Belag.—News of the First Party.—A Deserted Village.—Omri.—The Belgian Doctor. —Halt at Khor Rassay.—Pharaoh's Lean Kine.—Desolate Tract of Country.—Scorpions 34

CHAPTER VI.

Arrival at Fillik.—The Gash.—Abundance of Game.—Cassala reached.—Encampment in the Dry Bed of the Gash.—Caravans on the Cassala Road.—The Governor of Cassala.— Servants sent from Sanheit.—Death of Jules . . . 40

CHAPTER VII.

Purchase of Camels.—Expedition to the Atbara.—The Village of Naouri.—Mosconas and his Son.—White Ants.—Dinner with the Governor.—The Town of Cassala.—Hyænas.— Pariah Dogs.—Collections for European Zoological Societies. —Departure from Cassala.—Bashi-Bazouks . . . 47

CHAPTER VIII.

Journey from Cassala.—Game shot by the Way.—The dog-faced Baboon.— Arrival at Haikota.—The German " Animal-catcher."—Visits from two Sheiks.—Sheik Achmed Ageer. —Attack on the Beni-Amers by the Basé.—Fresh Supply of Camels.—Dinner to Sheik Achmed and the German.—Success of the Magic-Lantern 56

CHAPTER IX.

PAGE

Departure from Haikota.—Abundance of Game.—Halt at Toad-elook.— *Tétél.* —Adventure with a Lion on the Prowl.— A Shooting Expedition.—Fifty-seven Sand-grouse netted.— Night-watches in hopes of a Shot 66

CHAPTER X.

The Camp moves forward.—Scarcity of Game.—Water easily obtainable.—Baby Crocodiles.—Sheik Achmed rejoins the Travellers. — A *Battue.* — Mimosa - trees. — Road - cutting through the Jungle.—A Buffalo Adventure . . . 72

CHAPTER XI.

Arrival at Wo Ammar.—First Interview with Basé.—A Basé Village.—Giraffe-stalking.—The Village of Koolookoo.— Deputation from the Village.—The Sheik's Son makes him-self "generally useful."—Presents for the Deputation.—The Koolookoo Villagers much interested in us.—Visit to the Village.—Women of Koolookoo 78

CHAPTER XII.

Scarcity of *Dhurra.*—A number of Basé join our Camp.—Water carriers.—Another deserted Village.—Ceremony of making Peace.—Friendliness of the Basé Women.—The Mareb.— Buffaloes seen for the First Time. — More Basé join the Camp.—Exciting Stalk after an Ostrich.—Game abounds.— Aylmer and I start for Ma Ambasah, and find Water.—A Chase after Buffaloes.—Both Barrels at once.—A nasty Recoil.—A Visit from Sheik Kudul.—He departs, promising to return.—The Camp moves to Ma Ambasah.—Two Bull Buffaloes killed.—Some of the Camel-drivers sent to Amedeb for *Dhurra* 89

CHAPTER XIII.

PAGE

Disastrous Adventure with Abyssinians.—Akabah brings the Alarm.—Two of our Party surprised by a Hundred armed Abyssinians. — Making friends. — Treachery of the Abyssinians.—Mahomet fearfully wounded.—The search for him. —The Dembelas Tribe.—Contemplated Expedition against the Dembelas abandoned 105

CHAPTER XIV.

We leave Ma Ambasah.—Arrival of Mahomet.—Doubts of the Basé.—A Picturesque Scene.—Sport or Exploration ?—The Medicine-Chest.—Death of Mahomet.—Two of the Party start for Amedeb. — Difficulty of keeping Camels. — The "Guffer" Disease.—Dilatoriness of the Arabs.—Poverty of the Basé.—The Barea Tribe 114

CHAPTER XV.

Our Journey to Amedeb.—History of Sheik Said Carcashi.— The Bombashi.—Promises aid in recovering the Stolen Property. — Ras Aloula. —Town of Amedeb.—Mahomet's sister. —Return to the Mareb 122

CHAPTER XVI.

Alarm of an Attack by the Basé.—Our Camp moves on.—Independence of the Basé.—Elephant-tracks.—Most of the Basé leave the Camp.—A Shot at a Lion.—Difficulty of shooting while riding Camels.—The Arabs strike.—Abundance of Quail.—Return to Haikota.—Departure for the Settite.— The Village of Sogada.—Arrival at the Settite . . . 127

CHAPTER XVII.

The Road to the Settite. —The Everlasting Forest. —Sheik Achmed's Deception.—Fishing in the Settite.—The Camp moves on.—The Guides and Camel-drivers refuse to proceed.—The Return to Khor Meheteb.—Adventure with a Crocodile.—A Scare.—Encampment at Khor Meheteb.— Good Fishing.—The "*Kelb-el-bahr.*"—Capture of a *Baggar*. —A Visit from Basé of Lacatecourah.—Tracking Buffaloes. —Arab Escort sent back to Haikota.—Baboons.—Exciting Night among the Buffaloes 139

CHAPTER XVIII.

PAGE

A Visit from two Hamran Sheiks.—A *Shereker.*—A Second Visit from Hamran Sheiks.—Three Basé join the Camp.—They are attacked by the 'Hamrans.—Departure for Om Hagar.—Arrival at Om Hagar.—Capture of the First Hippopotamus.—Visit from Hamran Sheik's Son.—The Last Hippopotamus.—Marabou Storks.—Purchase of a Tortoise.—A splendid Buck *Nellut* shot 157

CHAPTER XIX.

Extracts from Diary.—Bait set for Lions.—Mosquitoes.—Among the Buffaloes again.—Beginning of the Homeward Journey.—Journey towards Lacatecourah.— The Village of Lacatecourah.—A *Bonne-Bouche.*—Encampment at Abou Sellal.—A Native of the Basé Settite.—A Dabergoum Sheik offers to conduct us to the Basé Settite.—Basé Villages on the Settite.—Capture of a Boa-constrictor.—Arrival at Haikota.—The Beni-Amer's Raid on the Basé.—A Visit from Sheik Achmed Ageer 170

CHAPTER XX.

Immense Flocks and Herds.—Night Watch for Lions.—Two Panthers killed.—Two Lions bagged.—The Camp moves on.—Religion of the Basé.—Origin of various African Tribes.—First Day's Journey towards Amedeb.—A False Alarm.—Arrival at Amedeb.—Journey continued.—Khor Baraka.—Another Watch for Lions.—Thrilling Adventure with a Lion 183

CHAPTER XXI.

Perilous Ascent of Tchad-Amba.—The Church.—The Monks.—We move on again.—An Old Acquaintance.—Arrival at Sanheit.—The Town of Sanheit.—A Visit to the Church and Schools at Sanheit.—We start for Massawa.—Dra's sad Story.—The Anseba Valley.—An Attempt to make India-rubber from the *Quol-quol* Plant.—El Ain.—Bashi-Bazouks and their Prisoners.— We encamp at the Water-course Camphor.—Occasional sudden Rising of the Water in the *Khors* 202

CHAPTER XXII.

PAGE

Arrival at Massawa.—Comfortable Quarters at the " Palace."—
Situation of Massawa.—Water Supply of Massawa.—The
Town is guarded at Night.—Camel Sale by Auction.—The
Start from Massawa.—Perilous Position of Mahoom.—Ar-
rival at Souakim.—A Visit to Mr. Bewley.—Our Fellow-
Passengers on the " Messina."—Arrival at Suez.—Accounts
of Abyssinian Raid in English and Egyptian Press.—Sulei-
man's History.—We leave Cairo for England .   .   . 220

CHAPTER XXIII.

Berber.—Native Entertainments.—The Bazaars.—Visit to the
School.— Fine Breed of Donkeys.— Population.—Start for
Wady Halfah.—Pacha Gordon's Shelters.—Wells of Abou
Kereet.—Pyramids of Nourri.—Ruins of Gebel Barkal.—A
Sheik's Hospitality.—Voyage to Debbeh.—Plague of Midges.
—Journey to Dongola by River.—Across the Desert from
Merowi to Dongola.—Visits to the Mudir.—The Third
Cataract.—Temple at Tolib.—Meet Caravan of Manchester
Goods.—Cataracts of Dal and Tangour.—Wady Halfah.—
Return to Cairo 230

INDEX   259

LIST OF ILLUSTRATIONS.

	PAGE
ON THE MARCH	25
GEBEL CASSALA	42
HAIKOTA	61
CAMP AT KOOLOOKOO	83
BED OF THE MAREB AT AIBARO	85
BASÉ WOMEN	87
BASÉ AT AIBARO	128
BASÉ HUT AT KOOLOOKOO	131
BASÉ	137
CAMP AT SETTITE, NEAR KHOR MEHETEB	143
THE SETTITE, NEAR KHOR MEHETEB	147
THE SETTITE	149
HAMRANS AT OM HAGAR	160
HAMRANS DRYING HIPPOPOTAMUS MEAT	163
HIPPOPOTAMUS AND SALEE	167
SHEIK ACHMED AGEER AT TOADELOOK	182
LION AND LIONESS	189
BAOBAB-TREE	192
DHOUM-PALMS AT GARGI, KHOR BARAKA	198
KEREN (SANHEIT)	207
PASS ON THE ROAD TO EL AIN	215
MAP OF EGYPT AND THE SOUDAN	*At End.*

POLITICAL ASPECT OF THE SOUDAN.

THE "Soudan" is a name that conveys no idea of defined
frontier, or of civilised territory; it is a vague term signifying "a country of blacks," which might include any portion
of Africa from the Red Sea to the Atlantic.

To the Egyptian understanding the Soudan commences at
Assouan, and thence continues to the Equator; while from
east to west it is bounded by the ocean or the sea.

An area of such enormous extent must exhibit important
variations, both in soils, climate, and fauna, in addition to
examples of the human race. The Egyptian Soudan is
intersected from south to north by the river Nile, which
divides the Nubian from the Libyan desert of the West.
With the exception of the Delta, one vast stretch of sandy
waste, interspersed with rocks and mountains, extends in a
direct line for fifteen degrees of latitude, through which the
Nile silently winds in a never-failing stream, without a
tributary to increase its volume, which diminishes in its
passage north by the exhaustion of intense evaporation and
the absorption of burning sands.

This inhospitable region is inhabited by various races of
obscure origin. There are numerous tribes of Arabs speaking Arabic, which no doubt were successful invaders from
Arabia. There are other tribes which speak a distinct
language, although the type is Arab, *e.g.* the Hadendowa, and
the inhabitants of Dongola; those would claim a more
remote descent from races which might have been aboriginal;
but in the absence of written history the ethnologist may

c

vainly attempt to solve the mystery of hidden ages, and must be content with the illustrations upon the temple walls of four thousand years ago, which depict the Arab tribes of that distant date precisely as they appear at the present day, even to the fashion of their hair.

Although the vast extent of deserts would denote an absolute waste of the earth's surface as unsuitable for human habitation, nature has adapted the requirements of the Arabs and their animals for the wilderness of their occupation. There are at distant intervals oases of rough pasturage where coarse grasses and thorny bushes supply a sufficient nourishment for goats and camels. Among those solitudes the Arabs rear their flocks, and drink from the same wells which watered the herds of their ancestors five thousand years ago. The hard slabs of basalt which frame the mouths of those deep wells are scored to many inches depth around their margin, by the friction of Arab ropes which have drawn water from the same springs since the days when the shepherd kings represented the authority of Egypt.

The most ancient history of Egypt recalls the chronic struggle between that country of advanced civilisation and the barbarous tribes of the surrounding deserts, which, like the wolves and hyænas of the arid mountains, made constant raids upon the valley of the Nile. It was the natural consequence of immediate contact between sterility and fertility; wherever the Nile water irrigates the desert, a green margin marks the limit of production, beyond which all is wilderness. Hunger and thirst are there confronted with a land of plenty—that land being a temptation which has ever induced pillage and invasion. It therefore became necessary to defend the long line of vegetation which fringes the channel of the Nile; to effect this defence, offensive action was important, and as the barbarians were driven from the Nile valley, the stronger power remained master of the barren ground.

From time immemorial anarchy existed throughout the deserts of Nubia and of Libya; although the Egyptians, under the leadership of Moses, drove back the Ethiopians out of Egypt and stormed their capital (Soba) on the banks of the Blue Nile ;[1] and again the Persians followed the active enemy across their waterless deserts with fatal precipitation, no power could actually subdue the various races of the Soudan until the reign of Mehemet Ali Pacha, great-grandfather of the present Khedive, his Highness Mahommed Tewfik. That great ruler of Egypt determined to suppress the chronic anarchy of the Soudan which had hitherto existed as a standing menace upon Egyptian frontiers, and to insure tranquillity by the establishment of a permanent government throughout those vast deserts which were the area of continual strife between opposing sheiks.

About sixty-four years ago the first expedition started from Egypt for the conquest of the unknown Soudan. Many sharp reverses and cruel vicissitudes of warfare delayed the progress of the conqueror, but, through slow degrees, with great courage and perséverance, the Soudan was won, and Khartoum was founded at the junction of the Blue and White Niles as a strategical point that would command the passage of both rivers. The troops employed in these arduous expeditions were composed of Turks, Albanians, with very few Egyptians, and were invariably officered by Turks and Circassians.

The chief points of the new provinces.had been carefully selected. Khartoum and Senaar dominated the Blue Nile, while Shendy and Berber were the principal stations upon the margin of the main river. Dongola formed an important province to the north, and commanded the desert routes from Kordofan. Cassala, situated upon the river Gash, was a fortified position which held in subjection the wild Arabs of the Hadendowa, Beni Amer, and many others.

A necessary sequence to territorial conquest in savage countries is the gradual extension that is forced upon the dominant power by events that are unforeseen and beyond control. Continual raids upon the frontier necessitate a resort to force, the enemy is driven back, and the victorious

---

[1] *Vide* Josephus.

party occupies the recently contested ground. Retreat would be construed as the result of fear, which would en-- courage renewed aggression ; therefore the result of victory is annexation, and the frontier thus continues to extend through force of circumstances. In 1861, during the reign, of Saïd Pacha, Egypt was in the possession of Kordofan, in addition to the Soudan east of the White Nile. In 1865 the Red Sea Ports of Souakim and Massawa were trans- ferred from the Sultan to his Highness Ismail the Khedive, who thus became ruler of an unbroken line of territory throughout the western border of the Red Sea to the con- fines of Abyssinia. Boghos had been annexed, and Gella- bāt, which had been an Abyssinian town on the extreme frontier, became the limit of Egyptian possessions. In 1869 Ismail the Khedive completed his scheme of conquest by the annexation of the entire Nile basin to the Equatorial Lake Albert N'yanza, and thereby embraced the enormous area of thirty degrees of latitude from the Nile sources to the Mediterranean. The slave-hunters, having been driven from the Equatorial Provinces, had taken refuge in Darfour, and it became necessary to crush the power of the Sultan of that hitherto impenetrable country, lest a formidable combination of malcontents from the slave-hunting interests should, with the assistance of Darfour, threaten the security of the Soudan administration. Zebeehr, who had been the chief of a vast company of slave-hunters, was subsidised and employed by the government to command the forces for the subjugation of Darfour. His long experience of the country, added to the renown of his position, enabled him to collect a considerable force from those parties whose profession of slave-hunters had conferred a knowledge of rough military tactics that were eminently adapted for savage warfare. Darfour was conquered and became an Egyptian province. A study of the map will exhibit the vast territorial extent of the Khedive Ismail's dominions, and, had he remained in power, I have no doubt that by degrees the several new provinces would have been de- veloped. Unfortunately the financial position of Egypt was in confusion, which led to foreign interference and the

lamentable complications which necessarily ensued. The rebellion of Arabi, a colonel in the Egyptian army, destroyed
the power of Mahommed Tewfik, the eldest son, who had
succeeded upon the abdication of his father Ismail. England interfered by force of arms to restore the authority of
the lawful ruler, and after the battle of Tel el Kebir Arabi
was exiled to Ceylon, while his Highness Mahommed Tewfik
was re-established upon the throne.

In the meantime a fanatical revolt had widened into
insurrection in the Soudan, under the guidance of a holy
personage named Mahomet Achmet, who had previously
been well known to the authorities. In several conflicts
the government forces had been destroyed, and Darfour and
Kordofan were entirely lost to Egypt; while the garrisons at
the Capital Obeyd and other places were hopelessly invested
by the rebels.

At this critical period the rebellion was encouraged by
the peculiar attitude which England had assumed in Egypt.
She had interfered nominally in defence of the Khedive, but
although the programme was rich in melodramatic power
and philanthropic declarations, there had been an extraordinary contradiction in her acts which exhibited a complete absence of any well-considered policy. The salient
facts were known to the whole world; the Khedive
Mahommed Tewfik was the lawful ruler. Arabi, a colonel
in his army, had rebelled against him, together with powerful confederates and the entire army. England bombarded
and destroyed the forts of Alexandria, but declined to
protect the city after she had destroyed all native authority;
the result was the pillage and destruction of the town, for
which Egypt has to pay an indemnity of nearly five millions
sterling. This was clearly the fault of England.

The rebel Arabi was taken prisoner with his confederates
after Tel el Kebir, and they were tried by the native courts,
and should have suffered the extreme penalty of the law
as a warning to others, and in vindication of the authority
of the Khedive. Instead of this, England interfered, and
arranged that a *pro forma* sentence of death should be
passed upon Arabi and others, but that an exile to Ceylon

should be substituted for the extreme penalty. As Ceylon is considered to represent the Paradise of the East, a banishment to the land of coffee and spices, with a liberal annual allowance of money, was an extraordinary punishment for the crime of rebellion, which the Egyptians could not understand, and which certainly did not increase their respect for the authority of the Khedive, with whose prerogative England had directly and bluntly interfered. England at the same time declared that her troops would be almost. immediately withdrawn from Egypt, and that she had no concern or responsibility for the Soudan; but she concocted a reformed administration for Egypt which the Egyptians neither wanted nor understood.

Every act on the part of England tended to destroy the authority of the Khedive, which she had interfered to re-establish, and her integrity was more than doubted by every class of the Egyptians, who witnessed the miserable position of their ruler shorn of all power, and obliged to act according to the dictation of British officers.

It was ridiculous to expect that under such conditions the power of the Khedive would be restored; at the same time that we vaunted our intention of re-establishing his authority we fettered every action when he wished to move, and we determined that no foreign material should be enlisted in his army. The Khedive was obliged to submit to the humiliation of absolute control; although he was himself aware that no dependence could be placed upon Egyptian troops, he was prohibited from the enlistment of Albanians, who would have formed a reliable force in an emergency, and his army was officered by Englishmen entirely independent of his option. At that time a British force of 8000 men in addition to the Egyptian army of 6000 were idle in Lower Egypt, while a dangerous insurrection was spreading in the Soudan. It is scarcely credible that the English Government determined upon inaction and still adhered to their extraordinary policy of non-intervention beyond Egypt proper—thus directly encouraging the Soudanese to rebellion. Nine thousand Egyptian troops had been destroyed in various conflicts with the rebels, and a total loss of confidence on the part of the soldiers necessitated the employment of British officers in command. General Hicks, together with several English and German officers of tried ability, were engaged by the Khedive to reorganise the forces in the Soudan; they left Cairo with reinforcements of about 1000 men, the same which had run away from Lord Wolseley's attack at Tel el Kebir a few months before. The Egyptians in this arrangement were perplexed by the anomaly that, although England declared herself free from all responsibility in the Soudan, she nevertheless permitted British officers to command the Khedive's forces against the rebels; at the same time that she sanctioned the employment of officers, she refused the employment of men!

The real fact was concealed; this was the crass ignorance of our authorities in all that pertained to the Soudan; they neither understood the country and its inhabitants, nor the danger or degree of the insurrection. England merely sought to shirk responsibility instead of manfully seizing the helm and boldly navigating the vessel through the storm.

There could not be a more convincing proof of this ignorance upon the part of our authorities, than the determination of withdrawing all British forces before the result of General Hicks' expedition had been made known. The orders had actually been given for the retirement of the British army from Egypt, and Sir Evelyn Wood had expressed his confidence in the sufficiency of the Egyptian troops to insure security, when suddenly the terrible news arrived "that General Hicks was massacred, together with his force of 10,000 men in the deserts of Kordofan."

Panic and consternation usurped the place of ignorant false confidence. If the Khedive and his ministers had been unfettered, they would have immediately recruited an army of Turks and Albanians to march direct upon Khartoum, and thereby crush the insurrection; instead of this, the British Government, which had declared itself determined to hold aloof from the affairs of the Soudan, now exhibited itself in the hour of peril, not as the ally and supporter of the Khedive, but as obstructor-general, and most positively interfered to prevent all aid from Egypt proper to the garrisons of Khartoum and other stations. England who had arrived in Egypt in the guise of knight-errant to redress the wrongs of an unfortunate Khedive, now bound him hand and foot, preventing all action, refusing all support, and determined to re-establish his authority by a forcible dismemberment of his empire! Against the protests of the Khedive and his ministry, England enforced her order that "the Soudan *in toto*, including Khartoum the capital, should be immediately abandoned." The Prime Minister Cherif Pacha, and his cabinet resigned rather than submit to this act of cowardly despotism.

By this rash and panic-stricken act, England who had declared herself free from all responsibility for the affairs of Soudan, became immediately and solely responsible for everything pertaining to the Soudan. It is in vain for guilty and conscience-stricken ministers to prevaricate and protest, and to endeavour to slip through some broken mesh in the entanglements of the net around them, the whole world is both judge and jury, and they are universally condemned for a policy of panic and consternation which has entailed misery and ruin upon thousands, and disgrace and humiliation upon all Englishmen.

Here was a picture of the aid and support of England to reform the administration of Egypt, and to re-establish the authority of the Khedive! By our act Alexandria had been absolutely destroyed. We had killed many thousands of Egyptians. We had dispersed an army of mutineers, and we had created another army out of the same worthless material; this army we had taken out of the Khedive's hands, and nevertheless we declared that in six months the British troops would be withdrawn, and the Khedive would be left to the protection of 6000 men, who had been against him to a man only twelve months before. Then, when the moment of extreme danger arrived, we not only declined to aid, but we prevented the action of the Khedive himself, and we enforced the abandonment of a Soudan Empire; that Empire which had been won by the Great Ruler of Egypt, Mehemet Ali Pacha.

The declaration of abandonment spread like wildfire, and drove the loyal Arabs in self-preservation to the ranks of the insurgents. The Soudan was in a blaze of insurrection. It was impossible for the various garrisons to escape; the announcement that the Soudan was to be forsaken, raised every arm against the government authorities.

From the Red Sea to the remote province of Darfour, the cowardly policy of England armed every hand and sharpened every spear. The unfortunate garrisons were closely invested by a pitiless enemy. Sinkāt and Tokar were starving, although within five days of 8000 British troops in Cairo, and 6000 of the Egyptian army under Sir Evelyn Wood.

The horses and camels had been consumed at Sinkāt, where Tewfik Bey was bravely holding his position with 600 faithful troops. They were at the last mouthful, the dogs had been all eaten. Still not a regiment moved to their relief. This was the value of British support to the Khedive. That unfortunate ruler who would be held responsible by his subjects for all calamities, now in the agony of despair requested Baker Pacha to attempt the relief of Sinkāt with 4000 police and ragamuffin blacks kidnapped for the service in the streets of Cairo.

Upon this forlorn hope Baker Pacha started for Souakim, where every attempt against the enemy had been defeated with terrible loss to the government forces.

In the meantime public opinion was exasperated in England. Parliament was about to assemble, and it was necessary that something should be done to allay the excitement of the British press. General Gordon, accompanied by Colonel Stewart, was sent post-haste to Khartoum, with instructions to evacuate the country and to secure the retreat of Egyptian garrisons. In hot haste those devoted officers urged their camels across the Korosko deserts upon this inglorious mission—a mission which, if fulfilled, might bring honour upon their individual names, but would assuredly add a stain to the British reputation. It was a policy of abandonment, and of retreat before a threatened danger. Baker Pacha's forces were cut to pieces in an attempt to relieve Tokar, 2300 men being slain. Here again was consternation! followed by contradiction and spasmodic action. It was impossible to allow the beleaguered garrisons to perish. Every hour was all-important; the whole world was yelling execration at the British policy and cowardice.

Orders were suddenly issued for a British army to advance from Cairo to rescue the garrisons of Tokar and Sinkāt. General Graham assumed the command of 4000 or 5000 British troops and started for Souakim. This was totally opposed to the British declaration that England would by no means interfere in the Soudan, and the Egyptians naturally concluded that if a British force could be despatched when too late, the same force might have been despatched at the proper time without any extraordinary derangement of policy. Not being sufficiently advanced in civilisation to understand the mysteries of Downing Street they imagined that a deep plan had been arranged to permit the total destruction of all Egyptian troops, in order to avoid all danger of resistance to our future occupation of their country.

The troops, under General Graham, arrived at Souakim too late for the object of the expedition—Sinkāt had fallen, and Tewfik Bey, with his brave garrison, had perished to a man. Tokar had surrendered to the rebels under Osman Digna, and a portion of the garrison fought the guns *against* the British troops in the sharply contested struggle of Teb. The battle of Tamai was fought a few days later, with a loss of 130 killed on the British side, and about 3000 of the enemy.

It would have been a natural conclusion that upon this total defeat of the rebels the opportunity would have been immediately seized for an advance to Berber, which was then held by Hussein Khalifa Pacha and an Egyptian garrison. Such an advance might have been easily effected, and the route thus opened to Berber would have at once assured the safety of Khartoum. Instead of this bold move the British Government fell back upon its usual policy of retreat, and General Graham had the mortification of retiring with his victorious troops to Cairo, where they began to wonder, and to ask themselves the painful question : " Was it not wilful murder to destroy some 5000 Arabs without any definite object except slaughter, especially as we had already declared the abandonment of the Soudan, and Mr. Gladstone had officially stated that the Arabs were '*rightly struggling for their freedom*'?"

The retreat of the British forces was naturally attributed to fear, and to the severity of their losses. A few Marines had been left to occupy the earthworks of Souakim, where Osman Digna quickly rallied his Arabs and insulted the garrison by a succession of night attacks. The effect of this was most damaging to the reputation of the government, and imperilled the position of Berber and Khartoum, as the Arabs concluded that the British were powerless to advance. The result was quickly visible. General Gordon was helpless at Khartoum, and in the absence of military support he was deserted by the various tribes upon whom he had relied for aid. Common sense would suggest that a policy of abandonment and retreat must alienate friends and encourage enemies, while it would insure the contempt of all. Khartoum was menaced ; Berber was attacked, and was taken by assault, the greater portion of the garrison being massacred. This was a direct blow at Khartoum, as it destroyed the base should reinforcements be sent across the desert from Souakim.

Khartoum was quickly invested, as the fall of Berber encouraged all tribes, and liberated the attacking force for action against the capital.

The British envoy, General C. G. Gordon, R.E., C.B., who had heroically obeyed the summons of the government for the forlorn hope of evacuating Khartoum, where impassable deserts would render a retreat impossible for a multitude, now found himself cruelly abandoned by that same government which he had assisted in its hour of need ; he was left to the care of Providence, together with his brave companion Colonel Stewart and a number of Europeans, including the French, Austrian, and British Consuls. The English Government adhered to their determination of non-intervention in the affairs of the Soudan. Although they had permitted General Hicks to march to slaughter, although they had employed General Graham to destroy 5000 Arabs, although they had despatched General Gordon and Colonel Stewart to Khartoum to enforce evacuation, still they persisted in their illogical and contemptible attitude, and abandoned their own Envoy to his fate.

Once more public opinion became outraged, and in spite of all former assurances of non-intervention—precisely as they had acted at Souakim when General Graham was sent *too late* to save the garrison—Lord Wolseley was despatched with a British force of 6000 men *too late*, as the Nile was already falling; and before a British regiment could reach Dongola the distressing news was telegraphed by Major Kitchener, R.E. (the gallant officer farthest in advance) —"That the unfortunate Colonel Stewart had perished— massacred with all his party, including the French and English Consuls—after the wreck of their steamer in the cataract north of Berber." Surely the ghosts of these victims must haunt the galleries of Downing Street!

Lord Wolseley is an able general, and I do not pretend to criticise his movements, but the distance by the river is immense, the passage against the stream is slow, and when the hostile country shall be reached, the difficulties will be increased tenfold. Nevertheless, under his guidance, there must be well-placed confidence, which means success in the endeavour to reach Khartoum. At the same time those who are experienced in the country must be well aware that the short route from Souakim to Berber would be an easy march of fourteen days, that would relieve Khartoum almost immediately if troops were despatched from Cairo without delay. The time is rapidly passing, and Gordon, if alive, must be short of ammunition and supplies. The catastrophe of Colonel Stewart's party is a proof that the Khartoum garrison was in great straits, otherwise General Gordon would not have risked the lives of Colonel Stewart and the European Consuls in an attempt to reach Dongola by steamer. With every confidence, and the best wishes for General Lord Wolseley's expedition, we cannot forget the motto of the British Government— " *Too Late.*"

Should Lord Wolseley be successful, what is to be the result of his expedition? He has instructions to abandon Khartoum and the entire Soudan south of Wady Halfah; thus Dongola, which is the gate of Egypt, is to be included in that dastardly policy of abandonment.

It is to be hoped that, if England is sufficiently base to wrest from defenceless Egypt the provinces so hardly won by the illustrious ruler Mehemet Ali Pacha, and to throw open the slave trade to the very heart of Africa, that Germany will not hesitate to occupy the deserted ground, and exhibit a wholesome contrast to our decrepit attitude.

Whatever Power shall hold Khartoum will dominate Lower Egypt. That is a consideration which may not have occurred to her Majesty's advisers.

The drainage of Abyssinia is the cause of the annual inundation of the Egyptian Delta. If any person will refer to the map, and especially to the *Nile Tributaries of Abyssinia*, published after my careful exploration of every affluent in 1861, he will find an exhaustive account of the hydrography of that region, which may be summed up in a few words.

The Delta, *i.e.* Egypt has been created by the deposit of mud brought down from Abyssinia and the Soudan by the river Atbara, known by the ancients as the Astaboras.

That river and its numerous tributaries, the Settite, Royān, Salaam, Angrab, and many smaller torrents, have cut through a vast area of rich loam, thereby widening their original channels by scooping out deep valleys in an otherwise level surface; the cubic contents of these depressions have been deposited to create Egypt.

The rainfall begins in May upon the mountain-ranges of Abyssinia, but the main channel of the Atbara river does not fill until the middle of June. From the middle of February until that time the bed of the Atbara is dry, from its mouth twenty-four miles south of Berber, throughout its desert course of about 260 miles. The channel in that distance is about 400 yards in width, and 30 feet in depth;

it passes through flat sandy desert, the course being marked by a fringe of dome palms and mimosa upon the margin.

Nothing would be easier than the construction of a dam during those months when the channel is dry, which would arrest the torrent upon its arrival at the commencement of the rains, and would divert the stream by the overflow of its banks, and disperse the waters over the absorbing surface of the deserts. The mimosa bark is used for the manufacture of immense sacks for the transport of gum-arabic and senna; the Arabs have the materials upon the spot, also the dome palms for the necessary piles; the construction of a dam sufficient to deflect the Atbara would be a simple engineering feat that only requires the force of many hands. It has occurred to me that the seven years of famine described in the Old Testament, when Joseph hoarded the corn of Egypt, might possibly have been occasioned by a stoppage of the Atbara river through the hostility of the Ethiopians, who were the chronic enemies of Egyptians.

The Rahad and the Dinder could also be deflected in a similar manner, as their beds are dry during the summer months. The Blue Nile would offer greater difficulties, as there is always water in the channel, although fordable waist-deep in March and April; but the stoppage of the Atbara would alone be sufficient to ruin Lower Egypt.

The whole system of mountain drainage of Abyssinia exhibits a struggle for the mastery between the impetuous torrents and the thirsty sands of the lower plains, which suck the productive bosoms of the hills, and exhaust the supply before it can reach the sea. Only the Nile, that one extraordinary river, can overcome the absorption of 1400 miles of sand; that Nile depends upon the Blue Nile and the Atbara rivers, which are commanded by Khartoum; and Mr. Gladstone's Cabinet would abandon Khartoum, at the same moment that they pretend to a paternal sympathy for the Khedive's authority.

Between the course of the Atbara and the Blue Nile to Fazoklé, extending throughout the south bank of the Blue Nile to Senaar, there is a vast tract of the most fertile soil, eminently adapted for cotton cultivation and all other tropical productions. A great portion of that country is within the influence of the rainy zone, and is independent of artificial irrigation; but, should railway communication be established from Souakim to the Nile, the whole of that immense area now in the barren grasp of nature would become of immediate value. When it is considered that the Egyptian Delta represents a mere handful of mud brought down by the rivers from this wonderful region through which they have cut their way, it appears impossible that England, having interfered for the assumed improvement of Egypt, should not only counsel, but enforce the abandonment of such a territory, which requires the simple development of a railway to awaken its vast resources. The British Government, when represented by Lord Dufferin in Egypt, recommended the true English policy of development; but the same government, after the departure of their able representative, determined upon a policy of abandonment, that change of attitude being the direct result of terror, after the defeat and annihilation of the unfortunate General Hicks. The British public cannot be deluded, even by a magician, but after the first bewilderment of legerdemain they will exercise the old English property of common sense. They will look upon the contradictions of policy, which in so many quarters of the world have entailed disaster; they will regard South Africa, and reflect upon the consequences entailed by that cowardly policy of retreat after Majuba Hill, which necessitates another costly expedition under Sir Charles Warren to retrieve a blasted reputation. They will open their eyes to the consequences of the retreat from Candahar when they see Russia advancing with rapid strides upon the Afghan frontier, while England has been lulled into a false security by Russian promises. They will also be awakened to the force of their responsibility should Germany or France claim an equal right with England to interfere in the Soudan, and to occupy the ground which we force the Khedive of Egypt to abandon.

In the original instructions given to General Gordon the

order was distinct, he was to *evacuate the garrisons of Khartoum and other places.* There were no orders to form a government; this is only a subterfuge raised since public opinion has awakened to the monstrous iniquity of abandoning Khartoum and the Soudan to anarchy and the slave trade. If Khartoum is to be abandoned, we have no right, neither have we the power, to exercise a dog-in-the-manger policy, and to prevent the occupation of the forsaken ground by others who have a better sense of duty. I have, after nine years' experience of those countries, never changed my opinions upon their value. The wealth is there; the treasury is the soil which has created Egypt, the infant of the great mother earth, from the womb of fertility which will produce all that the human race can desire. That treasury is like a strong locked safe that can alone be opened by its own key. That key is a railway from Souakim to the Nile, which could be made for one-third the cost of the expedition now slowly working its way against the current of the Nile in a forlorn hope to rescue the one man who has represented the ancient chivalry of England.

SAMUEL WHITE BAKER.

SPORT AND TRAVEL IN THE SOUDAN.

CHAPTER I.

We leave Cairo for the Egyptian Soudan.—The Basé Country.—
Egyptian Officials.—Quarantine Regulations.—Our Party.—Ser-
vants of the Party.—Ali the Cook.—Shereef the staid and stately
Waiter.—Mahoom.—The Agra's Passengers.

ON December 1, 1881, we left Cairo for Suez, *en route* for
the Egyptian Soudan, with the intention of exploring the
Basé country, a small tract lying between Taka (an Egyptian
province, of which Cassala is the principal town) and
Abyssinia. We were going chiefly for sport ; and, the
Basé country being almost if not entirely unknown to
Europeans, we hoped to be successful, especially as it had
not previously been shot over, and, moreover, lies in a part
of Africa abounding in many different kinds of game. We
knew that in all probability there would be considerable
difficulty to encounter in exploring the country ; as only a
small part of it, and that a part where there is little or no
game, belongs to Egypt, and consequently no help could
be expected, but rather hindrance, from the Egyptian
officials in endeavouring to carry out our programme.
They naturally dislike the possibility of sportsmen running
the risk of getting into trouble with tribes bordering on
their frontier.

The Basé are the *bêtes noires*, moreover, of all that part
of the Soudan, and have the character of being a very
treacherous and unfriendly people ; so that it was not only
on the part of the Egyptian officials that we expected to
have obstacles thrown in our way, but we felt sure that we

B

should have considerable difficulty in getting camel-drivers and servants to undertake the journey. Then, too, the Basé, dwelling as they do between Egyptian and Abyssinian territory, would naturally be jealous of any one entering their country through that of their powerful Egyptian neighbours, and might think that, instead of being bent purely on travel and sport, we were really come on behalf of the Egyptian Government to endeavour to squeeze taxes out of them, and reduce them to submission.

On our arrival in Cairo we heard that we should probably be delayed for some three or four weeks before we could find a steamer to take us to Souakim (the port on the Red Sea from which we wished to make our start into the interior), owing to the existing quarantine regulations. In consequence of the prevalence of cholera in India and at Aden, all steamers going from an Arabian to an African port were subjected to quarantine on their arrival.

The only *regular* steamers calling at Souakim are those of the Khedivial Company; and they, as a rule, call at ports on both sides of the Red Sea, in their voyages up and down. The steamers of the Rubattino Company are also advertised to stop at Souakim, but they are, at the best of times, most irregular; and when we wished to go, their "fleet" had been reduced to one steamer, the "Messina," and even she had, for the time being, been withdrawn from the service, owing to the quarantine.

Most of the steamers, moreover, were keeping to the Arabian ports, while several were being done up at Alexandria; so that there was only one steamer, the "Zagazig," performing the service between Suez and the African ports, and she had started before we had collected our party together.

In this dilemma we fortunately were able to induce the captain of the British India Company's steamer "Agra" to stop for us at Souakim on her way out to India. This was most lucky for us, as we grudged spending more of the cool weather at Cairo than we could help; the heat in the Soudan becoming very trying by the spring.

The "Agra" was delayed in the canal, and instead of

leaving Suez on December 2, as she should have done, did not start until the 7th; this was, however, fortunate, as one of our party (Colvin) was to join us there from Australia, and had she started on the right day he would have been too late, as he did not arrive until the 4th, running it rather fine. He had come straight from Adelaide, in the "Chimborazo," one of the Orient line, without touching anywhere; and she had been a few days late in starting.

Before embarking at Suez I may as well introduce our party to my readers. It consisted of seven, besides servants, —G. Percy V. Aylmer, R. B. Colvin, E. Lort Phillips, my two brothers, the Doctor, and myself. Of these, all except Colvin and the Doctor had made an expedition together, during the previous winter, into the Bogos country, on the Abyssinian frontier; and my brothers and myself had, four years previous to that, travelled *viâ* the Nile and Atbara Rivers, as far as the River Settite: so that we were not novices in African travel, and, moreover—a most important consideration in undertaking such an expedition—we felt that we should get on well together.

As we were so large a number of Europeans, we thought that it would be prudent to have a doctor in the party. I undertook the task of finding one, and found it no sinecure. As I could not hear privately of any one willing to accompany our party, who seemed suitable, I considered the best thing to do was to advertise in the principal medical journals; I also put an advertisement in the *Times* and *Athenæum.* The result was, I was inundated with replies. Some of these were most amusing.

The evident difficulties some of my correspondents found in describing their personal qualifications may be best illustrated by the following extracts from some of their letters, which I here subjoin. One, after stating that his age was forty-three, and that he had never had a day's illness, went on to say that he possessed "a disinfectant, unknown to the profession, for the prevention of fevers; also, the means of curing the same without medicine." He had had more experience in the treatment of fever than most medical men in England. His concluding sentence we all thought delicious, and felt he was quite the man to rough it in Central Africa. I again quote from his letter : " I like a cigar after my dinner and supper, with a glass of mild ale, *and meals at regular hours;* so that I call myself an abstemious man, and one to be depended upon day or night." Another applicant kindly observed : " If the expedition is of a scientific character, I should not object to take professional charge, provided that I am allowed to obtain a sufficient stock of Jaborandi (?) Warburg's tincture, and other prophylactics against marsh-fever, without which it would be unsafe to venture into that country, *or to permit others to do so.* Furnished with these, I would, using proper precautions as regards sanitation, food, and clothing, face the Terai or the Gold Coast without fear or hesitation. I have an excellent constitution, delight in tropical climate (barring swamp), am never sea-sick, and accustomed to rough travel, and to carry my life in my hand. Like all old Westminster scholars of my time, I can cook, do any kind of rough-and-ready housework, row, fish, shoot, and, I'm sorry to admit, *fight*, if occasion demands it, and also keep my temper under almost any provocation. I have the reputation of being a scholar, and I believe I may say a gentleman. I forgot to state that I pick up languages rapidly, am a tolerable *connoisseur* in art and cookery, play whist, piquet, and chess well for an amateur, and don't drink or gamble ; and that I am a member of the Church of England, as my father's son should be."

We felt that the field for this gentleman to display his taste in art as well as in cookery would be somewhat limited in the countries we proposed visiting, although his pugilistic skill might prove of value. We, however, fully appreciated the kind care he was anxious to take of us. His concluding sentence was most cheering in case of any sinister accident : " I am engaged in devising a series of tests to determine whether people are really dead before they are buried ; and Egypt is a good country to make observations of this sort in."

One applicant wrote in praise of a man whom he eulogised as follows : " It will be found on inquiry, that

Dr. ———— is highly and most respectably connected. He is good-looking, though unassuming, jovial yet refined, and strictly abstemious. He is about to commence practice for himself. When he does, his unpretending amenity, simplicity of manners and deportment, combined with his great acumen and high professional attainments, are sure to meet with success."

We felt that this gentleman's "deportment and unpretending amenity" would be quite thrown away on the wild tribes of the Soudan ; and passed on to another letter in which the writer, after enumerating every place marked on the most extensive map of the West Coast of Africa yet published, all of which places he stated he had visited, went on to say he had "attended Ocko Jumbo's son, made the acquaintance of King Ja Ja at Opobo," and that he was "on the most intimate terms with King Ockei." We felt that this gentleman was accustomed to altogether too high society for us, and we could promise him no royal acquaintances in the part of the Soudan we were about to visit. I shall only trouble my readers with one more quotation, and that from a telegram I received from a French doctor ; in which after stating his terms, which were "*quatre mille francs pour deux mois, payés d'avance, et tous les frais du voyage,*" he went on to say that he required "*une chambre à part, et ne veut pas être obligé de suivre ces messieurs dans leurs excursions de chasse !*"

For servants we had with us George Reason, an Englishman who had accompanied us during our journey into the Bogos country; and two Swiss, Jules Bardet and Anselmier; these made up the European contingent. The native servants that we took from Cairo consisted of Suleiman Daoud, our head man and a most excellent fellow ; he had been with us on our last expedition, and was for nearly five years with Sir Samuel Baker when he went as head of the Egyptian Government expedition to the White Nile and equatorial lakes ; Shereef the waiter, very staid and stately, never ruffled or put out by anything, slow, but an excellent man in his particular line, keeping the canteen, his special care, in first-rate condition throughout the entire journey ;

Ali the cook, a native of the Soudan, a most important functionary and a very good servant. He was with us during the winter of 1877-78, and on one occasion, when at Cassala, he asked leave to get drunk, urging as his excuse that some gentlemen, with whom he had travelled several times previously, always allowed him to do so at that place; he had consequently got to look upon it as a sort of local privilege; a lecture was delivered to him on the sin of drunkenness, which I believe he regarded as a sort of permission to get drunk; for he got very drunk, but not before he had sent us up a most excellent dinner, and, as far as I know, he never afterwards offended again in this respect: Mahoom, a coal-black negro from the White Nile, a boy of sixteen, speaking both English and Arabic. Mahoom was originally captured by some slave-traders on the White Nile, in a raid that they made against a village; he was freed by Colonel Gordon, the late governor-general of the Soudan, and given to Dr. Felkin at Khartoum. Dr. Felkin was the medical man in charge of the Church Missionary Society's expedition to Uganda, and took Mahoom with him to that place. He had returned with the doctor to England, where he had spent some months; hearing that we were going to the Soudan, Dr. Felkin was glad that we should take the boy with us, in order that he might escape the cold of an English winter.

Of these servants, the only one who did not speak English easily was Shereef. On asking him, at Cairo, if he spoke English, he replied in the negative, but added that he spoke "too much French." His powers, however, in that respect, we found were very limited; but, as most of us spoke a little Arabic, "too much French" was not required.

We brought with us from England two dogs,—a setter and a fox-terrier, "Tartar." The former, when he was put in the dog-box of the train at Cairo, to go to Suez, was in perfect health and spirits; but when we came to take him out at Zagazig, a station about half-way between the two places, where we had to change trains, he was dead. They had been poisoning a great many dogs at Cairo; and he must have been poisoned, probably, on the morning we left. "Tartar" stood the climate very well: he would run with the camels all day, and sometimes, when tired, we let him ride on some of the baggage. He would often run on ahead of us, and rest under the shade of some tree; and then, after we had passed him some distance, he would catch us up again. Once or twice we feared we had lost him. He was very fond of chasing gazelles,—which it is unnecessary to add he never caught,—and he sometimes went so far after them that we lost him for hours. Several times he reached the camp long after the last of the caravan had arrived; he had, no doubt, found and followed the scent of the camels.

Among the "Agra's" passengers we had two officers of the "Blues." They had come out to Egypt hoping to be able to make an expedition into the interior, from either Berbera or Tajourah, ports opposite Aden; but had been obliged to give it up, and had decided on landing at Souakim.

There were also three or four saloon-passengers, bound for India, who had come out in the "Agra" from England, and were not at all delighted, after their long delay in the canal, at the prospect of a further delay through going to Souakim, as it would cause them to be two days longer on their voyage to Kurrachee, to which port they were bound.

We found eight or ten Persian pilgrims, deck-passengers, far more interesting than the Anglo-Indians. They were dressed in parti-coloured robes resembling dressing-gowns, and wore the high felt Persian hat; and, though extremely dirty, were decidedly picturesque.

These unfortunate men had set out on a pilgrimage to Mecca from Bushire, at the head of the Persian Gulf; and some of them had saved up their money for years with this object in view.

After about a month's voyage, they had arrived at Jeddah, the port for Mecca, only to find that they might not land there. There was, at the time of their arrival at Jeddah, cholera in the Persian Gulf; and as it had not reached the Arabian ports, they were not permitted to land.

They consequently had to go on in the steamer; but were not allowed to disembark either at Suez, Algiers, or Lisbon, at all of which ports they touched, and so were carried on to London.

There they had spent three or four weeks; and the British India Company had sent them to the Aquarium, Crystal Palace, and other sights, keeping them at the expense of the Company. I should say they had a far more agreeable time of it in London than they would have had at Mecca; and surely, under the circumstances, it would help them as well on their road to paradise as though they had in reality been enabled to say their prayers at the sacred shrine, and to have drunk, at their source, the sacred waters of Zem-Zem.

As the pilgrimage season was over, it was of no use for them to land at Jeddah when the " Agra " called there after leaving Souakim; and consequently they were on their way back to Bushire. Two or three of the original band, better off than the rest, had, we were told, left London for Paris, intending to travel overland; and one had discovered a *houri* in London, with whom he was living in Bayswater.

CHAPTER II.

Arrival at Souakim.—The *Wakeel*.—Thieving Propensities of Egyptian Officials.—Encouragement of Slavery.—Souakim.—Caravan-routes from Souakim.—Ala-ed-Deen Pacha.—The Governor's "Palace." —Bedouin Government Prisoners.—Omnipresence of Greeks.— *Dhurra.*—"Hôtel du Soudan."—Curious Manner of dressing the Hair.—An African Hurlingham.—Story of the Seven Virgins.— Departure from Souakim.

AFTER a very uneventful voyage we reached Souakim about noon on December 11. The day before we had had heavy rain; and the day we landed was very cloudy, with occasional heavy showers. We were much surprised at finding wet weather in that part of the world, but afterwards discovered, that, although rain by no means always falls at that time of year, yet it is the season of coast rains.

On our arrival we called on the *Wakeel*, or government agent, Achmed Effendi; he offered us rooms in the "palace," which we were very glad of, though it was decided to remain for that night on board ship.

Mr. Brewster, the custom-house officer, and Mr. Bewley, were at that time the only English residents in the Soudan. The former had been there some time; but the latter had only just come from Jeddah, where he had lived as partner in a trading firm that had set up a branch establishment at Souakim. On our return to Souakim in the spring, we found Mr. Brewster had left, and that a native had taken his place, whose pay would perhaps be less, but who would in all probability far more than make up for that by well lining his own pockets at the expense of the government. As a rule, Egyptian officials, both high and low, go to the Soudan only in order to rob for themselves as much as possible during the time they are there; and, when they have feathered their own nests as well as their opportunities allow them, they give place to others, whose ambition it is to follow them in the same noble course.

It is this system of pillage and oppression that has been carried on so long in the Soudan that has caused the present rebellion. Gordon gave the country about five years of just government,—at least he did all that one most upright and honourable Englishman could do in such a country, and with such men for his lieutenants as he had to deal with. I travelled in the country both during his rule and afterwards, saw the difference that had come over the Soudan, and heard the groans of the poor people after he had left them. As Gordon himself says : " The egg of the present rebellion was laid in the three years during which I was allowed to govern the Soudan on other than Turkish principles."—(*Pall Mall Gazette*, 9th January 1884.) After Gordon left the country, the people were treated as badly or worse than they were before his arrival. They felt the difference. Then came the chance for the slave-dealers ; they, wishing to regain their power and revive their trade, which both Sir Samuel Baker and General Gordon had done so much to stop, stirred up the Soudanese against their rulers, the wretched Egyptian officials, and in order the more effectually to accomplish this, pushed forward the Mahdi, if they did not actually *create* him. The cry rang through-out the country, a cry emanating from the slave-dealers : " Drive your wretched oppressors the Egyptians into the sea, and govern yourselves." The movement has spread, and the Mahdi, originally a dummy figure-head, is now be-lieved in by thousands. Suleiman Daoud, head servant during our last two expeditions in the Soudan, and now chief native servant to General Stephenson at Cairo, the only Egyptian of my acquaintance I can implicitly trust, writes to me at the beginning of October in the present year : " The Egyptian people are in the full belief and hope that the Mahdi is going to kill all the English people both in Egypt and the Soudan." This hatred of the English used not to be,—at least it certainly *was* not common among the lower classes ; lately, however, owing to our extraordinary policy or rather want of policy in the country, a strong feeling of hostility to us as a nation has sprung up, and is growing stronger every day. Is England to reply to the cry of the slave-dealers by giving up the Soudan to all the horrors of slavery again? · In the interests of common humanity and civilisation I trust not!

To return to my narrative. We saw very little of the *Wakeel* Achmed Effendi, and did not hear at all a good report of him. We were told that he was doing anything but discouraging the slave trade; that, on the contrary, he took a bribe of two napoleons for every slave that he permitted to leave the port, and that the chief of police took one in addition. Some slaves had been lately seized, and a great to-do made about them; but this was because the hush-money was not forthcoming.

The entrance to the harbour of Souakim is narrow and long, and steamers can only go in by daylight; the entrance is well marked out by beacons, but there are dangerous reefs outside. Our captain had never been to the port before, and did not seem at all to relish taking his vessel in. There is not anchorage in the harbour for more than four or five steamers at a time.

The town, which is built of coral, is rather picturesque-looking, though of a glaring white; and it boasts of one or two minarets. The carving of some of the doors and window-shutters of the houses is most elaborate, and of a different pattern from any I have seen in Cairo. I was told that there was a great deal of the same kind of work at Jeddah.

The town is built on an island, which is united to the mainland by a causeway which Colonel Gordon had made when he was governor-general of the Soudan. Its population is about eight thousand; it is the chief port of the Soudan, and the outlet of the great bulk of the trade of the White Nile and Khartoum.

The great caravan route from Souakim is that which, crossing the desert, strikes the Nile at Berber, a distance of two hundred and forty miles; not the road to Cassala, which we followed. Its trade, however, is not increasing, owing to the present low price of gum, its chief export to Europe, and to the restrictions on the slave-trade.   Formerly slaves could be purchased with cotton-cloth imported from Manchester, and the slaves were made to carry ivory, ostrich-feathers, etc., to the coast; now this "branch of industry" is done away with, although more merchandise finds its way to Europe by Souakim than by the other great outlet, that *viâ* Berber and Korosko on the Nile.

I made the journey up the Nile, from Cairo to Korosko, during the winter of 1877-78, and from thence across the desert to Abou Hamed, following the banks of the Nile to Berber.   The desert journey from Korosko to Abou Hamed is a most severe one: the distance is two hundred and fifty miles of the worst desert imaginable, with nothing for the camels to eat, and only one well the whole way.   The heat, too, during the greater part of the year, is terrific; and the consequent mortality among the camels that make the transit very great.

In crossing this desert we saw two regular slave-caravans, consisting of boys and girls, probably from the White Nile or Darfour, travelling in the direction of Korosko.   They were all trudging wearily through the heavy sand, while their owners rode on camels which the slaves led.   Many, doubtless, perish on the journey.

Besides the Berber and Korosko route, and that from Berber to Souakim, there is a third road much used by Soudanese traders.   This road follows the banks of the Nile to Wady Halfah: it is chiefly made use of by caravans coming from Darfour and Kordofan, provinces to the west of the White Nile that produce great quantities of gum. The Nile is struck at a small village called Debbe, about latitude 18° north, whence goods are conveyed by boats as far as Dongola, where the cataracts render further navigation impossible; and then camels carry them to Wady Halfah at the second cataract.   The journey is then resumed in boats to the first cataract, where a railway five miles in length carries the goods below the cataract to other boats waiting for Cairo or Alexandria.

The Egyptian Government had just separated the Red Sea ports Souakim and Massawa, together with the country between them and Cassala, Sanheit, the town of Cassala itself, Gedariff, the Hamran country, Gallabat and neighbouring provinces, from the rest of the Soudan. Ala-ed-Deen Pacha, who had been for a long time governor of different parts of this country, was made supreme governor; and Ali Reza Pacha, formerly governor of the Red Sea ports, was deposed. The latter was much hated by the people. Our steamer brought this news to the inhabitants of Souakim; and, Ala-ed-Deen being much liked, the people testified to their joy at this change of government by getting up an impromptu illumination, chiefly by means of little oil-lamps which they hung in front of their houses.

We were very glad to be able to live in the "palace" during our stay at Souakim, instead of being obliged to live in tents, as it rained more or less every day. We were given two rooms on the first floor, in one of which we slept, while the other was assigned to our servants and luggage. Our meals we took either on the verandah—which was very broad, and looked on to the sea—or in the large passage, or rather hall, out of which our rooms opened. Although everything was open, the huge windows being without glass, but with shutters in its place, and plenty of air stirring, we found Souakim extremely hot and "muggy," and were anxious to leave it with as little delay as possible. The "palace" is built at one end of a large courtyard, one side of which faces the sea, and forms the sea-wall. On the right-hand side a double staircase led to our apartments; and the courtyard was entered from the street by an imposing gateway guarded by soldiers, over which a most formidable-looking lion carved in stone held sway; his tail, which was of extraordinary proportions, stuck out straight. I think the idea of the lion was chiefly ornamental, though, guarding as he did the entrance to the divan, he may have been intended as a symbol of power likewise : he was certainly looked upon with admiration by the inhabitants.

We encountered a very sad sight every time we either entered or left the courtyard. In one corner were huddled together some forty Bedouins, mostly men, with a few

women and children. They were all from the neighbourhood of Jeddah, and were government prisoners : they had
chains on their legs, and were living in a state of captivity
from no fault of their own.

It appeared that a number of Bedouins had crossed
over to Souakim with their camels, intending to settle in
the neighbourhood, and breed camels. As, however, they
quarrelled with the Arabs of the country, Colonel Gordon,
who was then governor of the Soudan, gave them nine
thousand dollars[1] compensation (they having originally
obtained permission to settle where they were), and sent
them back to their own country. On Colonel Gordon giving up the governor-generalship of the Soudan, and leaving
the country, a number of them returned, determined to try
again what they could do. Ali Reza Pacha, who was then
governor of Souakim, thought this an opportunity not to
be lost for raising a little money. As he could only squeeze
two thousand dollars out of them, and this did not satisfy
him, he put them in irons.

When we arrived, they had been living a year in the
courtyard in this way, and, although government prisoners,
were obliged to provide their own food. Their camels had
died off in great numbers, and many of the men also had
succumbed to the bad treatment they had received. Some
of them (guarded by soldiers) were allowed to live with
their camels, a few miles out of Souakim, where there was
food for their beasts. Achmed Effendi had actually made
them lately believe that, if they would give him forty dollars,
it would help towards freeing them. They subscribed this
amount between them, which of course went to line the
worthy Effendi's pockets, the result to the Bedouins being
nil. They had no shelter from sun or rain ; and some of
the poor little children were suffering from fever, which our
doctor did what he could to alleviate. We left forty dollars

---

[1] The current coin throughout the Soudan and Abyssinia is the
Maria Theresa dollar, which is worth nearly four shillings. A large
number were coined especially for the Abyssinian expedition. No gold
coin is in circulation, but one occasionally comes across the Turkish
medjedie, but only in the chief towns of the Soudan.

with Mr. Brewster, who promised to expend it during the
winter in food, which he kindly offered to distribute among
them.

On our return in April he told us he had been able to
buy a great deal of rice and *dhurra* with the money, and
that the poor people had been most grateful. We were
glad to find the wretched prisoners flown on our return, as
the first act of Ala-ed-Deen Pacha, on his arrival in the
spring, had been to set them all free, and this he had done
before being an hour in the place: he had, moreover,
allowed them to live somewhere to the north of the town,
if they wished to do so; and many of them availed themselves of this permission, instead of returning to their own
country. It is to be hoped that, in the many changes that
have recently taken place in the country, they will not have
been oppressed again.

We found a number of Greek shops in the town, and
the place was well supplied with meat. Greeks are to be
found everywhere: there is no place too out-of-the-way for
them to thrive in, and they make money wherever they
go. A great many of them, besides selling bad spirits,
beer, and groceries, add considerably to their incomes by
lending money to the natives, of course at usurious rates
of interest.

No vegetables are grown, and the whole of the surrounding country is desert. The nearest village is Tokar on
Khor Baraka, two days' journey away; and there, after
the rains, a little *dhurra* is grown. *Dhurra* (the *sorghum
vulgare* of Linnæus) is the staple article of food throughout
the Soudan; it contains a great deal of starch, and is said
to be more nourishing than wheat flour. The natives cook
it in a variety of ways, and add beans or onions, when
obtainable, to it. Horses will not thrive unless they get
a daily supply of it, and a small quantity is of great use in
keeping the riding-camels in good condition. In crossing,
too, such a desert as that between Korosko and Abou
Hamed, it is necessary to carry some for the baggage-
camels as well: it is wonderful on how little food they can
do, when pushed to it.

A Greek has set up a small shanty, which he dignifies by the title, " Hôtel du Soudan," and advertises hot and cold baths.   Fortunately we had no occasion to try its merits, otherwise than by sending some clothes to his wife to be washed : for these she charged us at the rate of two dollars per dozen, counting a pair of socks as two articles ; so that what they lacked in custom, they evidently tried to make up in their prices, when, as they say in America, " a stranger happened to come along."

Beyond the island on which the town is built, Souakim continues for some distance in suburbs, containing a somewhat extensive if not very inviting bazaar.

The camel-drivers, who mostly belong to the Hadendowa tribe, live on the mainland.   Most of them wear long hair standing up straight on the crown of the head, and of a fine but woolly texture, while that at the back of the head generally reaches to the shoulders, and is sometimes worn in plaits ; when properly dressed the whole is covered with fat, and a wooden skewer, by way of comb, stuck in it. We saw one or two men with their heads covered with fat that had been mixed with grated sandalwood, and presented a red-ochre appearance : these, we were informed, were about to enter the marriage-state.

The hair is, with all Arabs, a source of pride ; and the men of various tribes may frequently be distinguished by little differences in their mode of dressing it.

No traveller in these parts can fail to be struck by the great similarity in physique, and general appearance, of many of the wandering tribes of Arabs, to the ancient Egyptians as depicted on the walls of their temples and tombs.   The mode of wearing the hair is identical ; the curious little wooden pillows they use for their heads when sleeping are exactly of the same form and make as those which may be seen in museums containing ancient Egyptian curiosities ; as, too, are also the chairs that they use.   A very intelligent Greek, whom we afterwards met in Cassala, and who had given some attention to the study of the language spoken by the Hadendowa Arabs in the neighbouring country, and had, moreover, some knowledge of

hieroglyphics, told us that there was often a striking similarity in many of their words.

My brother Arthur in 1877 made the journey from
Souakim to Cassala; meeting the rest of the party, who
had taken the Nile route, in the interior. He had with
him a Hadendowa Arab, who had originally started as guide
to the caravan from Souakim to Cassala; and this Arab
accompanied him all the way to Cairo. Throughout this
journey his hair was a constant source of anxiety to him.
He could not dress it himself, and on leaving Cassala was
soon beyond the region of his own tribe. His delight was
unbounded when he met a woman of his own people on
the Atbara River, who, on being rewarded for her pains by
the promise of an empty beer-bottle, undertook to dress his
hair—a process that occupied a good two hours. He
reclined, during the process, with his head in the lady's
lap; and the crowning joy of all was anointing the plaited
tresses with the musky fat of the crocodile, the horrible
odour of which clung to him for days, to *his* great satisfaction, but to the great discomfort of our olfactory nerves.

The largest building in Souakim is a storehouse and
caravanserai in one, built on the mainland. It was erected
by a native for the merchants to leave their goods in while
waiting for transport, and cost eighty thousand dollars. It
was built almost entirely by slave-labour, otherwise it would
have cost fully a third more. The builder and owner was
formerly a government employé, at a hundred and fifty
piastres (or about thirty-one shillings) a month.

During our stay at Souakim, we were, of course, very
busy arranging and re-arranging our luggage. Sir Edward
Malet, H.B.M.'s consul-general in Egypt, had very kindly
telegraphed from Cairo to have camels ready for us. His
telegram, I have no doubt, hastened matters; but there is
always considerable delay in making a start.

Sheik Attman Galani, the sheik of the camels that
traverse the Cassala road—a very fine-looking Arab, with a
great idea of driving a bargain—paid us several visits before
we finally arranged matters.

We went out fishing once or twice, but did not catch

C

much—our chief capture being a ground-shark weighing eleven pounds. The amount and variety of fish in these waters are something extraordinary, and many of them are of the most gorgeous colours; but to meet with much success it is necessary to go some little distance outside the harbour, where we found the water often unpleasantly rough when anchored and fishing from a small boat; and we were, moreover, so busy making preparations for our departure, that we had no time for lengthy excursions.

One afternoon some of the Greeks of the place, together with Mr. Bewley, went off to a sandy island to shoot sand-grouse that some Arab boys had caught. It was quite Hurlingham in Africa; but the birds were thrown up in the air, instead of being released from traps, and very difficult shots they proved.

The derivation of the word Souakim or Souakin (for it is spelt indifferently both ways) is a curious one. In the language of the country it is called Sowagin (*Anglicè*, "together with the *gin*, or fairy"). The story runs that seven virgins inhabited an island in the Red Sea, where there were no men or people of any kind except themselves. Some fishermen one day visited the island and found the women *enceintes*. Their offspring colonised the mainland and founded Souakim; and the present inhabitants are descended from them. The ladies declared that genii were the fathers of their children.

We were very glad to turn our backs on Souakim, and make a start for the interior, which we did on December 15, about two o'clock in the afternoon. We left behind the two officers of the "Blues," who had travelled with us from Suez: they were busy buying camels, always a very slow and troublesome undertaking. They got off, however, soon after we did, and by following the bed of Khor Baraka and the Anseba reached Keren. From thence they made their way to Furfur, on the borders of the Dembelas country (where we had been the previous winter), but were rather disappointed with the sport they obtained. One of them succeeded in penetrating to some of the Dembelas villages,—a feat that had only been previously accomplished by the Marquis Antinori, the Italian traveller, the country being almost *terra incognita :* he reported it to be very hilly and impassable for camels, but found the people friendly, possessing better houses than their neighbours who were under Egyptian Government, and he observed more appearance of cultivation. He saw very little game.

Most of our provisions we had brought from England, which we found more economical than getting them in Cairo. Our outfit had been chiefly obtained from Silver in Cornhill, and nearly everything we got from him proved satisfactory.

We paid five dollars and a half each for our camels to Cassala, a distance of about two hundred and eighty miles. Our *personal* property in beasts of burden, which was destined afterwards to increase to considerable proportions, commenced from this date. My brother Arthur bought a very good *hygeen*, or riding camel, at the upset price of a hundred dollars. He had formerly belonged to Ala-ed-Deen Pacha, and though slow, was very easy in gait—a great desideratum. His name was "Bellus;" though what "Bellus" means, I am sure I don't know. My other brother also bought a *hygeen* from an Arab, who rode after us with it when we had gone an hour from the town; for this animal he gave forty dollars, and forthwith christened him "Snodgrass." These camels brought them both back eventually to the coast, but they were about done for when they arrived.

Colvin and Aylmer each bought a horse, the only specimens of the equine race of which Souakim could boast; they were wiry little animals and came from the Hamran country. Although they carried them to Cassala, they never recovered from the hardships of the long desert-journey, and one of them died soon after its arrival there.

Most people, after they have once become used to them, find camels far less fatiguing to ride than horses for long desert-journeys; and they are certainly much more suitable to the country.

A most uncomfortable start we made from Souakim:

the rain, which we had been daily favoured with, came down in torrents soon after our departure. Although in the winter months rain is unknown in the interior, at the time we landed in Africa it was the season of coast rains; and rain might be daily expected until we could put some miles between us and the sea.

CHAPTER III.

The First Halt.—The Rainy Season.—The Camel-sheik comes for *Baksheesh.*—Three Caravan-routes to Cassala.—Disputes with the Camel-drivers. — Gazelles. — Management of Camels. — Halt at Siterabb.—A Piteous Tale.

IN a regular African deluge, and wet to the skin, we pitched the tents. Some of the provisions became saturated with rain, which got, too, into our portmanteaus. The drivers were all quarrelling about their loads, and our halt for the night was made only an hour and a half's march out of the town. The camel-drivers always try to accomplish this, as they say it enables them to run back if they have forgotten anything; it means, of course, too, a late start on the following day.

The Egyptian tents we had had made in Cairo were decidedly fine-weather tents, and, although admirably adapted to a dry climate, were not so agreeable for a wet one. Tents soon spoil if often packed up wet, as they get mildewed and rot. We consoled ourselves with the reflection that the bad weather could not last long. The rain stopped before we went to bed, but came down faster than ever in the night; and we had to jump out of bed to rescue bags and clothes, and set to work to dig trenches round our tents to drain the rain off—a precaution that had been neglected before going to bed.

The natives were delighted with the rain; for, although it was the season when they expected it, it often happens at Souakim that there is none, or next to none at all, during the whole year.

The desert was carpeted with the most beautiful grass of a very vivid green; the dwarf mimosa-bushes, of which there were plenty, were bursting into leaf; and the plain was covered with cattle, goats, and sheep, while numbers of camels wandered from bush to bush, or grazed on the fresh grass, a rare treat to all animals in these regions.

The cows in these parts often prove very obstinate when they are wanted to keep quiet in order to be milked. The natives often resort to the expedient of holding a calf-skin, which the cow to be milked has previously smelt, at some little distance from her nose; she will then keep quiet, and submit to the process of milking without any further trouble.

The next day, although we rose at dawn, it was nearly noon before our camels were loaded, and a fresh start made; more rain falling during the process of packing. The camel-sheik, intent on *baksheesh*, arrived while we were at breakfast; we gave him a small present, and promised him the same on our return if our camels and the men in charge of them proved satisfactory.

There are three roads between Souakim and Cassala, all more or less traversed by caravans. The one we took kept close to the telegraph-wires the whole way, and is the shortest. A second follows, for the greater part of the way, Khor Baraka,[1] and although considerably longer is probably more agreeable, as there is more shade and water by this route. Khor Baraka runs into the sea a little to the south of Souakim, near Taka.

The third road follows almost all the way a mountain-range a little to the west of our route. The Arabs said there was more water on 'that road than on the one we took; but it is rather longer, and very stony, which is trying to the camels, with their spongy feet, especially when they are laden. On our route there was scarcely any grass the whole way; and what there was, was, of course, at the season of the year in which we travelled, completely burnt up; it was mostly very fine in texture, and as brittle as spun-glass. The grass that had sprung up in consequence

---

[1] *Khor* signifies a stream or river that only flows during the rainy season, and is quite dried up during the dry. *Bahr* means a flowing river that never dries up.

of the rain lasted only for twenty or thirty miles after leaving the town, by which time we got out of the rainy zone.

The greater part of the country was sparsely covered with mimosa-bushes, mostly leafless during the dry season, and affording no shade. In some places there were bushes covered with leaves of a most brilliant green. The branches, and especially the roots of this shrub (*Capparis sodata*) are much prized by the Arabs as tooth-brushes ; they are very fibrous, but I doubt if they have any special cleansing properties.

The teeth of these dark-skinned people are nearly always very white ; this is, no doubt, partly due to their very simple diet, and also it is certain that the strong contrast afforded by their dark skins makes them appear whiter than they are in reality.

We began to have trouble with our camel-drivers on the second day's journey from Souakim. The caravan had been allowed to go on ahead, as we had stopped behind with the camel-sheik, trying to bargain for another *hygeen*, but without coming to terms ; and, on overtaking it, we found the camels were off feeding, and their loads on the ground. We were anxious to get out of the rains as quickly as possible, and had given orders that they were to make a late march. Suleiman and the other servants had done all in their power to make them continue their journey ; but the camel-drivers had insisted on stopping at four o'clock, after a march of less than five hours. On being pressed to go on, they had threatened Suleiman with their spears, which had been taken away from them, and tied together in a bundle.

It was not only important that we should get out of the rains as quickly as possible, but more so, that we should let the men see, at the very outset of our journey, that we were the masters, not they, and that they were to do as they were told. Accordingly, we insisted on their loading up again, which they did very quickly ; and just at dusk we resumed our march, not halting until 9.15.

On our right was a high range of mountains, through which led the road to Berber ; while on our left a level,

sandy plain covered with green grass and low scrub stretched
to the sea.

We experienced great difficulty in pitching our tents in
the dark, as most of the men were new to the work ; and
as we were only just commencing our expedition no one
knew where anything was, nor what was required of him.
Everything was wet, and it was very difficult to make charcoal burn ; so that it was 12.30 before we had dined and
could go to bed.

We had seen a few gazelle (*Gazella Arabica*), and a
herd of ariel (*Gazella Dama*), but all very shy.   Each year
they become less numerous on the caravan routes ; and my
brother Arthur, the only one of the party who had made
the journey before, said they were far less common than
when he passed over the same road four years before.

The following day we got an eight hours' march out of
our camels, and without any great difficulty with the drivers :
they had begun to know their loads, and the inevitable
squabbling that takes place at starting was nearly over.

An eight hours' march for the caravan is as much as
can be accomplished with comfort.   As soon as the loads
are taken off at night the camels are turned out to feed ;
at dusk, unless there is a moon, they must be collected in
camp again, to be driven out to feed at break of day.   To
accomplish more in the day than eight hours, means getting
up at a more than abnormally early hour, and continually
hustling the camel-drivers to bring in their camels ; or it
means pitching your tents in darkness and getting dinner
very late.   In eight hours the caravan will accomplish
twenty miles, and the same distance can be got over on fair
hygeens in about four or five.   The start should be made
in advance of the baggage-camels so as to allow plenty of
time for shooting and for the mid-day halt.

Besides the discomfort to the traveller if camels are
constantly pressed to do more than eight hours, they do
not get sufficient time to feed ; as, when on the march, all
they can get, of course, is a mouthful of food snatched now
and then as they are travelling, and they *ought* to have
time given them to feed morning and evening.

ON THE MARCH.

The country gradually became less green as we augmented the distance between us and the sea; heavy clouds hung about, the air was close and sultry, and we had some heavy showers. We wound through some rocky hillocks before pitching our tents, and finally encamped in the sandy bed of a *khor* at a place called Siterabb, near the first water out from Souakim, and where there were a few huts belonging to the telegraph people.

The following morning a very wretched-looking old woman came to us with a piteous tale of how she had been robbed of her all—a few dollars she had saved—by the telegraph people. I gave her a dollar, and her joy was unbounded: she insisted not only on kissing my hand, but my boots; and I began to feel that there was such a thing as excess of gratitude—at any rate, that it could be expressed in too demonstrative a manner.

CHAPTER IV.

Journey continued.—Buck Gazelle shot.—More Trouble with the
Camel-drivers.—A rose-breasted Shrike.—Sand-storm at Ellegua.
—Jules taken ill.—Death in Camp.—Takroori Woman abandoned
by her People.—We divide the Camp.—Mishaps of those left
behind.—Christmas Day at Wandi.—"Molly."

THE country, as we travelled on, was monotonous, but not
unpicturesque, owing to the hills to our north and south,
and the glorious tints caused by the setting sun in a tropical
climate.

First, we traversed a sandy stretch with no bushes growing on it, only tufts of dried grass here and there; then
a patch of stony ground, covered with low mimosa-bushes
without leaves, but furnished with horrible thorns; followed
by a similar waste, with the addition of very occasional
nebbuk-bushes (*Rhamnus lotus*). This tree bears a fruit
very much resembling minute apples in appearance, about
the size of a hazel-nut: it is, however, not very palatable,
being dry. Juicy fruit is, perhaps, too much to expect in
such a burnt-up land.

In some parts of the country *nebbuk*-bushes are extremely
common: they are covered with very formidable thorns, as
are most of the bushes and trees of these regions; the
leaves are always green, and, when growing thickly together,
form an all but impenetrable jungle. The fruit is relished
by the Arabs, as well as by guinea-fowl, monkeys, and many
other animals.

We saw very little game, and what we did see was very
shy, and rendered additionally difficult of approach from
the very open nature of the ground, which made stalking
anything but an easy process. Aylmer was the first to draw
blood, having shot a buck gazelle the day before.

The next day we had some further trouble with our camel-drivers. We had started ahead of the caravan, and shot a couple of gazelles, when one of our native servants suddenly appeared to tell us that three of the camels were lost. This was all nonsense in reality, and only a ruse in order to give the camels more time to feed and to let the men dawdle about. We turned back, and when we met a number of the laden camels that had just started we unloaded some, and over-loaded others, so that we got two empty ones; with these we returned to our late camp, and loaded them with the baggage that was left, and which belonged to the camels supposed to be lost. We started them after the others as soon as possible; but it delayed us very much, and we only accomplished a six hours' march. The lost camels were soon found, and the baggage re-arranged.

We passed some huts in the afternoon, near to which water could be obtained, although two or three miles off the road, at a place called Sankereet: accordingly a camel was left behind to bring a supply, and we travelled on some distance farther before halting for the night.

Birds of any kind were very scarce; but Lort Phillips shot a rose-breasted shrike, a kind of butcher-bird I had never met with before.

December 20 was a blazing hot day, and the last on which we had any rain, and that only a slight shower early in the morning. We marched rather over ten hours to make up for lost time, journeying along a plain from twelve to fifteen miles wide, between the ranges of hills. *Khors* became rather more numerous, and were wider, showing that we were nearing a country where there was a greater rainfall: otherwise it wore much the same aspect, except for occasional *dhoum*-palms (*Crucifera Thebaica*), a new feature in the landscape.

A long halt being made in the middle of the day, darkness overtook us; and, losing what there was in the way of a path, we began to think the night would be spent in the open without any dinner. Our servants lighted great fires to guide us to the tents, and fired shots, so that at last camp was reached, but very late, as we had gone a considerable distance out of our way, the direct road having left the telegraph-poles some distance on its right. As a rule, the camel-path and the wire kept close together.

In the night a tremendous wind got up ; and all hands were busy driving in extra tent-pegs and tightening the ropes. The sand blew about in all directions, and half smothered us. Sleep was impossible, and I never spent a more disagreeable night. The name of this enchanting spot was Ellegua.

The following morning Jules complained of a bad attack of vomiting and diarrhœa. Our men declared that they must stop until noon to water and feed their camels, so that we did not feel that we had gained much by the long march of the previous day. The water was three miles away, in a gorge in the mountain. In order to hurry their movements, two or three of us faced the blinding storm, and went with them to the water ; and what with the heat and sand it was anything but a pleasant task. Had this operation, however, not been superintended, we should have been at Ellegua all day : as it was, we managed to get eight miles farther on our way, and pitched our tents near Khor Langeb.

The sand-storm continued, and we had the greatest difficulty in finding a spot where the ground was sufficiently firm to admit of our pitching the tents : the tempest, if possible, increased during the night.

Except that it was not so hot, it reminded me of my experience once in travelling by rail from Suez to Cairo. Then a violent Khamseen wind got up after we had started ; and, although all the windows were kept close, the sand on the floor was over a quarter of an inch deep. Some of the carriages ran off the rails, owing to the driving sand ; and in some places men had to go on ahead to sweep it off the rails before it was possible to proceed. The heat, too, was terrific, the thermometer in the wind marking 113° F. The sun was, of course, obscured by the sand, which rattled against the carriage-windows like hail. It is no joke to be living in tents in such a tempest, and it must be undergone to be thoroughly understood and appreciated.

There were a great many *dhoum*-palms near our encampment : previously we had only found them in ones and twos. There were, too, plenty of tamarisk-trees, which were here met with for the first time, and which we were glad to see, as they are a very favourite food of the camel.

We had to remain where we were the next day, as Jules was not well enough to go on. George, too, was unwell, and lay down all day in the tent ; and Suleiman, who was never ill, complained that "his stomach bite him plenty." The storm rather increased than decreased as the day wore on ; and we had considerable difficulty in securing the tents. To add to the general cheerfulness, a death took place in camp.

A day or two previously, a small band of Takroori pilgrims, returning from Mecca, had attached themselves to our caravan. The Takrooris came originally from Darfour. They have now, however, settled in the neighbourhood of Gallabat, on the Abyssinian frontier ; and the Egyptian Government has given them some land on a number of years' lease, where they cultivate *dhurra*.

The day before, the Takroori band had been joined by two more men of their tribe, whom we had overtaken on the road. We had not noticed them, and knew nothing of their presence, until Suleiman came to tell us about them, as one was ill. The doctor went to see what he could do for him, and found him lying on the ground, smothered in sand, and evidently *in extremis*. We administered brandy, and did what we could ; but he only lasted an hour. The man who was with him, and who said he was his brother, borrowed a spade from us, and buried him there and then. He had died, literally, of starvation and fatigue.

It appeared that these people had walked all the way from Gallabat to the coast, a distance of some hundreds of miles. On their return from Mecca, owing to cholera at Jeddah, and in order to escape quarantine at Souakim, they had landed on the African Coast, about a hundred miles south of that port. They were entirely without funds, and had lived on what they could beg from the Arabs, who are often kind to passing strangers. Such deaths in the desert

are doubtless of frequent occurrence, and are bound to be
so, while these long pilgrimages are undertaken, as they
often are, by old men and women almost totally unprovided
with means, and frequently possessing nothing but the strong
wish to see Mecca and die, which seems to bear them up,
and help them through apparently insurmountable difficulties.   The dead man's brother we looked after until our
arrival in Cassala, where he left us, and continued his
journey south to his home.   This event brought to light a
still more shocking occurrence that had taken place a few
days previously.

Among the Takrooris who had joined us soon after
leaving the coast, were two women, one of whom was rather
lame.   As she could not well trudge along with the rest of
the party, they simply left her behind to die in the desert;
although her husband was with her, it appeared that he
was perfectly satisfied to do so. · Unfortunately we knew
nothing of it until so long after she had been left behind
that it was impossible and quite useless to send after her.
She could quite well have ridden on one of our camels;
but such is the callousness to suffering, and total disregard
of life among these people, that no one of the drivers had
thought of asking her to do so.

A similar event took place when we were crossing the
Great Nubian Desert from Korosko, four years before : then
it was one of the camel-drivers that had been left behind
to die.   We knew nothing of it for several days after; and
when we expressed our horror at what had happened they
considered they had behaved in a really generous manner
by leaving him a small quantity of water and *dhurra*-flour.

The sand-storm continued the following day, and Jules
was too ill to move.   We decided on leaving him behind,
as we could not remain any longer at a place where there
was no water, and scarcely any food for the camels; for,
though fond of tamarisk-bushes, they would not live exclusively upon them.   Lort Phillips and the doctor remained
behind with the invalid.

After five and a half hours' march through a decidedly
less sandy country, we arrived at a *khor* called Wandi;

where there was more food for the camels than at the last
place, and, moreover, wells of tolerably good water. It
was only the second watering-place on our *direct* route we
had come across; and there were a few tents there, and
Arabs with sheep and goats.

The next day we spent in camp, hoping that the rest of
the party would overtake us. There being no signs of them,
on the following day, which was Christmas Day, I started
off by myself, on my camel, to see how they were getting
on; and in an hour's time I found them under a tree.

They had left the camp the previous afternoon late, so
as to avoid the heat of the sun. Their camel-men had
deserted them, and they had lost their way; so they slept
out under a tree, which was no hardship, as the nights were
warm, and there was no dew. On the morning that I
encountered them they had made a farther march of two
hours.

When we had left them at Khor Langeb, I had reminded
the doctor to see that he had plenty of medicine with him,
as I told him that, although the Arabs informed us water
was near at hand, I knew well from former experience that
they were not to be relied on to speak the truth, and that
we were bound to push on to water, even if it were two
days' journey distant. He had assured me that he had
kept plenty with him when we parted; and yet, thirty-six
hours after our departure, all the medicine was finished.
Lort Phillips had accidently discovered the presence of
dysentery, and told the doctor of it; when he found that
he not only had no medicine to check it, but had none of
any kind left.

I remained with Lort Phillips while the doctor went to
the camp for medicine : it was, however, eighteen hours
after the discovery that the disease had turned to dysentery,
before poor Jules had any medicine whatever.

In the cool of the afternoon, we went on to Wandi,
where we spent the rest of anything but a "merry Christmas."

Mahoom's master had presented him, before leaving
England, with a plum-pudding, and requested us to let the
boy know when it was Christmas Day, in order that he

might regale himself upon it. We did so; and he devoured it with evident satisfaction, doubtless considering the consumption of plum-pudding on that day to be one of the religious ceremonies of the British nation, to which he was exceedingly anxious to conform. He was a perfect specimen of the *genus* heathen, trained on the lines of Exeter Hall. He had brought with him, all the way from Edinburgh, a magnificent Christmas card, a veritable *chef d'œuvre* of De la Rue's. Intent on presenting my brother with this work of art, he entered his tent about midnight on Christmas night, waking him out of a sound sleep. I fear his kind intention was not appreciated; as, being only half awake, my brother was not able to take in what it all meant, and greeted him with language that would be anything but approved of by Exeter Hall. Poor Mahoom retired very much crestfallen; but, the *amende honorable* being made the next day, he was happy again. Mahoom was very much given to collecting wild-flowers; and, wearing a huge straw hat *minus* part of the brim, and clad in what we imagined to be a complete suit of his late mistress' underclothing, which he wore with a cord round his waist, he presented a well-dressed and decidedly original appearance, as he wandered about intent on his botanical pursuits. In consequence of the eccentricity of his attire he received the *sobriquet* of "Molly."

CHAPTER V.

We divide the Camp.—Part start for Cassala.—The Rest remain at
Wandi.—Continued Illness of Jules.—*Dhurra* runs short.—De-
parture from Wandi.—Khor Belag.—News of the First Party.—A
Deserted Village.—Omri.—The Belgian Doctor.—Halt at Khor
Rassay.—Pharaoh's Lean Kine.—Desolate Tract of Country.—
Scorpions.

WE decided on splitting camps; one-half of the party, with
the bulk of the luggage, to go on to Cassala, so as to
arrange, as far as possible, for another start by the time the
rest arrived. On the 27th they commenced their journey;
leaving Lort Phillips, my brother William, and myself
behind, with the doctor, of course, and Jules. It was very
dull waiting at Wandi: the heat was very great, and the
flies most troublesome. There was no game, with the
exception of a chance gazelle and a few sand-grouse, which
used to come for water morning and evening, when we shot
a few for food. They are not very good eating, being dry
and tasteless, and are grouse only in name as far as the
cuisine is concerned, though true grouse from a naturalist's
point of view.

We were at our wits' end to know what to do; sometimes Jules appeared to be getting better, and then again
he seemed weaker. We thought at one time of sending
him back to Souakim with George and the doctor, but
eventually decided to take him on to Cassala. We were
about half-way between the two places; and one objection
to sending him back to England was the voyage home, as
he suffered fearfully from sea-sickness.

We felt a move would have to be made soon, as the
dhurra was getting finished; the camel-drivers, who supply
their own, had exhausted their supply, and we had to give

them ours. The party that had preceded us to Cassala had promised to send us some as soon as they could procure any; but we knew it was not at all improbable that they would not be able to do so until they reached that town themselves. A breakdown had occurred in about the worst place where such a thing could have happened. Those that had gone on ahead had decidedly the best of it; for, although they had left us the cook and were obliged to do their own cooking, they were spared all anxiety as to what was to be done with Jules.

At last, finding that we could not remain any longer where we were, and by the advice of the doctor, who considered him rather better, and thought that it was important to get him to a place where such things as milk and eggs were obtainable, the order was given to continue our journey; and we left Wandi on the 31st.

We managed to purchase an *angareb* from an Arab. An *angareb* is a native bedstead made of wood, with strips of raw-hide stretched tightly across it. This we fastened to a camel, at right angles to the animal's back, and supported on two boxes; Jules' bed was placed on it, so that he could lie at full length; and, as a protection against the sun, some men we had hired at Souakim made a matting-cover stretched on sticks, and fastened it to the *angareb;* doors were made in it, which could be opened or shut at will. In this way he rode as easily as a sick man could well ride over such a country. We tried hard to get him and the doctor off very early in the morning; but the camels had been out feeding all night, and took a great deal of catching.

We made a six and a half hours' march, and encamped in a *khor* called Belag. Jules was not as much exhausted after the journey as we expected to find him : the dysentery had nearly stopped, but he was, of course, still very weak from its effects.

The country was most uninteresting and dreary, very sandy, with small hillocks covered with friable rock. We scarcely saw a living thing all day. The next day, the first of the new year, was very cool, with a high wind blowing, but no dust, a great relief after the heat we had lately been experiencing. The country, too, although anything but beautiful, was rather less monotonous than most of that we had lately traversed. The road wound in and out between low hills, so that one could not look far ahead. This, when travelling in an unpicturesque country, is far more agreeable than journeying over a level plain where you can see miles and miles before you ; there is always the excitement of a turn in the road, and the traveller can indulge in wonder as to what fresh object that turn may show him, in even the tamest landscape.

The post arrived from the other party, in the shape of a note fastened to a telegraph-pole, telling us where they had encamped the previous night, and that they were all well, which we were glad to hear, particularly as Colvin had been rather indisposed when he started.

We saw a few gazelles, and shot three, to the great delight of our men, who had not been troubled with a plethora of food for some time.

We halted awhile in the middle of the day at a place called Hadaiweb, where there was a palm-grove and water ; a most agreeable change after the country we had lately passed through. A short distance above the palm-grove, and on a slight eminence, we came upon a deserted village, or rather cluster of huts, which had evidently been inhabited at no distant date. The last occupants had left behind them cooking-pots, very neatly made mats, and chairs. These chairs were exactly like many of those made by the ancient Egyptians, to be seen in the Boulac Museum in Cairo, and which I have already mentioned. Some of the huts had holes in the ground where the women burn perfumes, over which they crouch in order to scent their bodies.

We soon came to *nebbuk*-bushes, for the first time in any number ; and also came across the aloe, besides passing several *khors* bordered with *dhoum*-palms. There were scarcely any birds : doves, which usually abound everywhere, were conspicuous only by their absence.

We made a march of nine and a half hours, and pitched our tents in a *khor* called Omri. There was a considerable

difference in the temperature of the nights about this time :
instead of the mercury falling no farther than 68° to 70°,
it varied from 50° to 55°, which was far from disagreeable
after the hot days.

On January 2, while on the march, we met a Belgian
doctor returning to the coast. He had been shooting with
a gentleman whom he had left in the neighbourhood of
Cassala, and had under his care a professional *chasseur*
who was suffering from sunstroke, and was very anxious to
return to his native " happy hunting-grounds " in Belgium.
He gave us a dreadful account of the heat and mosquitoes
at Cassala, and the unhealthiness of the place ; but as I
had once spent a fortnight there I was not alarmed by his
report.

Khors increased daily in number. We crossed one very
wide one called Aredey : it must have been fully two
hundred yards in breadth, with a thick belt of *dhoums* on
either bank. As there was water a little distance from
where we passed over, a camel was left behind to bring
some on. We encountered a jackal that the Arabs declared
every night set up an unearthly howling at the grave of a
man lately dead, who had murdered a number of his fellow-
creatures.

After an eight and a half hours' march, we spent the
night near a *khor* where there were more birds than we had
yet met with, and we saw green paroquets for the first time.
They flew about from one *dhoum*-palm to another, uttering
the most discordant cry. They are of the species so common
in India.

The following day we contented ourselves with a six and
a half hours' march, halting near Khor Rassay, a more than
usually wide river-bed, with a perfect forest of *dhoum*-palms,
and wells forty feet deep, dug in the sand. Here were
some huts, a few soldiers, and the Arabs about had plenty
of goats, so we revelled in fresh milk—a great boon for
Jules. We observed a few cattle much resembling
Pharaoh's lean kine, and thinking to give our men a treat,
sent Suleiman to bargain with their owners with a view to
the purchase of one of them. He very soon returned

saying that "the black people no sell hen bulls, only men bulls, this time of year." Although of a decidedly dusky hue himself, he invariably evinced a supreme contempt for those he was fond of designating as "black people."

A camel with *dhurra* met us here; the driver bringing a note from my brother to say he had paid five dollars for the camel's hire, and two and a half for the *dhurra*—very good pay; but the Arabs are sharp enough in finding out when you must ·have things, and one sometimes has to pay accordingly. The camel had come from Fillik, the only village on the road, and about forty miles from Cassala.

The day's work had been more than usually uninteresting. We crossed several *khors*, the country between being as desolate as it is possible to imagine. The mountains we had left, and saw no more till we came in sight of the great mountain at the foot of which lies Cassala, and found ourselves in a wide and stony plain, with a few stunted mimosa-bushes growing here and there. The heat, too, was very great, and we saw no game. The next two days' journeys, however, were even more trying. We had thought the country could not become uglier or more monotonous to traverse; but we soon found that it could —a perfectly level stretch of country to our right terminating in the horizon to our left, and in front of us a range of hillocks at a distance of some ten or twelve miles.

We occasionally crossed a *khor* bordered with a few bushes and sickly-looking *dhoum*-palms; the heat being intense, with a total absence of shade. For miles we passed over country without a bush, and covered with a perpetual mirage; then we would come to a strip on which grew a few dwarf mimosa-bushes. In parts the desert was covered with loose stones : as we neared Cassala, however, this gave place to a fine loamy soil, which, no doubt, with rain would be very fertile. Once we passed through what had been, after the rains, a *dhurra*-field. Of animal life, .we came across a few guinea-fowl, and saw a fine buck ariel, the first of the species we had seen since passing the herd near Souakim.

While the camels were being laden we observed a kind

of butcher-bird perch itself on the back of one of the camels, and make three darts, one after the other, for something hidden between the bags with which the animal was laden ; at its third dart, the bird fished up a scorpion, with which it flew off in great satisfaction, to devour at its leisure. Although we often came across scorpions, we were fortunate in never being bitten by any of them ourselves. Some of our servants, however, who slept on the ground, were not so lucky ; and Ali the cook was so badly bitten by one that the place did not heal for weeks. On the Cassala road we found a villainously ugly lizard, that lived in dead wood, and which the natives declared to be poisonous.

CHAPTER VI.

Arrival at Fillik. — The Gash. — Abundance of Game. — Cassala reached.—Encampment in the Dry Bed of the Gash.—-Caravans on the Cassala Road.—The Governor of Cassala.—Servants sent from Sanheit.—Death of Jules.

ON the 5th we arrived at Fillik, after two very long marches. This place is quite a town, or rather a collection of hamlets, built in a treeless, dusty, waterless plain; all the water required by the inhabitants has to be fetched from wells sunk in a *khor* some distance off, and below Fillik. The town, or village, is composed of conical-roofed huts, thatched with *dhurra* stalks. Being very straggling, it covers a great deal of ground, and is the permanent head-quarters of the Hadendowa tribe; the families of many of our camel-drivers lived there.

In the distance, a long way off, we saw a range of low mountains; the Cassala mountain was ahead, and just in sight; to our left, and all around us, was a great dismal plain, perfectly flat and without any vegetation. We halted inside the telegraph compound. Soon after our arrival, a telegram came from the governor of Cassala, ordering the authorities to send five soldiers to Wandi to our assistance.

The following day, as soon as we had seen the caravan off, we started to look for the Gash, the important *khor* on which Cassala is situated, and which, according to the map, runs very near Fillik. The ground fell a good deal for some distance after leaving the village. We soon came to a narrow *khor* bordered by very thick bushes and some good-sized trees; and, as there was considerable evidence of game, we did not trouble ourselves about the Gash.

The natives told us that a lion prowled about Fillik, and

had killed several people. We saw no signs of it; but when we met the rest of our party, they told us they had heard its roar quite distinctly, having passed at dusk within a couple of hundred yards of it, but, their rifles not being handy, they had concluded that discretion was the better part of valour.

There were swarms of doves of several varieties; and although, as a rule, these birds are extremely common throughout the Soudan, I am sure we had not seen more than half a dozen since leaving the coast. Guinea-fowl were plentiful, and there were many kinds of bright-plumaged birds—a most refreshing change. The only species of guinea-fowl we ever came across in Africa is the one with the blue comb and wattles. There were plenty of gazelles; and we saw for the first time the beautiful Dorcas gazelle (*Gazella Dorcas*), which, throughout the remainder of our journey, was far more numerous than the common variety (*Gazella Arabica*), which prefers the most arid desert. We saw, too, several herds of ariel, and had no difficulty in securing abundance of venison for our larder.

Three Houbara bustards were shot, and on our arrival in camp we found the cook-boy had caught one in a noose: we were glad to discover sporting tendencies in our servants. I never ate a more delicious bird than the bustard. It is but too frequently the case, that the game of these countries is dry and unpalatable—at any rate, it would be thought so in civilised countries—but this bird would be a great delicacy anywhere: its flesh when cooked is dark-brown and firm, very much resembling that of a goose, and it has a flavour entirely its own. Those we shot were very fat, in excellent condition, and were very good eating either hot or cold.

At a place called Miskenab in the *khor* we found deep wells of excellent water sunk in the sand; and we sent a camel with the water-skins to fetch some. We made a march of nine and a half hours, having an excellent day's shooting on the way.

Another long day's march of eight and a half hours brought us to Cassala, which we reached on the evening

GEBEL CASSALA.

of the 7th, twenty-four days out from Souakim. If there had been nothing to delay us, the journey should not have occupied more than twelve or thirteen days. My brother had accomplished the journey in thirteen days four years before we passed through the country; and that had allowed him a whole day's rest on the way.

Jules was, of course, much exhausted after the long journey; but the doctor declared that the dysentery had stopped, and he hoped with good food and rest he would soon begin to pick up his strength.

The day we arrived we spent in looking for game to the right and left of the path, but did not meet with nearly so much success as on the previous day. The aspect of the country was different from any we had passed through: it had, in fact, become quite park-like, and was dotted with numerous dark-green bushes very like laurels, and so neat-looking that they had quite the appearance of having been trimmed, the only drawback being that they sprang from dusty soil instead of from green grass.

We found the rest of our party quite well. They had been four days in Cassala, and had encamped about a mile from the town in the dry bed of the Gash, where it was some three or four hundred yards wide, close to the shade of a huge fig-tree, covered with dark-green leaves that afforded most grateful shade. We pitched a tent for Jules under it. Close by was a garden containing orange and lime-trees, watered all day long from a *sakeeyeh*, of exactly the same kind as the wheel so well known to Nile travellers by that name. The others had not been able to do anything towards buying or hiring camels, and of course all those we had brought from Souakim had to return to the coast: their drivers probably knew no other road, and spent their lives in going up and down. Arabs are wonderful fellows for getting into one groove and sticking to it, and are not at all fond of "fresh woods and pastures new."

We had met extremely few caravans on our journey; in fact, I never went over a beaten track in Africa and saw so little evidence of traffic or commerce. One day we met a caravan of seventy camels laden with *dhurra* and mats made of the fibrous leaf of the *dhoum*-palm. These are made by the women; they are very cheap, and used for many different purposes. Some of our servants slept upon them. We always spread them about the floor of our tents; but great holes were soon eaten in these by the destructive white ants, and they fell to pieces. When we stopped any length of time anywhere, and the trees did not afford us sufficient protection against the sun, we erected temporary shelters by sticking poles in the ground, on which, in a very short time, a kind of arbour could be formed by means of this matting; this was far cooler and preferable to sitting in our own tents during the daytime. The caravan in question was accompanied by about fifty men, besides women and children,—by far the largest we encountered. Sometimes several days elapsed during which we hardly met a camel. This was a very different state of things from what I had seen during previous visits to the country, when in travelling we frequently met long strings of a hundred, and even two hundred camels at a time. The road between Souakim and Cassala, however, though an important one, is not one of the main arteries for the commerce of the Soudan.

The natives had, so far, only brought an odd baggage-camel or two for sale; and for these, though not worth over twenty to thirty dollars apiece, they asked fifty or sixty. We had decided that, in order to visit the Basé country, it would be needful to buy our own camels, as the people had such a wholesome dread of the whole tribe that we knew it would be hopeless to endeavour to hire camels and drivers to take us there.

We found the governor of Cassala very polite. He was a small, insignificant-looking man, who spoke French fairly well, and seemed to give more energy to the management of his affairs than most of the Soudan officials we had previously encountered.

On leaving Cairo we had telegraphed to Père Picard, one of the priests belonging to the Roman Catholic mission at Keren (or, as the place is more usually called, Sanheit), asking him to send to Cassala certain servants that he had found for us the winter before. On our arrival we found a small army already assembled, four being old hands, and several having accompanied them on the chance of being employed. We were glad to see Salee, a most excellent tracker, who had proved his usefulness the previous year, among the number. The Abyssinians had come down during the summer near to Keren; and one of our old retainers had had a father, and another a brother, killed by them.

The afternoon after our arrival at Cassala the doctor informed us that he considered Jules' condition to be most critical; his pulse was very feeble, and he had been obliged to give him egg, milk, and brandy, beaten up together, to try and keep up his strength. This was the first intimation we received of his being in a really critical condition; we had all hoped that, as the dysentery had stopped, he would soon regain his strength, as he was of a naturally robust constitution. We had been discussing the advisability of sending him to Sanheit with one of the European servants and the doctor, if necessary, to await our arrival there, as we knew the climate to be cool, and, moreover, were sure that he would receive every attention at the hands of the priests. The next day he was weaker, and gradually sank, dying about half-past ten on the evening of the 9th.

I walked up to the town immediately afterwards, and informed the governor of what had happened, so as to make arrangements for the funeral, which we knew could not be long delayed in so hot a climate. They made a rough deal coffin, covered over with dark-blue cloth; and our native servants carried him to the grave the next morning. A Greek merchant, long resident in Cassala, had given a piece of ground for a Christian burial-place in a corner of a palm and lime grove inside the walls of the town; and there we laid him, covering the coffin with the British flag. The heat was terrific and the dust suffocating. To me fell the painful duty of reading the burial-service— a sad office, which I had never expected to be called upon to fulfil. Two Greeks were the only people present besides our own party and servants.

Jules had lived in Lort Phillips' family for over seventeen years; and he was greatly distressed, as we all were, at the death of an old and faithful servant, so far from his home and friends.

CHAPTER VII.

Purchase of Camels. — Expedition to the Atbara. — The Village of Naouri. — Mosconas and his Son. — White Ants. — Dinner with the Governor. — The Town of Cassala. — Hyænas. — Pariah Dogs. — Collections for European Zoological Societies. — Departure from Cassala. — Bashi-Bazouks.

As we found it impossible to purchase camels at Cassala, Colvin and my brother Arthur started off with Suleiman at seven o'clock on the evening of the 10th of January for the Atbara River, where they had heard plenty were to be obtained. They were back again by half-past one on the afternoon of the 15th, having purchased a number of baggage - camels, which, taking one with another, had averaged thirty-four dollars apiece; a rather high price, as there were some poor ones among them. The Arabs had not been at all keen to sell, and they had experienced great difficulty in coming to terms with them. They had ridden across a flat, ugly country, overgrown with mimosa-bushes, and, after following the track leading to Khartoum for about twenty miles, bore to the north-west, and encamped for the night. After a very early start the next morning they separated, and went in different directions in order to acquaint the inhabitants of the various villages with the object of their journey. This had to be done circumspectly, and the subject introduced in the most off-hand and careless manner. After considerable time had been spent in "pow-wows" with the sheiks, or head men, of the different villages, they met again, and pitched their tent near a village called Naouri, on the edge of a cliff overlooking the River Atbara,—truly a magnificent stream, and the most important tributary of the Nile. Naouri, belong-

ing to the Shukreeyeh tribe, is forty-five miles from Cassala.
It was a very large village when they saw it, containing
some thousands of Arabs. The houses consisted of mat
huts. These huts the natives take about with them ; and
during the rains there would be no trace of Naouri, as the
inhabitants move farther north, with all their goods and
chattels, to return to the same spot the following year,
when Naouri would again be called into existence. This
place is only a few miles north of a large permanent village,
called Kourashi, chiefly inhabited by fakirs, a kind of
dervishes, who have schools there. The following day,
about noon, camels and their owners began arriving from
all quarters. A trade anything but brisk followed. The
Arab, like all Orientals, delights in long bargainings, time
being of no object to him. We had already lost a great
deal of time, and were impatient to get on ; so, Colvin
and my brother having given a good price for the two first
camels offered for sale, it quickly opened the market : and,
acting on the system of buying at once, or sending the
animal away, by evening they found themselves the posses-
sors of about five-and-twenty camels. Although they
selected the best they could find, most had the hideous
wounds on the back and hip-bones that the majority of
baggage-camels have; these they at once doctored with
carbolic acid. At length they came to a very fine animal,
without mark or blemish, which they had purchased at an
apparently reasonable price, and which they were consequently rather proud of. However, they noticed a derisive
grin on the faces of the natives standing by ; and, on seek-
ing an explanation for their mirth, were informed that the
prize was an *abou gamāl,* or father of many camels, but
being old and of no further use in that capacity, he was
sold to us to do what we could with. At night a severe
sand-storm arose, which nearly capsized their tent, and,
of course, filled everything—beds, water, and food—with
sand.

The following day the purchase of camels was continued.
More cripples were brought in, which their owners attempted
to impose on our party, inexperienced in camel-flesh. When-

ever an offer was made, the invariable reply, accompanied by a jerk back of the head, was " Efta Allah," literally, " God open," and so, " May God open your mouth so that you may speak bigger words." However, by about mid-day they had completed their purchases, paid over the money, and struck camp. They then noticed a disposition on the part of the late vendors to abstract their camels : so revolvers were drawn, the camels tied as well as possible in the usual manner—nose to tail—and the homeward march commenced about 5 P.M.

A great deal of trouble was experienced in following the track, which they occasionally missed entirely ; and it was only by observing the stars that they were enabled to keep in the right direction, as the natives, having sold their camels and having nothing further to expect, refused to render any assistance, and in all probability hoped they would lose both their way and their camels. They pushed on all night, only stopping to re-fasten the ropes, which, for the first few hours, the camels were continually breaking ; and halted for a few minutes at daybreak to allow time for eating a few biscuits and dates, and reached our camp at Cassala about two o'clock the next afternoon. After a march of over twenty hours, and having been almost without food for twenty-four, naturally they were much exhausted.

During their absence we had not passed a very lively time : we had shot a few doves, and I obtained a marabou stork, the first seen. A more ugly, ungainly bird does not exist, and he is a regular scavenger ; but the beautiful white feathers that grow underneath the tail-coverts are much prized by ladies. Marabous must be endowed with marvellous digestive powers. An Englishman told me that when he was shooting in the Soudan he shot a lion, and soon afterwards missed his claws. He suspected some marabous that had been lurking about to be the thieves ; and, on shooting and dissecting two or three, found most of his lion's claws in their stomachs.

We saw a good deal of a very intelligent Greek, named Mosconas, and his son, the latter suffering greatly from

E

rheumatism.[1]   They were endeavouring to sink some wells
between Cassala and the Atbara, and also between that
river and Gedariff, a town to the south-west, in the midst
of a very rich district, where a great deal of *dhurra* as well
as tobacco is grown.   Although they had gone to a great
depth they had not succeeded in reaching water; and they
felt that success was very doubtful.

Lort Phillips made a cross of mimosa-wood, which is
very hard, for Jules' grave, to remain until he could send
a stone out from Egypt.   All wood perishes after a short
time in consequence of the white ants, which are nowhere
more persistent than at Cassala.   We had met with them
on the road, but to no great extent, and had been able to
regard them more in the light of entomological curiosities
than as plagues; here, however, we had to be very careful
not to leave anything that could be injured by their attacks
on the ground for any length of time.   Canvas sacks, or
such things as socks, they would eat through in one night,
or damage so [much that holes would very soon appear in
them ; they were particularly partial to leather, and com-
mitted great havoc among our gun-cases and portmanteaus.

Before commencing their depredations they cover whatever they intend to eat with earth, and work from inside
this covering : this I believe they do in order to protect
themselves from their natural enemies, the black ants,
which are always to be found not far off, on the look-out
for them.   The longer we stayed the more persistent they
became in their attacks; and it was only by occasionally
shifting our tents that we could obtain any peace.   The
boxes that contained our provisions, etc., had been made
with little legs to rest upon, so that they had to build up
these legs before they could obtain a footing inside : nevertheless they *would* get in, and we often found quantities
of them, and the earth they had brought, covering whatever the boxes contained, the paper used to wrap up various
things being frequently entirely destroyed.   In this way,

---

[1] This poor fellow was afterwards killed when with Baker Pasha
at El Teb, and his father described to me how he identified his body
on the battlefield days after his death.

unless great precautions were taken, cartridges would sometimes get spoilt. In many parts of the country they are so
troublesome that it is found cheaper to use iron telegraph-
poles instead of wooden ones, as the latter have so frequently
to be renewed.

One evening we dined with the governor, in Turkish
fashion, eating with our fingers instead of using knives and
forks,—a not very delectable form of entertainment. The
dinner was served on a large brass tray placed on a circular
table, round which all sat, including some Egyptian officers
who had just arrived after a long march, and apparently had
not fed for a considerable time. Behind us, immovable as
statues and holding lamps above their heads, were some
five or six White Nile slaves. The sweet and meat courses
alternated throughout dinner, a rather trying ordeal for the
European palate; but, on the slightest sympton of flagging
on our part, the hospitable Bey immediately insisted that
we did not like our fare, upon which we were obliged to
renew our efforts. We were provided with an immense
number of dishes, twenty-five courses all told, including the
inevitable sheep roasted whole, head and all. Once, when
assisting at a similar entertainment, the attentive host gouged
the sheep's eye out with his thumb and finger, and was
anxious to put it in my brother's mouth, a mark of attention
he had some difficulty in resisting.

Cassala, next to Khartoum, is the largest town in the
Egyptian Soudan, and contains a population of about fifteen
thousand, besides a considerable garrison of soldiers. It
is a walled town, and presents a very animated appearance
every morning, when crowds of people, men and women,
resort to a large open space, where they hold a market,
sitting many of them under rough booths formed of matting supported on poles, as some protection against the
fierce rays of a tropical sun; here they sell various kinds
of food, cooked and uncooked, beads, gum, pepper, beans,
mats, etc.

The province in which Cassala is situated is one of the
richest in the Soudan. The country round the town is
very fertile, and a certain amount of cotton of excellent

quality is grown, besides onions, which are very large and mild, and somewhat resemble those grown in Spain; tomatoes also thrive well, and various nondescript vegetables are cultivated.

For some miles up and down the Gash there are a number of *sakeeyehs,* or water-wheels, of the same kind as those used so much in Egypt; by their means a plentiful supply of water for irrigation is obtained.

Anything would grow here, as the soil is very rich; but the people are very lazy and unenterprising, and all they care about is to produce enough for their absolute necessities: they do not attempt to grow anything new. The great drawbacks that any one would have to contend against, who wished to try and develop the resources of the country, where such a thing as cotton, for instance, might be cultivated to any extent, are the laziness and apathy of the inhabitants, hostility to innovation, and the cost of transit. As regards labour, I really believe it would be necessary to introduce fellaheen, a most industrious class, from Egypt; and I understand that the experiment has been tried to a very limited extent, and with success, on the White Nile. I am afraid that very few of the agriculturists of the Soudan have studied Adam Smith carefully.

A few years ago an enterprising Englishman, after great trouble and considerable expense, built a flour-mill at Cassala, with which he was able to grind *dhurra* for about one-eighth the price the natives are accustomed to pay for it. However, popular superstition was too much for him; they refused to have their *dhurra* ground in his mill, as they said it was "*affreet,*" or pertaining to the devil, so, after struggling on for some time, he was obliged to give it up; and the deserted mill now remains as a memorial to the ignorance of the inhabitants.

A great deal of *dhurra* was growing when we were there; and caravans laden with this grain constantly arrived from the south, a great deal of it being brought by the Arabs as taxes. The government often buy it, paying the Shukreeyeh Arabs, who bring it from the neighbourhood of Gallabat and Gedariff, and the Hamrans, when they send any from their country on the Settite River, with salt instead of money.

Cassala is rich in hyænas, chiefly the spotted variety, although we did not find them as numerous as we had done four years before; then we saw one night fully a hundred quarrelling over the dead body of a donkey. Aylmer's horse died, and we dragged its body out on the sand, some little distance from our tents: we had cause to regret having done so, however, as night was rendered hideous by the frightful noises of these animals. Nothing of the horse was left by the morning. They are often very bold, and would not only come close to our tents, but one night one of them had the impudence to walk inside while we were in bed; on another occasion, a hyæna absconded with one of a pair of hide sandals that had been left close by the tent-door.

Occasionally we shot one or two, whose attentions were a little too marked, in the neighbourhood of our camp; but we soon learnt that hyænas were a part of the sanitary arrangements of Cassala, where the whole refuse of the town is thrown outside the walls for these animals to devour at night. They live in holes in the ground, which they dig out for themselves; and we frequently came across them. Although most cowardly animals, they are said sometimes to attack people either when they can take them unawares or when they are in very large numbers. A short time before we arrived in Cassala a woman and child were killed by one as they lay asleep. The pariah dogs, too, were most troublesome. One night one of them entered our camp and abstracted two sand-grouse pertaining to Ali. Suleiman caught the culprit, and begged us the next morning to allow him to "give dog kill;" suggesting, as a means of getting rid of the animal, to give him "shield in stomach." Suleiman invariably confused a spear with a shield.

Cassala has for a long time been the headquarters of several Germans, who are engaged in collecting wild animals to sell in Europe to the various zoological societies and menageries. When we were there they had captured several young lions, an ant-eater, leopards, wild-cats, and various species of antelopes, to say nothing of quite a number of giraffes and ostriches. The giraffes used to be promenaded about the bed of the Gash very frequently for exercise. We were told they were very troublesome to get to the coast, as they had most decided wills of their own, and required several men to look after each animal. Formerly large sums were made by this trade; but, like many others, the number of people engaged in it has increased, and the natives who catch the animals expect more for them than used to content them. A few ostriches were kept for their feathers. We saw some that had lately been plucked: they had not a feather on them, and wonderfully ugly they looked.

It was the 17th of January before we turned our backs on Cassala, and the mountain at the foot of which it lies: this mountain rises behind the town, and is a conspicuous object in the level plain for miles around. Its sides are so precipitous that I doubt the possibility of getting to the summit.

On the day of our start we received two or three papers dated London, December 10: they had arrived *viâ* the Nile and Khartoum. No mail had reached Cassala by the Red Sea route for over a month, and we expected it would be a long time before we received any news from the outside world.

The governor gave us three soldiers; and it was arranged that they were to go with us as far as Haikota, where we proposed making a *zariba* [1] in which to deposit what baggage we wished to leave behind; and they were to remain there to guard it. We had fully determined to take no soldiers with us beyond Haikota, even if (which was more than doubtful) the Bey would have given us any for that purpose; for we knew well, from former experience, that nothing paralysed one's movements so much as soldiers when attempting to go off the ordinary beaten track. As a rule, they are a lazy, idle, good-for-nothing set, ever quarrelling with one's camel-drivers, and greatly hated and

---

[1] A *zariba* is a hedge formed of the prickly trees of the country, and is intended for a protection against wild beasts and men, should there be any of hostile intent lurking about at night.

dreaded by the independent Arabs of the country ; and no wonder, for the soldiers are perpetually bullying them, and think nothing of stealing their sheep, or anything they can lay hands upon.

By far the worst soldiers in the Soudan are undoubtedly the irregulars (Bashi-Bazouks) ; and I can fully indorse the opinion of Lieutenant-Colonel Stewart in his report on the Soudan recently presented to Parliament. In pointing out the great harm done by employing the Bashi-Bazouks in the collection of the taxes, he says : " Many, if not most, of these men, are very indifferent characters. They are mostly swaggering bullies, robbing, plundering, and ill-treating the people with impunity. Probably for every pound that reaches the treasury these men rob an equal amount from the people. They are a constant menace to public tranquillity. As soldiers they are valueless, having no discipline; nor, except in talk, do they exhibit any extraordinary courage."

CHAPTER VIII.

Journey from Cassala.—Game shot by the Way.—The dog-faced
Baboon.—Arrival at Haikota.—The German "Animal-catcher."—
Visits from two Sheiks.—Sheik Achmed Ageer.—Attack on the
Beni-Amers by the Basé.—Fresh Supply of Camels.—Dinner to
Sheik Achmed and the German.—Success of the Magic-Lantern.

THE first day from Cassala we accomplished a march of
four and a half hours, travelling for some distance in the
bed of the Gash ; then we crossed to its south bank, passed
through some fields in which excellent crops of *dhurra*,
nearly ripe, were growing; and encamped in a plain at
some little distance from a large village, composed of mat
huts, and tenanted by numerous hungry-looking dogs, that
barked savagely on our approach.

Not long after starting from Cassala we found it necessary to disarm one of our escort, and though thereby
diminishing our fighting force certainly added to our own
safety. Our three Egyptian soldiers were armed with guns
of a decidedly obsolete pattern, of the use of which they
were almost as ignorant as a militia-man of his Martini, but
having more curiosity on the subject ; one of them, while
we were on the march, desirous of exhibiting his prowess in
the use of fire-arms, fired at a crow that was sitting on the
ground. Owing to a slight defect in the sighting of his rifle,
the bullet just missed one of our baggage-camels, and grazed
George's arm, who was riding on another in the caravan.

The next day we followed a regular caravan-route, which
ran not far from the Gash, on its south bank. A thick
grove of *dhoum*-palms lined either side, and we passed one
or two small villages.

We came across game, and shot two ariel and a gazelle.
Partridges were seen for the first time, and one or two added

to the bag; a more acceptable addition to the larder, although they were not such good eating as chickens, notwithstanding the fact that the domestic fowl, as bred in the Soudan, is a most diminutive and skinny bird.

We saw, for the first time, the baobab-tree (*Adansonia digitata*). This well-known tree, so frequently described in books of African travel, became henceforth a familiar feature in the landscape : it is most weird and elfish-looking, having a gigantic trunk, giving out branches altogether disproportionate to its size, and, at the time of year we travelled, was entirely without leaves. The fruit, which is white and dry, grows in an oval green pod, and has a rather agreeable acrid flavour, but a little goes a long way. The natives are very fond of it, and we were told that the Basé frequently lived on it for a long time together; besides eating it raw, they pound it up, mix it with water, and cook it.

On the third day out from Cassala, as we were breaking up camp, we noticed a caravan loaded with *dhurra* going by; and soon after, hearing a great disturbance going on amongst the camel-drivers, we rushed down to the spot where the altercation was taking place, and found that the caravan had been stopped by some soldiers, who were endeavouring to levy black-mail. The camel-drivers resisted, but, although numerically superior, were no match for the soldiers, with their rifles and sword-bayonets, which they had no hesitation in using. They had already rendered one man *hors de combat* by a violent blow in the stomach when we interfered; and having heard all sides of the question—or rather the question from all sides, as they all spoke at once —we comprehended that the soldiers, having to support themselves when on the march as best they can, feel it incumbent on themselves to do so at the unfortunate Arabs' expense, backed by the tacit consent of the authorities; and, consequently, the appearance of a "tarboosh" (or fez) causes the Arab to fly with his property. We gave strict orders that none of our servants were to wear the "tarboosh" while in this country.

Almost immediately after leaving the camp we saw the fresh tracks of elephants, which we followed; they took us

to the Gash, where we found a good deal of water on the
surface where the bed was rocky, and narrower than we had
previously seen it.   This was the only place between
Cassala and Haikota where the water in the Gash rose to
the surface of its own accord—what the natives, in their
peculiar Arabic, call *moieh sarkit*. *Moieh* is the ordinary
Arabic for water; but it is difficult to find an English
equivalent for the word *sarkit*, an expression only made
use of in the Soudan, and employed in a great variety of
ways. For instance, when we once stood a chance of
being lost in crossing a desert, by nearly taking what appeared to be a path, but which in reality was not one, and
led miles away into the Sahara—on asking where the supposed path led, we were told *atmoor sarkit*, that is, "only
to the desert."   Again, on starting off alone anywhere, you
would be asked if you were going *sarkit;* meaning by
yourself, without taking any one with you.

Some natives, watering their goats, informed us that a
herd of elephants had drunk there the day before; their
marks led in the direction of the Settite River.   These
animals travel great distances, and when disturbed on the
Gash usually make for the Settite, and *vice versâ*.

I never saw more sand-grouse than at this place; the
ground was literally covered with them, packed so closely
together that it appeared impossible for another bird to
wedge itself in.   When they rose, as we approached, the
air was fairly rent with their peculiar guttural cry.   The
Arabs call them *gatta*, and this word is supposed to sound
like the noise they make when on the wing.

There were baboons, too, sitting on the rocks, the
Cynocephalus or dog-faced variety (*Cynocephalus hamadryas*),
hideous animals, which one frequently sees depicted in the
ancient Egyptian sculptures.   There are two kinds in
North-Eastern Africa, one much rarer than the other.   In
the spring of 1881 an Austrian travelled with us in the
same steamer from Massawa to Suez, who had with him
sixty-five of the rarer species alive; he was taking them to
Hamburg, where he made a large sum by their sale.   He told
us it was the first time that any had been brought alive to

Europe. Both kinds are very savage in confinement : in a wild state they are not very shy, and often approach pretty close to the traveller. They appear to be regular in their habits, visiting the same localities every day and at much the same time in quest of food ; and sleeping every night at the same place, usually on rocks in most inaccessible places, to be out of the reach of leopards or other enemies. We occasionally came across the pretty little green monkey (*Cercopithecus griseo-viridis*), generally met with only in thick jungle and near the banks of rivers. We had bought several in Cairo some years before, and taken them to England, where they proved most amusing pets. Two which I had thrived very well for three winters in a stable, after which I gave them to the Zoological Society in Regent's Park, where they very soon died.

The country gradually gave more promise of game, the trees became more numerous, and the covert thicker. To our right was a range of mountains clothed to their summits with trees, among them baobabs, as well as other varieties, some of considerable size.

We spent our third night in the dry bed of the Gash, close to a large encampment of mat huts, belonging to the Beni-Amer tribe, and called Ashbirah—a very picturesque spot. There was abundance of dry grass ; and numbers of sheep and goats, as well as large herds of cattle, were grazing on it for some miles round the village.

Our Arabs declared, for some reason only known to themselves, that Haikota was too far off to reach that night ; and the next morning we discovered it was only three-quarters of an hour farther on, at which we were much annoyed, as it gave us the trouble of packing up our traps only to unpack them again almost immediately.

Partridges were very numerous, a species of francolin ; and in the long grass and dwarf *dhoum*-palm jungle, where we found them, they rose well, and afforded capital sport. In open places they generally run on ahead of the sportsman, and are most unwilling to rise, reminding one of the habits of the French partridge at home. We shot, too, a fine male specimen of the Abyssinian hornbill (*Buceros*

Abyssinicus), or *abou gumba*, as it is called by the natives.
It is a most curious-looking bird, nearly the size of a turkey,
black, with a few white feathers in the wings. The beak is
thick, and over it protrudes a horn-like substance, the front
of which is hollow; it has enormous red-and-blue wattles.
It was the first time we had seen one, though we frequently met them afterwards, usually in parties of two or
three; but they were extremely shy, and rarely permitted
us to get within gun-shot. We also found quail for the
first time, but not in any numbers.

Haikota is a large village situated in the bed of the
Gash, and formed of the usual mat huts. We encamped
on the right bank of the *Khor*, some feet above the sand.
It took some time to clear a space for the camp, which
involved clearing away a number of bushes and cutting
down a quantity of high grass. This done, we set to work
to make a *zariba* to keep the Arabs off as much as possible;
former experience of such places having taught us that
we might expect them in dozens to inspect the "Inglees,"
their goods and chattels.

Our camp we placed close to that of a German animal-
catcher, a very agreeable fellow, who had spent eight
winters in the Soudan, and whose acquaintance some of
us had made four winters previously on the Settite. He
had built himself a house, as well as several sheds for his
animals; and when we arrived he had three young elephants and fifteen baby ostriches in his compound. He
told us that he had paid the Arabs as much as two hundred
and fifty dollars apiece for elephants. Every summer he
went to Europe; he obtained the best prices for his animals
in New York, which he had visited twenty-three different
times. As he very kindly offered to take charge of the
luggage that we wished to leave behind, we gladly accepted
his offer, and accordingly dismissed the soldiers, to the
evident relief of the population, who appeared to have a
wholesome dread of them.

The chief, and in fact only, wealth of these Beni-Amer
Arabs consists of flocks and herds, of which they possess
vast numbers. When the pasturage is exhausted in one

HAIKOTA.

part of the country, Haikota shifts its quarters, and moves, huts and all, to another.

Our first visitor was the Sheik El-belad, or head man of the village, a fine-looking old gentleman, with an immense head of gray woolly hair. We informed him of our wish to shoot in the Basé country, to which he raised no objection whatever, and seemed to regard it as a mere promenade. Later on, the sheik of the whole of that part of the country —a far more important personage—arrived. The German had informed us that he had had a good many dealings with him ; that he was by far the most powerful man in the country, much looked up to and implicitly obeyed by his people. His name was Achmed Ageer, and he was said to be the second sheik in rank of the Beni-Amer tribe, one of the largest and most powerful in Eastern Africa. A tall, lithe, wiry, well-built man of about fifty, he was in appearance a perfect specimen of his class, and was quite the best-mannered, most plausible Arab sheik I had ever met. I have often wondered during the present crisis in the country what course he was pursuing. In any arrangements entered into with the Beni-Amer tribe I feel sure he would side with us if properly approached, for he had a genuine admiration for Englishmen, and was actually so far well informed as to mention, without any prompting on our part, the names of public men, such as Lord Beaconsfield and Mr. Gladstone.

When we first disclosed our wishes to him he endeavoured to throw obstacles in the way of their attainment. He told us that no Englishman had ever travelled or shot in the Basé country before, with the exception of a Mr. Powell, who with his wife and child had been murdered by them some years before ; that the previous winter two Austrians had arrived in his country, to whom he had given guides to go some thirty miles up the Gash, but no farther. He suggested our writing to the governor of Cassala to ask his aid in the matter, and said that, through a sheik who lived near Amedeb (an Egyptian military station to the north of the Basé country), we should be able to penetrate into their territory. We knew, however, that this was the last way to set to work to gain our point, as the sheik in question was friendly to the government, and had nothing to do with the part we were anxious to visit. We told him that he alone could help us; that we had been in the Soudan before, and had come again on purpose to shoot and travel among the Basé, and we trusted to him to aid us. After a very long discussion, and a number of cups of coffee had been drunk and cigarettes smoked, he acceded to our wishes, and promised to help us. We explained to him that we were anxious to go along the Gash, or Mareb as it is called farther up, as far as the Abyssinian frontier, and then across country to the Settite, returning along the river, and crossing over to Haikota. He did not absolutely promise that we should carry out the whole of this programme, but he said we might follow the course of the river's bed as far as the Abyssinian frontier at any rate, and that then he thought we should have no difficulty in finding some Basé who would show us a road across to the Settite, as the banks of that river were inhabited by people belonging to that tribe, who, as we had already understood, lived to the east of the Hamrans, and between them and the Abyssinians.

As soon as Achmed Ageer had promised us his aid in travelling through the Basé country, he said that in order to go there it was essential we should take some of his horsemen; after much discussion we arranged to take four (he had at first proposed our taking ten !), and to pay them at the rate of twenty-five dollars apiece a month. Two or three of these braves were supposed to speak the Basé language, but we afterwards found that only one of them could do so; this man rejoiced in the euphonious appellation of Bayrumphy, and was supposed to have lived for two years in the country.

Although, of course, it was essential to have some one with us who knew the language, we were well aware that four horsemen would prove a great encumbrance; particularly as we should be obliged to feed their horses, as well as themselves. We knew, however, that it was a kind of tax paid to the sheik for his help in our plans, and regarded it accordingly.

The Beni-Amer Arabs about Haikota are the only people who have any dealings with the Basé, as it is only there that any are found who are conversant with the language. The Beni-Amers farther north, living on Khor Baraka, have no dealings whatever with them, and are much afraid of them.

Although, when travelling in the country, we came across one or two sheiks who, we were told, had jurisdiction over the whole country, I had not much faith in them; for each village has its own chief, and the people of the different villages are constantly quarrelling with each other, and I do not believe that any responsible heads exist.

Only a few days before our arrival at Haikota a number of Basé had come down from one of their villages and made an attack on some Beni-Amers. They were mostly boys or old men who were looking after their flocks, only two or three miles from the village itself. Twenty-seven of them they killed, and drove off about three thousand head of cattle. Sheik Achmed Ageer informed us that he was then meditating reprisals, and gave us a most pressing invitation to unite our forces with his. When we first heard this piece of news we thought it would entirely interfere with our going among them. We learnt, however, that the people who made the attack lived at some little distance to the south of the Gash, and off our intended route; and that, moreover, they were at enmity with that part of the tribe we proposed visiting.

As we thought it would be well to take with us more camels than we required for our baggage, knowing that some of those we had would be sure to die, or become useless, we arranged to hire several. In consideration of our paying for them at a very high rate—namely, twelve dollars a month each, as well as feeding the drivers—we induced some Shukreeyehs to accompany us with their camels. We hoped to add considerably to our *impedimenta* in the shape of skins and heads while in the country; and knew that no camels could be obtained from the Basé, who do not possess any. We were delayed to buy a further supply of *dhurra;* as with so many mouths to feed, both men and horses, it disappeared at a surprising rate.

On one occasion we exhibited the magic-lantern, to the intense delight of a large crowd who came after dinner on purpose to see it, and had never seen anything so wonderful before. We worked the lantern from the inside of a tent, with a sheet hung in front of the door. We always commenced the show by displaying portraits of the Queen and Prince of Wales : these were both very popular and invariably re-demanded. We had been careful before leaving England to choose subjects for the slides that we thought would interest them; and their exhibition was always successful. The most popular consisted of a series of animals found in Africa, such as the lion, hippopotamus, elephant, etc.; and when we displayed a representation of a man escaping up a tree from a crocodile, with the beast opening and shutting its mouth, and trying to seize him, they fairly shrieked with laughter.

Some of the slides represented the Suez Canal, English scenes, caravans in the desert, African villages, etc.; and all these were explained to them in Arabic, to their intense delight, while the Arabic was translated into their own tongue for the benefit of those who did not understand that language. As a termination to the entertainment we sent up one or two rockets, and lighted a Bengal light or two ; by which time our reputation as wonderful magicians was fairly established among them. As a hint that the show was over and that it was time for the crowd to retire, we hit upon the expedient of conducting the sheik by the light of a Bengal light to his horse, which was in waiting for him outside our *zariba*. The result was a most happy one ; a veritable *retraite aux flambeaux* took place, and the camp was cleared in less than five minutes.

F

CHAPTER IX.

Departure from Haikota.—Abundance of Game.—Halt at Toadelook. —*Tetel.*—Adventure with a Lion on the Prowl.—A Shooting Expedition. — Fifty-seven Sand-grouse netted.—Night-watches in hopes of a Shot.

WE left Haikota on January 22, and very glad we were to make a fresh start. So far our journey, owing to unavoidable circumstances, had been a very slow one; but delays are the inevitable adjuncts of African travel. We were getting very tired, too, of the crowds of natives that surrounded our tents more or less all day. We were fortunate, however, in not having any of our *impedimenta*, that lay about the camp in all directions, stolen: in fact, during such expeditions to Africa we have always found the Arabs whom we encountered wonderfully honest folk, and scarcely lost anything through theft the whole time.

Among other visitors at Haikota we were more than once favoured with a visit from an Abyssinian chief of the Walkait country, who was at Haikota "on business" connected with Sheik Achmed, and was accompanied by his son, a most amusing boy, who played on a curious stringed instrument and sang to us. He really had some slight idea of singing; but his songs were very monotonous and dirge-like compositions, and were sung in his own language, which none of us understood, but we were told they were redolent of the praises of the "Inglees."

Before starting we presented Sheik Achmed with a very good tent we had bought in Cairo, with which he was much pleased. I greatly doubt if he would make much use of it, as the sheiks generally prefer to live among their people, in the same kind of huts as they do, so that in case of an

attack by a bordering tribe, the chief's dwelling may not be
conspicuous.

During our last night at Haikota we heard two lions
roaring near the camp, which we thought augured well for
the sport we anticipated having in the Basé country. The
neighbouring country is more picturesque than any we had
seen so far. On either bank of the Gash was a thick fringe
of *dhoum*-palms, backed by a range of mountains, greener
than any we had yet come across; while in the river's bed
crowds of Arabs, men, women, and children, and immense
herds of cattle, sheep, and goats, lent animation to the
scene.

It was half-past four before the last of our caravan was
under way. We crossed the Gash, and, after riding for
some distance through a grove of *dhoum*-palms, recrossed
it, thus cutting off a great bend, and pitched our tents
above its bed, having gone only about six miles. There
were wells sunk in the sand close to where we encamped,
and Arabs watering large herds of goats. We were, luckily,
quite independent of the Arabs in regard to milk, as, in
addition to several sheep, we had a number of goats, all
presents from the sheik. He himself started with us, so as
to see us fairly on our way, appearing highly to appreciate
our " flesh-pots ;" and we began to think he intended spending the rest of the winter in our camp.

The whole country swarmed with guinea-fowl, and there
were plenty of partridges. We frequently shot the former
for the pot, and cooked them in a variety of ways, but
found them best of all curried. I think, too, they were
not quite so dry as those one eats in England, where I
regard them as the driest bird that comes to the table.
Shooting them is not much sport unless they chance to fly
over one's head, when they afford fine "rocketing" shots.
As a rule, they run; and it is often necessary to shoot
them on the ground, if they are to be shot at all. In this
way we sometimes obtained four or five at a shot. When
stalking antelope they are sometimes a great nuisance, as
they often alarm them by their sharp, metallic cry.

Our first night out of Haikota was the coldest we had

yet experienced, and there was a very heavy dew. We began to think we had started short of blankets; and I accordingly rode back for some, and returned just as the caravan was starting. The nights afterwards were often colder still, and we were many times glad of the extra coverings.

We made a six and a half hours' march, and formed quite a cavalcade. We all rode horses, and had as escort the sheik, some of his mounted retainers, and our five horsemen. Our next halting-place was Toadelook. About a quarter of a mile from the Gash were a hundred acres or more of tall, rank grass, growing in what, for a long time after the rains, is a swamp; but at the time we visited it it was all dried up, with the exception of a small piece at one end, where there was water, said to be much resorted to by game going to drink.

Water is always to be obtained in the Gash by digging, but it is often very far below the surface. At that time it fortunately could be readily obtained by scraping away the sand; we were not even obliged to do this, as some Arabs who had been there lately had done it for us, and had, moreover, made reservoirs of mud in which to put the water for their beasts to drink. Plenty of fine green grass grew in the river's bed, and coarse high grass lined either bank.

On the way to Toadelook we saw *tétél* (*Bubalis mauritanica*) for the first time. There are two varieties of this antelope, both of which were frequently encountered and shot. They are ugly, ungainly-looking beasts, but their flesh was the best to eat of all the antelopes we came across. In South Africa, where both varieties are found, it is called the hartebeest.

Immediately on their arrival my brothers took their light rifles and made for the marsh, thinking by chance to find some gazelle or *tétél* returning from the water. They had just arrived at the watering-place when they espied a lion lying on the top of a slight eminence, evidently on the look-out for any animal coming to slake its thirst. As the lion had not perceived them, and their rifles were of very small calibre, one of them lay down concealed under a bush,

about a hundred yards from the lion, while the other made
for the caravan, which had just arrived, to fetch a heavy
rifle. He returned as quickly as possible with a ten-bore,
and out of breath from running. The lion on the top of
the mound was partly hidden from them, and my brother
was unsteady from running in the heat : so that, what with
that and the excitement of firing at the first lion seen, he
either missed him altogether or wounded him very slightly.
With an angry growl it started up and trotted towards them.
They reserved their fire till he was at close quarters, in
order to make sure of him. Just as they were going to fire,
he turned off suddenly at right angles ; and, before either
of them could get a second shot, he disappeared in grass
eight or ten feet high. Dreadfully disappointed, they
followed him, but saw no more of him in the jungle to which
he had retreated. Returning to camp, my brother (who
had missed the lion) made a very long and successful shot
at a gazelle galloping. If it had only been the lion instead !

The next day we all went out in parties of two, with our
rifles, in hopes of getting a shot at buffaloes or other big
game. Aylmer and one of my brothers followed up a large
herd of buffaloes for some miles, only to see them disappear
full pelt in a cloud of dust a long way ahead. Antelopes
were not very plentiful, but we managed to secure a fine
bull *tétél* and a doe *nellut*. This latter animal is a most
beautiful creature, with a mouse-coloured skin ; it was the
first we had met with that year. It is common in South
Africa, where it is called *koodoo ;* while in Abyssinia, and
some parts of the Soudan, it is known as the *agazin*.

We spent another day at Toadelook ; and, although
finding no big game, secured three *tétél*, and so kept the
larder well supplied, and had besides plenty of meat for
our men. We had so many people about us that we were
enabled to shoot a great deal, and yet feel that nothing
would be wasted ; we were always very particular about
this, and never shot anything to waste. The sheik left us,
as he said, to go a little farther up the Gash, where he
expected to meet some of his horsemen returning from the
Basé with camels laden with *dhurra*. As none of the Basé

we ever came across grew any worth speaking of, this was only a polite excuse, invented on the spur of the moment, for leaving our camp.

As large numbers of sand-grouse arrived morning and evening to drink, Lort Phillips thought it a good opportunity to test a clap-net he had brought with him from England; and, accordingly, he set it close to the water, and in one haul caught fifty-seven birds. This net proved frequently useful, not only in catching sand-grouse, but pigeons and doves as well; and we often used it when we wanted them for food, and were anxious not to disturb the country by firing shots, in case by so doing we should frighten away any animals wont to frequent the watering-places near to which we were encamped.

At Haikota we had bought some fresh ostrich-eggs, the contents of which we placed in bottles to be used when required for making omelettes. *Omelette à l'autruche* was for some time quite a common dish with us for breakfast; I must acknowledge, however, that we found that, although eatable, they had rather a strong flavour, and we should have preferred the eggs of the domestic fowl had they been obtainable.

There being a moon, two of our party watched some hours by the water, perched more or less uncomfortably on the branches of trees, in hopes of getting a shot at some animals coming to drink. For the first two or three hours this kind of thing is exciting enough; everything is still, and the sportsman hears the least sound. After a time, however, a drowsy feeling steals over him; and it is only with a great effort he can keep awake or from falling off his perch. In fact, after a long day in the blazing sun, it is often more than he can do, as we sometimes found by experience. Occasionally, after watching in vain for a long time, a noise as of some large animal approaching is heard. To reach the water, it must pass within a few feet of where you are sitting. From the noise it makes in the bushes, it must be large game. At last the unknown animal stands out in the moonlight; and it is only a hyæna, after all! Such was their fate that night; but soon afterwards they heard a tremendous crashing through the jungle, which set every nerve tingling. They felt sure the noise could be caused by nothing less than a herd of buffaloes, and such was indeed the case. The animals, however, got their wind, and went off at a gallop, with their thirst unquenched. For some time longer they waited, in hopes either that they would return, or some other herd make its appearance; or, perchance, that a single bull buffalo might visit the pond; for often the largest and fiercest bulls separate themselves from the herd, and wander about alone. None, however, arrived. They heard a lion roar, and thought they were going to have a visit from the king of beasts; but the roar gradually became fainter and fainter, as he evidently made off in the opposite direction. At last a gentle rustling was heard in the grass, and a *dik-dik* (*Nanotragus hemprichianus*), the smallest of the antelope tribe, and not much bigger than a hare, made its appearance, looking timidly about it for a hidden enemy, before daring to drink, and at the same time uttering the peculiar cry from which it has obtained its name. They did not disturb it, but let it quench its thirst in peace; and then, having had sufficient excitement for one night, and the moon having gone down—it being then three o'clock in the morning—they returned to the tents.

CHAPTER X.

The Camp moves forward.—Scarcity of Game.—Water easily obtainable.—Baby Crocodiles.—Sheik Achmed rejoins the Travellers.—A *Battue.*—Mimosa-trees.—Road-cutting through the Jungle.—A Buffalo Adventure.

AFTER spending these two days at Toadelook we made a farther move forward, being anxious to get well into the country without more delay; for we felt all the time that Sheik Achmed Ageer might give us the slip, and our people refuse to proceed farther. We made a march of only five hours and a half, encamping at a place called Toadwan. We pitched the tents high above the river-bed. Although we had considerable difficulty in getting the camels up, as the bank was steep, and a good many bushes had to be cut down and grass cleared away before the tents could be pitched, we were glad we had chosen this position; for the next morning, on awaking, there was a thick fog—a most unusual phenomenon in this country. Whenever practicable, we encamped above the river's bed; for, though clean sand was very comfortable for the purpose when there was no wind, we felt that, if the water were near the surface, we might, by sleeping there, run the risk of getting fever. We readily obtained water by digging to the depth of about a foot; and in a rocky *khor* close by, a tributary of the Gash, there were some stagnant pools, but no signs of game, nor had we on the march seen any whatever. We were disappointed in not finding game at Toadwan, as our Arabs had held out great hopes of our getting rhinoceros there. On the spot we had chosen for our encampment there were the traces of many recent fires. It was evidently the place that had been selected by the Basé for their first

night's halt, after they had driven off the cattle captured
from the Haikota people; and there was plenty of evidence
of their having slain and eaten some of the beasts. The
next day we pushed five hours farther into the country; on
the way coming to another *khor* called Sobat, which we
explored for some distance, and found running water, which
very soon, however, lost itself in the sand. On either side
grew coarse grass, ten to twelve feet high.

We found too a good deal of water in the bed of the
Gash, containing small fish and two or three baby crocodiles.
It is extraordinary how these creatures are often found in
the smallest pools ; and we were informed that during the
rains very large ones are seen near Cassala. As the Gash
loses itself in the sand I am at a loss to know what becomes
of these animals; for any pools that remain in the dry
season are so small that they could not afford accommoda-
tion for any but the smallest crocodiles. Perhaps they bury
themselves in the sand and lie *perdu* till the next rainy season
comes round, as, I believe, is the habit of alligators in some
parts of South America during the dry season. We saw
a good many antelopes, and the fresh tracks of a herd of
buffaloes. Tamarind-trees were seen for the first time ; the
fruit is a very favourite food of baboons, and wherever this
tree is seen there are sure to be some not far off. We again
encamped above the Gash, at a point where its bed widened
considerably, and where the country looked less promising.

The sheik joined us on the march. He told us he had
been to look after the Basé who had made the raid on his
cattle and killed so many of his people; he had got a
number of them penned in a cave, and some of the Beni-
Amers had surrounded it, and were trying to starve them
out. He expressed his intention of returning the following
day to the place where they were, which was some distance
to the south of the Gash. According to his statement he
had at first applied for assistance to the governor of Cassala,
asking him to supply troops with which to attack the hostile
Basé. This request the governor had refused, and told him
to fight his own battles and to take vengeance on the Basé
in his own way. He was justly aggrieved at this, as he

said, and with some reason, that he paid yearly heavy taxes to the Egyptian authorities, and it was very hard that they should refuse him their assistance when he stood in need of it. He carried out his intention of leaving us, and took his departure the following day; at which we were very well pleased, for we were getting tired of his company.

Before moving any farther into the country we indulged ourselves in a *battue* of the quail and partridges, which were very numerous in the patches of dry grass that grew on what, in the rains, would be islands in the Gash. It was the only place, during the whole expedition, where we found quail in any considerable numbers. It was terribly hot work; but the most uncomfortable part of it was, that we got covered from head to foot with horrible black ticks. These creatures were in appearance exactly like those that infest the camels, and stuck so tightly to our clothes with their legs that it was often no easy work to dislodge them.

Our next march was at some little distance from the Gash, and through an open country, in which grew clumps of mimosa-trees, of a different kind from those we had hitherto seen, growing very straight to a height of about twenty feet,—trees, not bushes. The outside bark was generally wanting; underneath it was of a reddish-brown colour. This tree was easily distinguished from the other species of acacia so common all over the Soudan. It produced considerable quantities of gum; and we gathered some beautiful amber and white pieces, each weighing three or four ounces, and mostly round in form; they presented very much the appearance of preserved apricots. A good deal of it, however, was of a bright red colour, and, I should think, worthless, as it was gritty and by no means pure. Gum is not found in sufficient quantities in these districts of the Soudan to be worth exporting; the best comes from Kordofan and Darfour, provinces to the west of the White Nile, and some also from the Blue Nile.

We made a very bad march of not more than ten miles, and encamped in the Gash, where we had to dig seven feet deep for water before we could have our dinner cooked. We were greatly delayed by being obliged to cut a way for the camels through a great deal of very high grass in order to cross the Gash; it was literally necessary to fight one's way through it foot by foot. This tall grass, often attaining a height of from ten to fourteen feet, was a great nuisance : it usually fringed the river's bed on either side, and often ran a long way back; on horseback or on foot it was almost impossible to get through it, except by following paths trodden down by elephants or buffaloes. Although affording splendid covert for big game, it was often a source of great difficulty in shooting. Animals *would* get into it, and you might often pass close to them without being aware of their presence. If we wounded buffaloes in the open they would almost invariably make for it, when it was of course extremely dangerous to follow them, as by so doing one might receive a charge at close quarters. In fact, the grass was often so thick that it was quite possible to get within a yard or two of a buffalo without seeing anything of him. An instance of this occurred to my brother and myself when shooting in the Bogos country on the borders of the Dembelas territory the previous winter.

It was the first time any of us had seen these animals, and we had wounded two ; one of these made for the open, while the other had taken to the high grass; this one we followed by its blood-tracks until we reached the edge of the grass into which they led. During our pursuit, and before arriving at this covert, we had once or twice caught a glimpse of it disappearing among the thick trees that · grew in that part; but as it went off at a gallop on our approach we soon lost sight of it again. We were debating whether we should follow it, when, without giving us much time to think, the infuriated beast rushed out of the grass and charged straight at my brother. The grass was so high that neither of us had seen it until we were close upon it.

We were standing side by side when the buffalo charged; and as my brother could not see the beast until it was within four or five feet of him, he had to fire in such a hurry that he barely had time to raise his rifle to his shoulder. His bullet struck the animal's horn, which turned the brute sharply round to the right, and it disappeared into the grass again. I fired after it as it was disappearing. After this we concluded that we would not attempt to follow it farther, but try and drive it out. This grass formed a belt from fifty to a hundred yards in width, which bordered a *khor* called Furfur, where water flowed for about two miles, and then lost itself in the sand.

We threw stones and sticks after the buffalo without any result; and a native who was with us climbed a tree to see if he could catch sight of it, but could neither see nor hear anything of it, so that it was impossible to determine whether the animal was dead or not. About an hour after, on approaching the grass from the side of the *khor*, we heard something moving inside, and making a noise as though endeavouring to rise. The natives on hearing this were most anxious that we should set fire to the grass, and so drive the brute out; but the grass was too green for this to be done, and we did not attempt it. My brother finally climbed a tree, while I stood in the bed of the *khor* in case the buffalo should come out in my direction. I had not long to wait before I heard my brother sing out, "Look out, it's coming!" The words were hardly out of his mouth when I heard a noise in the grass, and the buffalo emerged opposite to where I stood, about sixty yards off, and made straight for me. A lucky shot in the ear turned it, and it fell on its side.

It proved to be a large cow; and my shot, though a fatal one, by no means finished her at once. She was game to the last, and several times tried to rise and charge me: the poor brute was, however, done, and a second shot soon put an end to her. On examination we found that the first shot had struck her rather far back. We then went after the other wounded buffalo. Salee was with us, and tracked it in the most wonderful way for over six miles. The track often became so faint that we lost it altogether; and the animal led us through very thick covert, several times across the *khor*, and over a hill. Just at dusk, as we were thinking of giving it up, Salee declared that he was sure from the appearance of its tracks that we were not far off; and very shortly we heard it bellowing, and soon found it lying down. A second shot quickly terminated its sufferings ; and both of us had the satisfaction of bagging a buffalo on the first occasion that any of these animals had been seen. Unfortunately they were both cows. A lion had scented the last one, as we found the fresh tracks of one following her footsteps for some distance.

CHAPTER XI.

Arrival at Wo Ammar.—First Interview with Basé.—A Basé Village.
—Giraffe-stalking.—The Village of Koolookoo.—Deputation from
the Village.—The Sheik's Son makes himself "generally useful."
—Presents for the Deputation.—The Koolookoo Villagers much
interested in us.—Visit to the Village.—Women of Koolookoo.

THE following day, January 30, we made a farther march
of five hours and a half, encamping high above the Gash,
where the river makes a great bend. This place rejoiced
in the name of Wo Ammar, and was a very pretty spot,
the banks of the Gash being thickly fringed with high grass
and *dhoum*-palms, many of them of great size and covered
with creeping plants; while on either side rose a chain of
hills.

A fine sunset completed a very pretty picture : as a rule
the sunsets were remarkably beautiful, owing to the
absence of clouds, but on this occasion there were a great
number.

There were plenty of guinea-fowl and partridges on the
banks; and in the river's bed we found several herds of
tétél on our arrival, coming upon them suddenly, having
been travelling away from the Gash all day, until we
abruptly struck it at this point. For the first time we
came across a very pretty little antelope, smaller than a
gazelle, called by the Basé *mora*, by the Arabs *oterop;* it
has a very rough chestnut skin, and I believe it to be the
Calotragus montanus. The country through which we
passed had all been burned; and there was, in consequence, very little game, there being no grass left. We
went through a large grove consisting entirely of *hegleek*-
trees (*Balanetes Ægyptiaca*), and extending for four or five
miles. The Arabs are very fond of the fruit of this tree,

but I must confess none of us found it very palatable.
Elephants also enjoy it, and will gather it one by
one; we several times found the trees overturned by
these animals, and it was evident from the amount of
trampling that had taken place that they had stopped to
eat the fruit. Sir Samuel Baker says that this tree is so
rich in potash that it is used as a substitute for soap. It
was the first time in our travels that we had ever come
across a country in which these trees were the sole kind,
though in parts they were common enough here and there,
growing with other species.

The previous evening some excitement had been caused
in camp by a report that some Basé had been seen skulking
about the tents during the night; and on this day, January
30, 1882, some of these redoubtable people were for the
first time seen by us, and, moreover, "interviewed;" but I
do not think even a *New York Herald* reporter would have
got much out of them. On the march we suddenly came
across a party of eight or ten engaged in collecting the fruit
of the baobab-tree. All took to their heels and made off
as fast as they could, except one, who was fairly treed, and
could not get down from his perch before we came up to
him. He appeared to expect to be instantly killed, and
stood trembling all over like an aspen-leaf, the picture of
most abject terror. He did not know what to make of us
when, instead of being led to instant execution, he was
presented with a knife by my brother, while Suleiman gave
him some food.

Bayrumphy called after the fugitives in their own language, and endeavoured to make them understand that
we were peaceably inclined; but it was no use; they only
ran the faster, and we soon saw them disappear over the
brow of a hill. They were much blacker than any of the
Arabs we had seen before, with very negro-like features, and
were evidently considerably behind the people of the adjoin-
ing countries we had visited in the scale of civilisation.
Their sole clothing consisted of a piece of skin fastened
round the waist.

Baobab-trees were exceedingly numerous. They nearly

all had sticks driven into their trunks, one above the other,
to enable the natives to climb them. This they do, not
merely for the purpose of gathering the fruit, but also to
collect the honey which is often found in large quantities
in these trees.

On our journey of January 31 we saw the first Basé
village, called Fodah, a small collection of conical-roofed
huts, perched, as all their villages are, on the side of a hill,
near the top. The Basé not only inspire terror in the
hearts of their neighbours, but are themselves very much in
dread of every one else. "Their hand is against every
man, and every man's hand against them." We passed by
some tombs, and through what had been *dhurra*-fields, but
saw no people. The Arabs were most anxious that we
should not fire our guns until we had "interviewed" some
of the natives, as they feared that by doing so they would
only be unnecessarily alarmed. There was fortunately very
little provocation to do so, as we saw scarcely any game.

The whole day's march was at some distance from the
Gash, and, as I before mentioned, through a country that
had been recently burned. We were at a loss to imagine
what could be the object of burning so much country. It
certainly had the effect of driving away every head of game.
At night we constantly saw fires on the hills; and were told
that, though we did not see them, there were plenty of Basé
living all about, and that they made these fires to telegraph,
as it were, that there were strangers in their country.

We saw the footprints of great numbers of giraffes that
had been there during the last rainy season, when the place
had been little better than a swamp; and their marks in
the mud had dried hard. We felt there was no chance of
seeing any of the animals when we passed through, as there
was simply nothing for them to eat. In our experience of
African game, with the exception of elephants, giraffes are
the most wide-ranging of all; and we frequently saw their
footprints at very great distances from water. They are
very difficult to shoot, their long necks giving them a great
advantage over the hunter, as they can see him long before
he is aware of their being in the vicinity, and thus frequently

make off without being seen at all. They are, moreover, very keen-scented. Their food chiefly consists of the leaves of the trees, which are, as a rule, so low that their long necks enable them to see over them.

One day my brothers had gone out to see what they could obtain in the way of game, and had fallen in with the fresh marks of a giraffe. They, therefore, ascended a hill to observe if any were in sight, and soon made out three or four, feeding in the plain below them. Quickly taking their bearings, they descended, but had to go a very long way round, to avoid approaching them down wind. After a very long stalk, in which they became much heated, they felt sure they could not be far off, and were advancing very cautiously, moving the twigs of the trees aside with their hands before pushing their way through them, so as to make as little noise as possible, when suddenly they heard the report of a shot, and at the same moment the sound of some heavy animals crashing through the jungle, which was so thick that they could not be seen, though barely a hundred yards away. One of the Arabs to whom they had entrusted an express rifle had let it off. It had been given to him locked, but he had been playing with the locks, and so managed to discharge it. They were naturally greatly annoyed and disappointed, but determined to return to the same place the following day; this they did, and were rewarded by shooting a very fine bull. Although there is not much of a trophy to be obtained from a giraffe, they are much valued by the Arabs. The flesh we found rather tough and strong, but we ate it cooked in various ways; and the natives were very fond of it. The hide is exceedingly tough, and is much prized for making shields; and the tails make excellent fly-whisks.

Whenever we shot a large animal, such as a buffalo or a giraffe, there was a great clamouring for a piece of hide to make a shield. Every Arab wanted some, and we endeavoured to divide the skin as fairly as possible; but it was often difficult, not to say impossible, to satisfy everybody, and we began to wish the animals had been born without skins. When they did not want to manufacture

G

shields out of the hide for their own use, they could easily obtain a dollar at the nearest town for a sufficient quantity to make one.

The trees along the Gash got thicker and more numerous the farther we plunged into the country, and we noticed several varieties we had not met with before; amongst others, some very like English pear-trees in appearance. There was, too, a very curious grass, with a head to it like cotton; and we regretted that none of our party were botanists.

After a night spent in the river-bed opposite Fodah we pushed five or six miles farther up, and encamped near a large village situated on the spur of a hill on the right bank of the Gash, and called Koolookoo; we suddenly came in sight of this place on turning a bend of the river. The inhabitants, as they saw our caravan winding along the river-bed, were seized with a panic; and with our glasses we could see them crowding to the summit of the hill on which the village was situated. We placed our camp, contrary to our usual custom, in the river-bed, as the Arabs were afraid to spend the night among the trees and bushes until we had interviewed and made friends with the people. Here it was necessary, before proceeding any farther, to have a " palaver " with the authorities. Accordingly, as soon as we arrived, Bayrumphy and two other horsemen rode up to the village. They very soon returned, bringing with them the sheik's son and three other men. The sheik himself was away. They carried spears and shields, as all do in these countries. These they left on the bank of the river opposite to that on which we were sitting discussing our luncheon, and crossed over to us, accompanied by Bayrumphy and the other horsemen.

Their costume was exceedingly simple and unpretending. It consisted of a scrap of dirty cotton cloth tied round the waist, with an undergarment of leather. These were, how- ever, the grandees of the village; and we afterwards found that scarcely any one not of exalted rank indulged himself in such an excess of raiment. We presented them each with a piece of Manchester cotton cloth, with which they were

CAMP AT KOOLOOKOO.

delighted, and proceeded without further delay to divest themselves of what little clothing they possessed, and to wrap our gifts round their waists instead. To the sheik's son we presented in addition a piece of maroon velvet, on which were fastened little silvery ornaments like buttons. This he put round his neck in place of a necklace of dried palm-leaf, which he discarded. On his wrists he wore palm-leaf bracelets, and as we had no better to give him he stuck to his own, which were indeed far prettier than any we could have given him in their place, their light yellow colour contrasting well with the glossy black of his skin.

This sheik's son, whose name was Longay, stayed with us the whole time we were in the Basé country, and was throughout most faithful and devoted. In alluding to him, George said one day, " The king's son is learning to clean knives ; " and, indeed, he made himself most useful in that capacity, as well as in fetching wood for the cook and drawing water. He often, too, induced others among his people to work for us, when without his help they would have done nothing at all. On parting from us he fairly shed tears, and altogether he was the best specimen of the completely " untutored savage " I ever came across.

We gave each of the men who came from the village a knife, a looking-glass, some pins, needles, and cotton thread. We had bought a great quantity of such things in England for the purpose of giving them as presents to the natives, and found them most useful. We regretted, however, that we had not bought more Manchester cotton and beads, as these are things they appreciate more than anything you can give them.

We could see from our camp part of the village of Koo-lookoo, some huts built on the spur of the hill ; and while this interview and dressing-up of the four Basé was in progress, their brethren, together with " their sisters, their cousins, and their aunts," had clambered up a great rock at the back of the village, and we could see great numbers of them looking down on us and wondering who we were and what we had come for. Our people did not at all admire the appearance of the Basé, who they declared resembled baboons. The Basé have a very peculiar way of resting (which is, I believe, common among many of the tribes on the White Nile) : they place the sole of the right foot against the left knee, a mode of repose which to a European seems most uncomfortable and almost impossible. The accompanying woodcut is engraved from a photograph which Aylmer took on the Mareb. The men had no idea

BED OF THE MAREB AT AIBARO.

at the time that they were being taken, so that the position is a perfectly natural one.

The next day Lort Phillips, Colvin, and I, with two of the horsemen and three or four Basé, rode up to the village of Koolookoo. Just before reaching the huts we passed on our right the remains of a house built of sun-dried brick, which had evidently been a much more substantial dwelling than any the natives ever build. This house, we were told, had been erected by Mr. Powell, an English gentleman, who with his wife and child had been murdered by the Basé some twelve or fourteen years ago. Mr. Powell was the brother of the unfortunate gentleman who recently perished in a balloon accident; he had spent some time at Koolookoo, and had entered the country from the north. They were massacred, not at Koolookoo itself, but by some people who lived not far off, the same who made the raid on Haikota, which has previously been mentioned. Koolookoo is a very small place, and the conical-roofed huts present much the appearance of large bee-hives. There was merely the semblance of a path leading up to it; and the latter part of the way was so steep we were obliged to dismount and proceed on foot.

The women were particularly shy, and most of them nearly naked; all wore beads and cowrie-shells, if they had little else; a few wore anklets made of the skin of some wild animal; one carried a skin cross-belt. We took a number of little things with us to give away, as we were anxious to conciliate the people as much as possible. I offered one woman some needles and thread; a gift she declined, complaining very sorrowfully that they were useless to her as she had no clothes, and consequently no mending of old garments or making of new to effect. Her remark was almost literally true, as her sole covering was a piece of goat-skin worn round the loins as an apron.

We ascended to the top of the hill above the village, and were rewarded by a most extensive view, and saw one or two other small villages on distant hills; on the top of this one were great boulders of granite, and on the very summit a hut. We found mats, cooking-pots, and other valuables stowed away in holes in the rock; as the natives when they first descried us had dragged them up there, fearing we might prove to be enemies.

In the afternoon those of us who had visited Koolookoo went out shooting, and those that had not went to see it. We killed two *nellut* and a *tétél*, to the great delight of some of the Basé who were with us. They ate the liver raw, first squeezing the contents of the gall-bladder over it to

BASÉ WOMEN.

give it a flavour; this was also what we had seen the Arabs do with whom we had formerly travelled. Great quantities of the flesh they cooked on the spot, and bolted in enormous mouthfuls. The inhabitants of these countries at their meals are not a pretty sight. I have seen our camel-drivers devour a whole bullock raw at a sitting, so that there was absolutely only the skin remaining. They waste nothing, and those parts that with us are thrown away are by many of them considered the choicest morsels.

We were anxious to give an entertainment with the magic-lantern after dinner; but the bidden guests did not at first feel sufficient confidence in us to trust themselves in our camp at night. The women, too, who were usually the water-carriers, did not dare for a day or two to come down from the village to the Gash to get water; and this duty at first devolved on the men. Very soon, however, curiosity overcame this fear, and they came to our camp in crowds.

CHAPTER XII.

Scarcity of *Dhurra.*—A number of Basé join our Camp.—Water carriers.—Another deserted Village.—Ceremony of making Peace.—Friendliness of the Basé Women.—The Mareb.—Buffaloes seen for the First Time.—More Basé join the Camp.—Exciting Stalk after an Ostrich.—Game abounds.—Aylmer and I start for Ma Ambasah, and find Water.—A Chase after Buffaloes.—Both Barrels at once.—A nasty Recoil.—A Visit from Sheik Kudul.—He departs, promising to return.—The Camp moves to Ma Ambasah.—Two Bull Buffaloes killed.—Some of the Camel-drivers sent to Amedeb for *Dhurra.*

ON February 3 we moved forward again. The *dhurra* was running short; at least, the time was not far distant when we should have none left. There were fifteen horses and from thirty to forty men to feed, and it was difficult to calculate how long it would last; for, although we had usually enough meat for the men, they could not live entirely upon it. Our guides told us that four or five hours' march farther up the Gash there was a village where as much as was required could be bought. On our arrival there *dhurra* was found to be very scarce and absurdly dear; and, while we wanted it by the camel-load, the natives only brought it literally in handfuls. In fact, very little, almost no *dhurra* is grown on the Gash much above Cassala. The Basé did not care for money, but wanted cotton cloth and beads, which they wished to exchange with us for *dhurra.* We soon saw, however, that scarcely any was to be obtained. We were obliged, moreover, to be very chary of our supply of cotton cloth and beads. I never came across any African tribe so fond of beads as the Basé, and the men are not far behind the women in this respect.

The village near which the *dhurra* was supposed to grow is called Mai-Daro. On our way numbers of Basé joined us, and when we arrived there must have been fully eighty to a hundred of them. They had fastened themselves on to us in the hope of getting meat; and we were obliged to explain to them that, having a large party of our own to feed, although we hoped to obtain sufficient game to supply them as well, it was impossible for us to promise to do so. They replied that, when they could get no meat, they would live on the fruit of the baobab-tree; that they were quite accustomed to doing so, and frequently had no other food to depend upon.

On our way to Mai-Daro Lort Phillips and I came across a party of Basé felling trees, clearing a space in which to plant *dhurra* against the next rainy season. On first beholding us they were much frightened, probably never having seen white men before, and were going to run away, but we both exclaimed "*Maieedah*,"—a Basé word, which we generally found acted on them as a kind of talisman; it seems to signify "How do you do?" and "We are friends" in one: its enunciation, at any rate, generally had a magical effect. On hearing "*Maieedah*" pronounced, the men in question insisted on our dismounting, and gave us some "beer," made of *dhurra*, which they were drinking. It was very sour and extremely nasty. They had a great quantity of it, and evidently thought it very good, judging from the amount they consumed; several of them were decidedly intoxicated. They carry all liquids in very neatly-plaited baskets, made by the women out of the leaves of the *dhoum*-palm—so finely plaited as to be completely water-proof. The women are the water-carriers generally, in fact, nearly always. The water is a long way from the villages, as there is never any on the hills where they are built. We frequently saw the women, in the heat of the day, carrying these baskets filled with water back to their huts; each woman carried two, fastened one at each end of a pole by means of cord made of the fibre of the *dhoum*-palm. The village of Mai-Daro was at some distance from the Gash, and we never visited it; I took a walk, however, up a hill at the back of our camp, and found the remains of a small village lately burnt. All that part of the country had suffered much from fire, it being impossible rightly to determine whether occasioned by accident or design.

On the top of a hill not far off was a deserted village, having evidently been abandoned in a hurry; very likely the inhabitants had been driven away by the people of a neighbouring town, as the Basé are anything but a united people, and are constantly quarrelling among themselves. Most of the huts were placed in small enclosures made of the dried stalks of the *dhurra*. In the dwellings we found cooking-pots, gourds for drinking, and roughly-made wooden bedsteads; our men appropriated some of the cooking-utensils for their own use. In one house was a huge earthenware jar, resembling one of the celebrated jars in the old story of Ali Baba, or the Forty Thieves; it had probably been used as a receptacle for grain, most likely *dhurra*. Terraces, looking quite like those built for the vines in France and Italy, were to be seen on the side of the hill on which this cereal had been grown.

In the evening the sheik of Mai-Daro arrived in camp; and we went through the ceremony of making *amān*, or peace, with him and his people. We had done the same before at Koolookoo with our friend Longay, the sheik's son. It consisted in the sheik placing his naked sword on the ground and drawing his foot along it, the blade passing between his bare foot and his sandal; after which he placed the palm of his hand on his sword, and uttered some cabalistic words indicative of peace and good-will towards us all.[1]

The women gradually became quite confiding, and displayed that passion for admiration and attention common to the sex over both the civilised and uncivilised world.

---

[1] Even the most ignorant and savage African tribes have some solemn form or oath for sealing a contract and making friends, and this once made they dare not break or infringe. Each tribe has its peculiar form, one throws a stone, as the western Somali; another swears by the bridle of his horse; a third in extinguishing a flame.

Numbers came to have their photographs taken by my brother, and were greatly delighted when we noticed their beads. Both men and women greatly appreciated the red tinsel capsules we had on some claret bottles : the men in particular greatly affected these as ornaments—some beating them into a square shape and hanging them round their necks, while others tipped the ends of the wooden skewers which all the men wear in their hair with the bright-coloured bauble.

We again proposed the magic-lantern ; and this time a number came to the entertainment, with which they seemed to be greatly delighted.

Our next camping-ground was about ten miles farther up the river's bed, on a burnt patch of ground between some high grass and the Gash. The natives declared we had reached the Mareb of which they had been talking for days. The Gash and Mareb are one and the same thing. The Arabs of the Soudan call it the Gash ; the Abyssinians, the Mareb ; and the Basé, the Sonah. It rises in Abyssinia, and flows only during the rains ; even then, although a very broad and swiftly flowing river, none of its waters reach the sea, being lost in the sands of the desert. The Arabs have the vaguest ideas of geography, and knew next to nothing of the countries immediately surrounding the places where they are living themselves. For a long time all the men we had with us, if they offered an opinion at all, insisted that the Mareb and Gash were perfectly distinct and different water-courses : they were, however, at last forced to acknowledge them to be one and the same. They also declared that we should find that the Mareb was a flowing river ; instead of which, all the water has to be obtained by digging, unless a small quantity appears above the level of the bed. I do not think that during the dry season it flows even far up in Abyssinia, although the water there, no doubt, appears more frequently on the surface.

The country improved in appearance as we travelled on, and gave promise of more game ; there were not nearly so many *dhoum*-palms, and the trees fringing the river's bank were often of an immense size and in full leaf, affording the most perfect shade; then, again, these trees would disappear for a time and give place to acres of very high thick grass.

During the night some of us were awakened by a great noise in the grass near our tents. Colvin and Aylmer jumped out of bed, and, hastily seizing their rifles, went to see what was causing the disturbance. Unfortunately it was not a very bright night, the moon being partly obscured by clouds. Suddenly they came upon a herd of about thirty buffaloes drinking at a small pool of stagnant water : the beasts either saw or heard them, and went off with a great noise through the grass, fortunately for them in the opposite direction from that in which they were approaching. Both fired as they galloped off, but it was impossible in the semi-darkness for them to do more than fire at the black mass; as they neither saw nor heard any fall they could not tell whether they might claim the first buffalo. Early the next morning they started off to see if they could discover anything further of them; and did not return to camp until 9 P.M., having enjoyed an excellent day's sport. They had not long left the camp before they found the blood tracks of a buffalo they had wounded during the night. After following these for some distance, all the way through high grass, they came to a slight eminence, up which they climbed, and gaining the summit saw the buffalo moving slowly along the margin of the grass. Aylmer obtained a snap shot at about a hundred yards, with the result of driving the animal farther into the grass, where Salee, who had climbed to the top of a tree, declared he saw it lie down. Step by step they cautiously advanced to the edge of the grass, sending Salee round to endeavour by throwing stones and clods of earth to drive the buffalo toward them; this was, however, of no avail, and thinking it possible that it was already *hors de combat*, they gingerly entered the covert, which in that part was sufficiently thin to allow of their seeing some six or seven yards ahead.

They had not proceeded many yards when a crash, accompanied by a warning shout from Salee, was heard; and turning quickly round they espied the buffalo making

for and almost on the top of them.   A well-directed shot
from Colvin brought the infuriated beast on to its head; it
quickly struggled to its feet, however, and endeavoured to
charge again, but feebly; and another bullet soon administered the *coup de grace.*   Unfortunately it proved to be a
female; the shot fired the previous night had only wounded
her in the hind-quarters.   The breath was hardly out of
her body when the Basé, who, like vultures, had been
watching the contest from afar, flocked to the scene.
Words fail to convey an adequate sense of the filthy spectacle that then took place.   No sooner had the head been
removed and the body abandoned to them, than with yells
and shouts they precipitated themselves upon the carcass,
struggling for the possession of what they looked upon as
tit-bits.   All was fish that came to their net, entrails and
every abomination included; and no pack of jackals or
hyænas ever left a cleaner skeleton.   Entrails, and all parts
that could not conveniently be transported, were devoured
raw on the spot; and their black hides were soon dyed in
gore as they wallowed in the horrible mess.

In the afternoon Colvin and Aylmer each shot a buck
méhédehet, or water-buck (*Cobus Ellipsiprymna*), a very fine
species of antelope, which we had never seen before.
They have red hair, much like red deer, and fine annulated
horns, and are very plucky beasts.   One of them when
wounded tried to charge Colvin when he approached it:
he had shot it at about two hundred yards range, having
hit it rather far back.

Two days later a dead cow buffalo was discovered that
had been shot on the night of the 4th.   It was found near
the back of the camp, close to a small pool of water; and,
although in an absolutely putrid condition, the Basé ate it
with relish, regardless of the fact that they had plenty of
freshly-killed meat in camp at the time.   With such a
crowd of natives about as we had it soon becomes desir-
able to shift one's quarters: scraps of meat are carelessly
thrown about anywhere, and the trees are soon festooned
with strips of meat drying in the sun.   The stench caused
by quantities of half-putrid meat about the camp can more

easily be imagined than described; it is, moreover, apt to breed fever and dysentery.

More Basé arrived and joined our camp, and we began to think it was possible to have too much of a good thing; we had again to explain to them that, while we should gladly do our best to supply them with meat, yet we could not promise to do so, as our own party was so large without taking into account the Basé; we could say no more when they urged that if there was no meat they would be perfectly satisfied with the fruit of the *dhoum*-palm and baobab-tree. They certainly added to the picturesqueness of the camp; we made them keep outside our *zariba*, and they slept in the river's bed, each man planting his spear in the sand, which, as they usually placed them all near together, had a very odd effect. Sometimes we had as many as two hundred of them, then there appeared quite a forest of spears. As they wore scarcely any clothing, and the nights were very cold, they were in the habit of lighting a great number of fires, which they placed very close together, each fire serving for two or three men. When well supplied with meat they became very merry and ardent votaries of Terpsichore; and what their dances lacked in grace they more than made up for by the wildness and picturesqueness which they added to the scene. Some of them began to make themselves useful as well as ornamental, fetching firewood for the cook and carrying our water-barrels down to the wells we had dug in the Mareb, filling them, and taking them back to camp; in fact, we became the best of friends.

On the same day that Colvin shot the buffalo William and I had a most exciting stalk after an ostrich. It was a fine black cock, and none of us had ever seen one of these birds in its wild state before. We had gone a long way from the Mareb, and on ascending a small hill, in order to get a good view of the surrounding country, we suddenly discovered the ostrich. It is at all times an exceedingly difficult bird to approach, generally keeping to the open and being always on the look-out for danger. The ostrich is supposed by the natives to be deficient in the senses of hearing and smelling, but to have abnormal powers of sight.

The one we saw was by no means an exception to the rule ; he was marching about in a great open plain covered with very fine dried grass not more than two feet high. To stalk it was next to impossible, owing to the almost total absence of covert ; however, we were most anxious to do our best, an ostrich being a prize one did not get the chance of obtaining every day.

For two mortal hours we crouched and crawled and wriggled ourselves along the grass like eels, during the very hottest part of a roasting-hot day ; once or twice we stopped to rest for a few moments under a *hegleek*-tree. There was only an odd tree or two in the grass, which we kept endeavouring to make use of as screens between ourselves and the ostrich. On crawling near the tree in hopes of finding the game within shot on the far side we discovered that we were no nearer to the object of our pursuit, as the ostrich had walked on all the time, and was probably farther than ever from us. At last, finding it hopeless to get at it in the open, we endeavoured to drive it towards a clump of trees to our left ; all to no purpose, as it was well on the alert, and would never let us get nearer than four hundred yards. And so we never even fired at it.

I don't think I was ever so hot in my life. My clothes were literally saturated with perspiration ; I sat under the shade of a tree while I took off my things and dried them in the sun. We never felt any ill effects from the heat, although constantly taking violent exercise during the hottest hours of the day ; in fact, we were always better when camping out shooting in the wilds than when stopping in towns where there was very little inducement to take exercise. Taking plenty of exercise is the only way to keep well in a very hot climate. Although we never feared the sun, we always treated it with proper respect ; our pith helmets were the very thickest that could be bought ; mine, an immensely thick one I had got four years previously at Benares, served me for two winters in the Soudan. We wore besides, down our spines, thick pads made of cotton wadding quilted, a good inch or more thick ; these were buttoned into our coats.

The days were intensely hot and very dry. I have seen as many as thirty-five degrees difference between the wet and dry bulb; for some hours every day the thermometer would range from 85° to 95° in the shade, usually nearer the latter than the former temperature. I had a thermometer made expressly by Casella of Holborn for testing the heat of the sun's rays, which, like all my thermometers, had been corrected at Kew; and I have seen it rise during the day to 164° Fahrenheit, the usual maximum being from 150° to 158°. The nights were very cold, especially in the early mornings. After dinner in the Mareb we frequently liked to sit round a blazing fire. About dawn I have seen the thermometer go down to 37°, and night after night it would descend to 42° or 50°. We found these cold nights most agreeable, bracing us up as they did to endure the heat of the day. The dews were frequently so heavy that the ground in the morning would be as wet as though it had been raining heavily; it was impossible to know when to expect them, as the night after one and in the same place it would perhaps be quite dry.

On our return to camp I saw some *tétél*, and missed one very badly. This was the only shot either of us fired all day. We saw the fresh tracks of more than one rhinoceros, an animal none of us had ever encountered. A great addition to the *cuisine* was made by Ali our cook in the shape of wild tomatoes, which he found growing near the Mareb; they were small, but of good flavour. Ali had travelled formerly along that part of the Mareb which runs through Abyssinia, where he said there was any quantity; and he had been on the look-out for them for days.

We spent two more days in shooting before shifting our camp. There was evidently plenty of game; but owing to the immense quantity of high grass it was often difficult to get at it. The only species of big game of which we were astonished to find a scarcity was the lion; we had neither heard nor seen any since leaving Toadelook, and had, moreover, come across hardly any of their tracks. Giraffes we had seen tolerably often, but had shot only one; and, as long as other meat was plentiful, we were not very anxious

H

to kill any more.   One day during the march, while halting
under a tree, we had allowed the caravan to get ahead of
us, and two or three ran across the river's bed, just ahead
of the camels.

One morning Aylmer and I started off for a *khor* called
Ma Ambasah, where there was said to be a good deal of
water; it ran into the right bank of the Mareb about eight
or ten miles above our camp.   On our way there we each
shot a *tétél*, after one of which we had a long chase before
finally securing him; these we shot soon after leaving camp,
so we sent them back on one of the two camels we had
taken with us for the purpose of carrying game.

On arriving at Khor Ma Ambasah we found that,
although there were no large pools of water such as we had
been led to expect, still a good deal of water filtered up
through the sand in several places.

There were plenty of very fresh tracks of buffaloes in the
sandy *khor*, and these animals had dug holes in the sand in
order more easily to obtain a supply of water to drink.

We had struck this *khor* at its junction with the Mareb,
which we had followed up to this point; and, after having
gone about a mile up its bed from this junction, we set off
to shoot our way back to camp, intending to cut off the
angle formed by the junction of the two *khors*.   We had
only just started, and one of our men had run on ahead to
the top of a small knoll on our left to look out for game,
when we saw him frantically gesticulating to us to follow
him; this we did at our best pace, and found some buffaloes
crossing the rising ground about fifty yards off, separated
from us by a narrow ravine.   We each singled out one
and fired; mine fell immediately to the shot, but Aylmer's
though hard hit went on.

Hearing the report of the shots some dozen or more
buffaloes that had been hidden from us by the trees rushed
past; we fired at them, but with no result, as far as we
could see at the time.   The buffalo I had shot, which was
unfortunately a cow, though a very large one, was nearly
done for and could not rise; so I put an end to her sufferings by a ball in the neck.   Then we lost no time in starting

off to see what had become of Aylmer's wounded beast;
there was no difficulty in finding a very distinct blood-track,
and on following it up for about a hundred yards we came
across another cow, this time stone dead.

It is all very well to talk about singling out the bulls,
but it is by no means an easy thing to do. Sometimes one
comes across single buffaloes that have separated themselves
from the herd. These are sure to be bulls, and very savage
bulls too. In meeting with a herd all that you can see, as
a rule, is a number of buffaloes, glimpses of which you
catch between the trees; for you are far more likely to find
them in pretty thick covert than in open country. You fire
at what you imagine to be a bull and the leader of the herd.
At your shot three or four more buffaloes that were in front,
hidden by the bushes, rush out; and you discover, to your
annoyance, that you have only fired at a cow.

I had been nearly deafened by the report of my rifle as
well as almost knocked down. For the first time I had
tried the effect of conical instead of spherical bullets (which
I had hitherto been using) in my ten-bore rifle; although
this rifle was supposed to be made to shoot both, the locks
were probably not strong enough, as the concussion caused
by firing the right barrel was so great that the left one went
off simply from the jar produced. The effect of firing from
one's shoulder fourteen drachms of powder and a good six
ounces of lead was by no means an agreeable experience;
and, had a buffalo charged me, I should have been in a
decidedly awkward predicament. The recoil was so great
that it had fairly spun me round like a teetotum, and my
hat had been sent flying. The conical bullets are far
heavier than the spherical. Exactly the same accident
happened to my brother Arthur's rifle a few days later, and
from the same cause; we decided that in future we would
content ourselves with spherical bullets, although the rifle
should certainly have been able to shoot both.

It was long after dark by the time we got back to camp,
and we found all the others had returned before us. Lort
Phillips and Colvin, who had been out together, had seen
a good many buffaloes, but had not succeeded in bagging

any. Salee, who had been with them, came across a
rhinoceros in high grass, which was, however, of such
extent and thickness that it was impossible for them to get
near it. In following game into high grass the utmost that
can be done is to have a snap-shot at an animal making off,
alarmed by the noise of approaching footsteps ; and oftener
than not it is heard running away without being seen,
although it may perhaps be within two or three yards of
one's rifle.

Neither of my brothers shot anything that day, though
they saw buffaloes, ostriches, and two giraffes, and they
might have shot *tétél* or *nellut* had they wished to do so ;
but it frequently happened that we felt obliged to abstain
from shooting antelopes, for fear that by so doing we should
lose a chance at bigger game. There were, in fact, no days
after we were once fairly in the game country on which we
could not have shot antelope, of one kind or another, if
desirous of doing so ; and there were such numbers of
natives about our camp that we felt we could shoot a great
deal and yet that no meat would be wasted.

A very bad piece of luck happened to us that same day.
While we were all out in different directions shooting, two
elephants passed within sight of the camp ; they were first
seen by some of our servants, who pointed them out to the
doctor. He did not shoot, but walked out some distance,
so as to get a good view of them. The next day some
of us took up their tracks, and, after going a very long
way and seeing nothing of them, gave it up and returned
to camp.

A country may fairly lay claim to being considered a
gamey one where elephants, rhinoceros, buffaloes, giraffes,
and ostriches are all seen on the same day, and where, in
addition, are found seven or eight varieties of antelopes,
wild boars (or rather wart-hogs), to say nothing of lions and
panthers, which, though scarce in that particular part at the
time of our visit, were nevertheless to be occasionally found.
As for birds, there were swarms of guinea-fowl, partridges,
pigeons, and doves, and many birds of brilliant plumage if
any one cared to collect them. Only once did any of us

obtain shots at ostriches, and then at such tremendously long ranges that it was, practically speaking, almost useless to fire. They invariably kept to the open, and were so extremely wary that we could never approach unperceived.

The following day my brother William had a shot at a wart-hog with a fine pair of tusks, one of four he came across in the bed of the Mareb; unluckily he missed it, so we had no pork for dinner that day. I must say it was no great disappointment to me, as the flesh of the wart-hog, though eatable when you can get nothing better, is not a thing to yearn after.

On the 7th, the day before we shifted our camp to Ma Ambasah, which was destined to be our farthest camp in an eastward direction, we had a visit from a peculiarly villainous-looking Basé sheik, rejoicing in the name of Kudul. We were informed that he was the most powerful sheik in those parts, and that it would be politic to propitiate him with some more valuable gift than any we had heretofore bestowed. Accordingly, from a box that we designated "the present-box," because it was full of things we had brought to distribute among the natives, we unearthed a very handsome *abba*, or cloak, of blue silk, with a great deal of gold thread worked upon it, which we had bought in the Cairo bazaars, and invested him with it. The ceremony took place in the presence of a great crowd of his people; and, although perhaps not so important an investiture as that of the Garter with us in England, it was, nevertheless, a very grand and solemn affair. Round his head we twisted a gaudy silk *kufeeyeh* of many colours, and wound a magenta *cumberbund* round his waist.

He was greatly delighted with his appearance as displayed in a looking-glass we gave him. It was most decidedly startling! I fear our gorgeous gifts would very soon become shabby, or covered with grease from the amount of fat he was in the habit of putting on his head; then, too, most likely he would become not only an object of admiration, but of envy, to his Abyssinian neighbours; and some of the more powerful chiefs among them would, doubtless, very soon deprive him of our gifts.

He informed us that, when he first heard of our travelling in his country, he thought we must be Turks come with
Sheik Said Carcashi (the powerful Basé sheik who is under
the thumb of the Egyptian Government, and lives near
Amedeb) in order to take possession of the country.   Had
that been our intention, he frankly informed us he had
made up his mind to obtain the assistance of some Abyssinians, with whom he said he was on friendly terms, in
order to repel us.   It was not until he had almost arrived
in our camp—at least, so he said—that he had learned who
we really were and our object in visiting that part of the
country.   Previously to our presenting him with these things
he had gone through the regular *amān* ceremony to which
we had become so accustomed of late.

The only sign of his exalted rank that he displayed on
first coming amongst us consisted of a singularly dirty and
very gaudy red cotton handkerchief that he wore twisted
round his head, and a kind of dressing-gown of the same
material.   We questioned him about the Basé dwelling on
the Settite; and he declared that he had nothing to do
with them, but that we could go among them if we wished
to do so.   He did not, however, appear to know anything
of that part of the country, and made us no offer of guides;
nor did he make any suggestions as to how we were to get
there.

The day after the "investiture" Sheik Kudul took his
departure, comforting us at the same time with the promise
of the pleasure of his company again in two days' time.
As far as his appearance went I never saw any one with
a more villainous cast of countenance, nor one I should be
more loath to trust.

On the 8th we moved to Khor Ma Ambasah, close to
where Aylmer and I had shot the buffaloes; and a prettier
camp we never selected.   Our tents were pitched some
three or four miles from its junction with the Mareb and
above its sandy bed, in a place where numbers of lofty
trees afforded us plenty of shelter from the sun, and where
a kind of natural arbours were formed by the bushes, in
one of which we placed our table.   The trees and bushes

were of many different kinds and in full leaf, and so thick
that no part of the camp was exposed to the sun for very
long at a time. As I have already mentioned, this camp
was destined to be our farthest in that direction; this, and
the place we had last left, showed more signs of game than
we had found anywhere else, nor did we subsequently find
any part of the country in which the chances of good sport
promised so well. It was most unfortunate that circumstances soon made it advisable for us to retrace our steps;
otherwise, if we had been able to remain longer on Khor
Ma Ambasah and could have penetrated rather farther into
the country, we should doubtless have obtained a far better
bag than we did. As it was we spent three clear days
there; on one of these days we shot two fine bull buffaloes.

One day two of our party went several miles farther up
the Mareb in the direction of Abyssinia, where they ascended
a hill, from whence they obtained a good bird's-eye view
of the country for some miles round. They reported that
the mountains came down to the river's bed, which was
fringed with *dhoum*-palms, but that the high grass decreased
very much in quantity farther up the Mareb. They saw
very little game, but came across a great many Basé.

The natives told us that the Basé villages extended
about a day's or a day and a half's journey in that direction
from the junction of the two *khors*, and then came Abyssinia. Probably their villages ceased about ten or fifteen
miles off, and between these villages and Abyssinia lay a
neutral piece of ground upon which neither Basé nor
Abyssinian dare live for fear of each other.

As we were running short of *dhurra*, and found that,
contrary to what we had been led to expect when leaving
Haikota, it was a very scarce commodity in the Basé
country, it became a very important question to decide
what was to be done in order to replenish our supply.
Our native servants depended greatly upon it for food;
and it was, moreover, an absolute essential for our horses.
After some difficulty, and on promising a handsome *baksheesh*, we found some of the more intrepid among our
camel-drivers willing to go with their camels to the Egyptian

frontier town of Amedeb to purchase some. Besides *dhurra* we told them to bring back some cotton cloth to distribute among the Basé. There was nothing we found they prized so much; for, as they were at constant logger-heads with the Egyptians, it was almost impossible for them to procure it. They started on their journey on the after-noon of February 10.

CHAPTER XIII.

Disastrous Adventure with Abyssinians.—Akabah brings the Alarm.
—Two of our Party surprised by a Hundred armed Abyssinians.—
Making Friends.—Treachery of the Abyssinians.—Mahomet fear-
fully wounded.—The search for him.—The Dembelas Tribe.—
Contemplated Expedition against the Dembelas abandoned.

ON the 11th a most disastrous event occurred, and one
which materially affected the remaining portion of our
expedition. We had so far got on very well, and had had
no serious drawbacks to the success of our journey, with
the exception of poor Jules' death at Cassala. We had
found our camp at Ma Ambasah the most picturesque and
agreeable that we had yet formed; and it promised to be
most successful headquarters from which to start in pursuit
of game. No Europeans had been there before us. The
Basé were entirely unarmed, with the exception of their
spears and shields; and it was sufficiently far from the
headquarters of the Beni-Amer tribe on the west and the
Abyssinians on the east to have allowed the game to
remain almost undisturbed.

Although it was only a small tract of country that
enjoyed these advantages to the sportsman, they were
advantages fully appreciated by us, who knew from the
experience of two former winters the great difficulty of
finding in this part of Africa territory containing an abundance of game; of the larger game, I mean, antelopes being
numerous in many other parts. A few years ago elephants
and rhinoceros were plentiful in places that the former
now visit only at rare and uncertain intervals, and where
the presence of the latter is a thing entirely of the past.
At Ma Ambasah there were plentiful marks of rhinoceros,
and elephants not infrequently visited the neighbourhood.

It was our custom to draw for pairs to go out shooting, and we had done so, as usual, on this occasion. Lort Phillips and Aylmer had drawn together. I was to go with Colvin; and my brothers decided on remaining in camp for the purpose of making observations and taking photographs. We also drew for trackers; Colvin and I got Salee, while the others took Mahomet, an excellent man whom we had engaged at Cassala.

We started up the dry river's bed and saw numerous tracks of rhinoceros. One or two of these animals had evidently been drinking during the night at some pools of water we came across; during the daytime they usually retire to the thick grass and almost impenetrable jungle that grows so thickly in this part of the country, and where they are almost un-get-at-able. On the Settite there is none of this grass; and, although it is much affected by the larger animals, their pursuit is rendered much more difficult where it abounds. One feels constantly sure of the presence of big game when it is impossible to see it.

A number of Basé had accompanied us, eager for meat; and we found it very difficult to keep them back. We had been on the fresh tracks of a large bull buffalo for some time, but owing to the chattering of these fellows we could not get near it, and at last, in despair, sat down and refused to proceed farther till all but three or four had set their faces in the direction of the camp; and we insisted that those we allowed with us should keep a long way in our rear, which with great difficulty we persuaded them to do.

I had caught a glimpse of a buffalo on the bank to our right, which had seen us and made off; and we had been following him for some time, when suddenly there appeared running towards us a Basé named Akabah (in their language, "the buffalo"), who we knew had that morning accompanied the other party. His face was torn and his legs bleeding from the thorns he had encountered in his flight. He called out to us, "*El Makadah, el Makadah!*" ("The Abyssinians!"), and made for the direction of the camp. Presently five or six more appeared; but we did not think anything of it, well knowing what cowards the much-feared

Basé really are, and feeling sure that it was only necessary for them to see, or imagine they saw, some Abyssinian on the top of a hill for them to bolt at once, without waiting to see whether their intentions were hostile or not. At this time no one was with us except Salee, as we had left the rest of the natives in the river's bed with our horses, and a camel we had taken with us to carry meat should we shoot anything.

We continued tracking the buffalo, but at last gave it up, as we could see by its marks on the ground that it had several times been frightened, doubtless by the flying Basé, and gone off at a gallop. Accordingly, we made for a shady spot and discussed our luncheon, and, that ceremony over, crossed the bed of the river, and looked for fresh tracks on the other side. We had not proceeded far when we espied Mahomet Salee and Bayrumphy galloping along on the opposite side : so we crossed over to them to see what was the matter. As soon as they perceived us approaching, they shouted to us, in a tremendous state of excitement, to return to the camp immediately as the Makadah had attacked the other party. On joining them we learned that Aylmer and Lort Phillips had been surprised by a large party of Abyssinians, who had taken their rifles and a horse ; and, worse than all, that Mahomet had been speared and was left behind dangerously wounded.

We made all haste to the camp, where we found every one in a high state of excitement and dreadfully anxious about us, as they knew we had gone in much the same direction that the others had taken when they were attacked. They were engaged in strengthening the *zariba*, and had fired the grass on the other side of the river's bed opposite the camp; as, in case of an attack, it would have been a grand shelter for our assailants. They had, moreover, dealt out all spare guns and rifles to those of our servants whom they imagined most competent to use them. I fancy, however, that if anything had happened they would most of them have been just as likely, perhaps even more so, to shoot some of us or themselves as to do any damage to the hostile natives.

We were, of course, most eager to hear full particulars of what had occurred, and were not long in hearing the whole story. Lort Phillips and Aylmer had proceeded some eight or nine miles up the dry bed of Khor Ma Ambasah, and were making for a mountain called Gala, which rose on the west bank of the *khor*, at the foot of which there were said to be some pools of water at which rhinoceros, buffaloes, and other animals were in the habit of drinking. They had nearly reached Gala, and were riding in the sandy bed of the *khor* keeping a sharp look-out for game, and feeling pretty sure that they would come across some either going to drink or returning from the water, when, on turning a bend, they saw first one and then another man run across, while a third, in a baobab-tree, was gathering fruit.

The Basé who were with them, without looking farther, immediately turned tail and fled. They had evinced no fear when starting from camp, and had said nothing about the Abyssinians; so that Lort Phillips and Aylmer were at first at a loss to account for their sudden consternation. These were the Basé that Colvin and I had encountered flying in the direction of the camp. After going a few steps farther they saw about a hundred men armed with spears, as all are in these countries, sitting under an over-hanging rock, beside a well they had dug in the sand. On seeing Lort Phillips and Aylmer they ran towards them. Achmet, our head horse-boy, whom we had engaged at Souakim, shouted, "*Edroop, edroop !*" ("Fire, fire !"); and it is a pity they did not act upon his advice, as there is little doubt that the enemy would have fled immediately if they had only fired a shot or two over their heads; it would have been quite enough to scare them away, without the necessity of firing *at* them. Mahomet, however, who had been in the country before (Achmet had not), and whose opinion might consequently be considered to have more weight than Achmet's, begged them not to do so, and urged them to make *amān*, or friends.

We had of late frequently heard the word *amān* applied to ridiculous ceremonies performed by the sheiks of various

Basé villages through which we had passed, and which were supposed to have the effect of making us friends for ever with those with whom they had taken place; and Sheik Kudul had informed us that he was friends with the Abyssinians : so that Aylmer and Lort Phillips imagined they would only have to go through the same performance again to make them sworn allies.

Accordingly, acting on Mahomet's advice, they dismounted when the Abyssinians got up to them; Mahomet and Achmet then placed the spare rifles they were carrying on the ground, and motioned Lort Phillips and Aylmer to do the same, in order to show that they were peaceably inclined. The Abyssinians (who afterwards proved to be of the Dembelas tribe, a semi-independent people living on the north-western frontier of Abyssinia, and whom I shall hereafter distinguish as Dembelas) commenced by kissing their hands and making every demonstration of friendship. Suddenly, however, they fell helter-skelter one on top of the other upon the rifles. Mahomet, Achmet, and the other three or four natives who were with them, on perceiving the tables thus unexpectedly turned, thought it was a case of *sauve qui peut,* and made off as fast as their legs would carry them. The Dembelas fought with each other for the possession of the much-prized rifles; and one or two made a rush for Lort Phillips' horse, which En-Noor, who usually looked after it, was holding. They stripped En-Noor, moreover, of Lort Phillips' revolver, which he had unfortunately given him to carry early in the day, and which was fastened to a strap he wore round his waist.

Aylmer had his revolver in his hand, and drew it, intending to shoot a man who was trying to obtain possession of his horse; but, for some reason or other, it would not go off—a fortunate circumstance for him I should think ; as, at the time he tried to use it, the Dembelas had, ten to one, the best of it. They managed, however, before the natives made off with the booty, to recover Lort Phillips' ten-bore rifle and Aylmer's horse, which they were also making off with. Hardly had they done so when Lort Phillips gave a view-halloo. This (to them) unearthly noise had a magical effect; they took to their heels up the hills that bordered the *khor* as fast as they could go; while Aylmer and Lort Phillips made the best of their way towards camp with the ten-bore rifle and one horse, having lost a ·500 and a ·450 express rifle, an eight-bore, a revolver, and a horse.

After going some distance on their return to camp they encountered the native servants who had run away; and from them they learned, to their horror, that Mahomet had been fearfully wounded in the stomach by a spear and had been left behind. As far as we could gather, after having started to run away he looked back, and, observing their struggle to regain possession of their rifles, turned round to render them assistance and was speared. The boy in charge of the camel took his hand and helped him for a short distance; but Mahomet, feeling he was hard hit, told him he was dying, and could go no farther, and urged him to look to his own safety.

One of the Dembelas threw a spear at him; which happily missed him, but killed the camel. They stripped the animal of the saddle-bags, containing luncheon, and about thirty or forty cartridges. These cartridges, however, would not have been much to divide between three rifles of different calibres. One of the horsemen with them, whom we had brought from Haikota, they robbed of his horse, and, having soundly thrashed him with the back of his own sword, took it away. He was an old man, and greatly distressed at the indignity that had been offered him; and he quite thought we should consider the loss of his sword as the most important of the whole affray.

As soon as Colvin and I arrived in camp we all resolved to lose no time in going out to search for poor Mahomet, or his body in case he were dead—a contingency that seemed only too probable, judging from the fearful description we had from the camel-boy of the manner in which he was wounded. We decided that this boy should be of the party, as we trusted to him to show us where he had left him. As it was impossible to leave our two European servants (who were in a state of great terror) or the camp alone, we drew lots for four, with the doctor, to go in search of Mahomet, and for the other two to remain in camp. Colvin and my brother William were the two who remained behind. It was four o'clock before we started, and we did not get back till after nine. Although we made all possible haste, it was almost dusk before we arrived at the spot where the boy stated he had last seen him. We searched everywhere, until darkness compelled us to desist; but we could find no trace of him, and all we saw were some thirty or forty huge vultures sitting together on the palm-trees; and the sickening fear came over us that he was dead, and that these birds, which in Africa so often act as sextons, had already devoured his remains. This seemed but too probable, for in these parts of Africa it is usually only a matter of a few minutes, or even seconds, for these birds to collect after one has shot an antelope or any other kind of game.

I remember, the first time I travelled in the Soudan, shooting two ariel, which fell not over a hundred or a hundred and fifty yards apart; and yet, although when I shot them I could see no vultures about, by the time I had secured the head of one and had come up to the other its head was already destroyed by the vultures, which had commenced to devour it. When we shot more than one animal at a time we always sent some one to keep the vultures off one while the men were engaged in cutting up the other.

On our return to camp there was a great discussion among our men as to whether the people who had plundered us were Tigré Abyssinians or Dembelas. We ourselves felt almost sure at the time, from the direction in which they came, that they were Dembelas, and we afterwards established the fact. I do not think that the attack was premeditated. In all this part of Africa there is a considerable tract of country which divides each tribe, and which it is difficult to assign to either, both of them being afraid to inhabit it.

At our camp on Khor Ma Ambasah we were, so to speak, wedged in between three tribes—the Basé, the Tigré Abyssinians, and the Dembelas; and none of these would go there unless in considerable numbers. The people we had encountered had some boys and three or four women with them, as well as goats and three mules; and it is not likely they would have taken such *impedimenta* with them had they started with hostile intent. They travelled a strong party to be prepared for hostilities with their enemies the Basé; and their object in going where they did was probably to search for honey, which is plentiful in the baobab-trees, and for the fruit of the baobab-tree itself; and they were, moreover, most likely furnished with traps to catch antelopes. The country being uninhabited would be favourable for their purpose. Seeing white men they doubtless took them for Turks, and thought they could not do better than try to possess themselves of their rifles. They are the most lawless and uncivilised of all the Abyssinian tribes— only nominally paying taxes and owing allegiance to King John. Their country is almost *terra incognita:* the only European that I could ever hear of as having travelled there at all being the Italian traveller the Marquis Antinori; and he had explored only a small portion of it.

The previous winter we had been on the northern boundary of their country and had gone into the neutral territory; but not so far as their villages, because we could never find any one of the neighbouring Arabs sufficiently intrepid to accompany us. On our return to England, however, we learned from Captain Gascoigne, of the "Blues," that he had penetrated to several of their villages with one of their own people, whom he had got hold of in some way or another. Although at first they wanted to keep him prisoner, his guide persuaded them to let him return. He found the villages much neater than those of the Arabs, and that they grew a great deal of millet and *dhurra.* The country was very mountainous and unsuitable for camels, of which they had none; and he saw very little game. The Dembelas Lort Phillips and Aylmer saw were quite light-coloured, and better clothed than most of the nomad Arabs; and, of course, far more so than the Basé, who are literally nearly naked. They had bare, shaved heads; and one man carried a gun, and actually wore a felt wide-awake hat, with the brim turned down like an Irishman's. It would be curious to know where he got it—possibly from the Marquis Antinori! They wore no sandals ; and this, some of our men declared, was a proof that they were Tigré Abyssinians, as they said they never wore them, and that the Dembelas did.

Some of our men also asserted that, while *"amān"* with the Basé and Arabs meant making friends or peace, these people understood the word to signify unconditional surrender : "take all we have, only spare our lives." Those of our men who pretended to know anything of the language of the Dembelas made this statement, and said that it was unfortunate that none of the men with Aylmer and Lort Phillips could speak the language. It is next to impossible to get at the truth in matters of this kind. It is very certain that none of the men with them knew anything of the " lingo," but I doubt whether any one in the camp did.

Our first impulse was to start off after these people, and we offered Sheik Kudul money for men to go with us ; but he would not give us any, and, on second thoughts, we decided that it was impossible to follow them into their mountains. At the least, it would have meant abandoning the baggage to the Basé, who would, of course, have walked off with everything left behind. This sheik stuck to it that these people were Tigré Abyssinians ; and, as he had previously declared they were his friends, we began to wonder whether he meant treachery by us himself. Moreover, it looked rather suspicious that, after having paid us a visit, he had left for two days " on business," and had returned only that very day.

I

CHAPTER XIV.

We leave Ma Ambasah.—Arrival of Mahomet.—Doubts of the Basé.
—A Picturesque Scene.—Sport or Exploration?—The Medicine-
Chest.—Death of Mahomet.—Two of the Party start for Amedeb.
—Difficulty of keeping Camels.—The "Guffer" Disease.—Dila-
toriness of the Arabs.—Poverty of the Basé.—The Barea Tribe.

ALL our servants and camel-drivers declared they would
not remain any longer on Khor Ma Ambasah; and we
ourselves found it impossible to do so, although we greatly
regretted turning our backs on what looked like an excellent
locality for sport. Had we attempted to remain our men
would all, or nearly all, have deserted, probably taking the
camels with them, and we should have had no means of
transport. Accordingly we decided on leaving the next
morning.

Very early, and before we had started another party in
search of poor Mahomet, we heard a cry that he was coming into camp; and running outside the *zariba* down to the
khor we saw the poor fellow. A more dreadful or pitiable
spectacle I never beheld. A fine healthy-looking fellow
when he left the camp the morning before, he was but the
wreck of his former self. When I first saw him he was
crouching on his haunches, in the manner of these people
when they wish to rest, and his face had become quite
drawn and thin. He had taken his sole garment—some
yards of cotton cloth, which he wore ordinarily round his
loins and across his shoulders—to support his entrails,
which he further did with his arms. He had been wounded
by a spear in four places—in two places in the back, one
in the arm, and this fearful wound in the abdomen. In
this state he had crawled eight miles from where the attack
took place to our camp. His first words were to ask if

Lort Phillips and Aylmer were safe. He told us that we had passed a few yards of him the previous night; and that, although he plainly saw us, he was too weak to call out for help; he had been lying under a bush at the time, quite close to the camp, unable to proceed farther. The night had been very cold, the thermometer having gone down to 43° Fahrenheit; and his suffering from cold and thirst, added to the fear of being attacked by some wild beast (hyænas especially being very numerous there), must have been something terrible.

We got an *angareb* and carried him into camp. The doctor did what he could for him, but from the first the case was hopeless. We wanted to give him a little brandy, which he refused to take, it being against his religion. However, we put some in his beef-tea, so that he took it without knowing it. The doctor declared it would make him no worse to carry him on the *angareb;* so we gave orders to strike the camp and return to our last halting-place, with which order our camel-drivers and servants were delighted.

The only member of our party who did not seem in the least excited by what had occurred was old Ali the cook. Nothing ever ruffled *him.* He was busy with his saucepans when the news of what had happened was first brought into the camp; and, amongst all the din and clatter raised by our numerous camp-servants, he continued calmly and quietly to proceed with his cooking.

We were beginning to have some misgivings with regard to the Basé. Between two and three hundred had attached themselves to us. We felt we could not trust much to Sheik Kudul; and, although so far we had had no cause of complaint of their attitude towards us, some of them were beginning to show signs of disaffection, and grumbling that they had no more presents made to them. We regretted that we had not brought a camel-load or two of Manchester cloth to distribute amongst them. The small quantity we had brought was much appreciated; and we parcelled it out with great care, the larger portion of course going to the sheiks. Our stock of razors, knives, and scissors—a large one to begin with—was rapidly diminishing; and as, of course, we could get no more, we had to be very chary of them. Our only fear of the Basé was, lest, emboldened by the success of the Dembelas, they should endeavour to surprise us at night. In order to guard ourselves against this possibility, we were very careful to surround our camp with an extra-strong *zariba;* keeping, moreover, fires burning at night in various parts of the camp, and having regular sentries, who were relieved at intervals.

At night the Basé slept all together immediately outside the *zariba.* Their innumerable small fires flashed upon a forest of spears thrust in the sand around them, occasionally lighting up their dusky forms; while in the centre of the camp our watch-fire illuminated the trees above, the tents around, and the dark background of the jungle, with its tangled creepers festooning the trees, gracefully draped by the faultless hand of nature—the *tout ensemble* creating an altogether fairy scene.

There is no doubt about it that exploration and sport are two very different things. If the traveller's object is the former, he pushes through the country as best he can, with his purpose—exploration—always in view, trusting to luck and tact to overcome the many inevitable obstacles that will beset his path. If, however, the latter is his main object, he wants to feel pretty free to move where he likes from the camp, and cannot expect to meet with much success with the game if he is constantly on the look-out for enemies in the people among whom he is travelling. He wants, when he chooses, to wander out alone some distance from the camp in pursuit of the object that has taken him to the country, and, when away from his goods and chattels, to feel that both they and his servants and followers are tolerably safe from a hostile attack. I think, however, that an Englishman, provided he treats the natives well and pays proper respect to their prejudices, can go almost anywhere. He must, above all, pay particular deference to the chiefs, and let them see that he regards them as important personages, as in their own country they undoubtedly are; at the same time letting them see that he is a person of consequence himself, and expects to be treated accordingly.

A medicine-chest is often of more use to the traveller than a revolver, for nothing gives an African savage greater pleasure than a good doze of medicine; but it must be a strong one, and rapid in its effects—none of your half measures with them. A good doze of croton-oil and colocynth, or four or five grains of tartar emetic, is what they like. They hold the European "medicine-man" in great awe and respect. But, although delighting in being physicked internally, they are almost invariably unwilling to submit to the knife. During our first journey in the Soudan we did more doctoring than on either of our subsequent expeditions. At some places, Cassala for instance, there were days when as many as two hundred people visited the doctor, who gave away, among other drugs, great quantities of Holloway's pills. These pills we found immensely popular, and we took a good supply with us, in half-pound boxes, on each of our expeditions; and I should never travel in Africa without a good supply.

Mahomet stood the journey very well, and seemed better when we arrived at our last camp. The doctor had given him some opium, and he travelled easily on the *angareb*. We had induced some Basé to carry him by promising them some cotton cloth when the camels we had sent to Amedeb for *dhurra* should return; for we had given the camel-drivers money to purchase it there.

We pitched our camp on the opposite bank of the Mareb, at the junction of a *khor* called Mai Sarsah, from that on which we had previously halted; partly to avoid being near some high grass, which grew at the back of our last camp, and in which an enemy could very easily have lain hidden, and partly because on the opposite bank there was more material at hand with which to construct a *zariba*.

We made Mahomet as comfortable as we could by giving him the doctor's tent; and Salee remained with the poor fellow all night. Although he took large doses of opium he hardly slept at all; he did not, however, complain of

pain until the following morning, when mercifully his sufferings were very short, and he died soon after nine o'clock.
The Arabs buried him on the same morning in a grave
which they dug at some distance above the Mareb. We
gave them some cotton cloth for grave-clothes; and Mahoom
stitched them together with the fibre of the *dhoum*-palm
leaf, fresh from the tree. The Arabs use this for the purpose when they can get it in preference to thread, which I
suppose they regard as European, and therefore unsuitable.
The doctor considered it fortunate that his life had not
been prolonged, because, had it been so, he must have
suffered terrible agonies, which he was mercifully spared.

After a considerable discussion as to what was to be
done next, we decided that Lort Phillips and I should go
to Amedeb to inform the Egyptian authorities of what had
happened; the rest of the party waiting for us on the Mareb.
There were two objects in doing this. We felt that, even
in that wild country, the news would probably travel to
Amedeb, and we feared that a greatly exaggerated account
might reach Cairo, and very possibly get into the English
newspapers and alarm our friends at home; and we were
anxious, if possible, to recover our rifles, and thought that,
as they would most probably get into the hands of some
Abyssinian sheik, there was a chance that by going to
Amedeb we might be able to put ourselves in the way of
regaining possession of them. Accordingly, we retraced
our steps to Aibaro, where we chose a good position for the
camp. On the way we found very little game, shooting
nothing but *tétél* and *oterop* (*Calotragus montanus*), a very
small species of gazelle, which is very easily shot and is
very fair eating; we only met with it on the Mareb.

On February 15 Lort Phillips and I started for Amedeb.
We decided to bring back more camels if possible. Camels
are very awkward things to own, or rather to have properly
looked after. Several of ours had died since leaving Cassala,
and a number were almost incapable of carrying loads.
The fact is that regular camel-drivers—and by that term I
mean the class of men who accompany the camels one hires
from place to place, as, for example, from Souakim to

Cassala—are not to be had by paying them monthly wages. They are either owners of camels themselves or the servants or slaves of owners; consequently, if one buys camels one is forced to employ men to load and look after them who are quite unaccustomed to the work, and, moreover, take no kind of interest in it. Camels are very delicate; and, if accustomed to a low hot country, will not thrive where the nights are cold, and *vice versâ;* and, if used to travel in a level sandy country, they cut their feet dreadfully when obliged to traverse rocky or stony roads. A camel, too, that inhabits a district where grass is plentiful will not thrive where it is scarce, but where trees with green leaves abound; while others, on the contrary, relish green leaves, and will not look at grass. They are very stupid animals, and require to be taken to suitable feeding-ground, as they are not always sensible enough to find it for themselves. It sometimes happened that there was grass to be found on one side of the river's bed and green leaves on the other; and our camel-drivers, unmindful of these peculiarities, would sleep in comfort, leaving these stupid animals to feed off whatever happened to come first.

On some parts of the Mareb a parasitic plant, which the natives call *hikabeet,* with a most brilliant green leaf, is very common. It is poisonous; but camels will devour it greedily whenever they get a chance. We lost a good many from this cause; and others, though they recovered, were for a long time unfit for work. Careless loading, too, caused many to suffer from sore backs; and we were constantly at loggerheads with our drivers.

There is a disease, very common amongst camels, which the natives call the *guffer.* We were never able to make out clearly what this disease was. Some of the Arabs declared it was catching; others that it was not; but all said that a number of the camels we had bought on the Atbara were suffering from it when they were bought. Whenever we had to complain of any of the camel-drivers having, through negligence, allowed a camel to run down, the excuse was that it was suffering from this mysterious disease, the *guffer.* We were once asked to look at a camel said to be suffering from this complaint. It was certainly in a miserably poor condition, and at the time appeared to have a fit or convulsion of some kind. It rolled on the ground, apparently in great agony, and was only induced to get up after much difficulty. ·Somehow or other it got through the day's march, but was never afterwards good for much. Some of the natives said this disease was caused by the bite of the tsetse-fly during the rainy season.

We were told that one long day would bring us to Amedeb ; but although we rose at five o'clock it was nearly nine before we were fairly off. It is impossible to hurry Arabs ; and, whether we started with a large or a small caravan, getting off was always a very slow process. We took with us Mahomet Salee and Bayrumphy, who rode on horseback ; one did not like to go without the other ; and, moreover, Bayrumphy was our interpreter with the Basé. He knew very little Arabic, and had first to translate Basé into the language spoken by the Beni-Amer tribe to Mahomet Salee, who re-translated to us into Arabic ; in this way, when any of the Basé wished to communicate with us, their original sentences were sadly mangled and distorted before we could understand them. Suleiman rode on top of the camel that usually carried our luncheon when on the march, and all necessary provisions, saucepans, etc., for the journey were stowed away in the panniers on which he was seated. We took two camels completely laden with heads and skins to be left at Amedeb, as we all expected to pass by there on our way to the coast, when we could pick them up again.

We carried the European servants' tent to sleep in. At first we thought of going without one, and sleeping in the open air ; but were afterwards very glad we had not done so, as the nights were intensely cold, with fogs in the early morning. During my first journey in the Soudan I slept without a tent of any kind, and both I and another of the party who did the same suffered from fever. I do not know whether we caught it in this way or not, but I think it very likely that the cold nights, and often heavy dews, after the intensely hot days, would induce fever. At any rate, none of our party suffered in this way during our last two journeys; and, except when lying out at nights on the watch for game, we always slept under canvas.

The road was at first very bad, and we had sometimes to cut our way through bushes in order to allow the camels to pass. We saw scarcely a bird or a gazelle, but we met a good many Basé, with fifty or sixty donkeys and a few goats, going to the Settite for *dhurra*, we were told; but I am sure that was not the case, as we found afterwards that the Basé on the Mareb had no dealings whatever with the people living on the Settite. Some idea of the poverty of the Basé may be formed from the fact that these donkeys and goats were the first we had seen since leaving Haikota, with the exception of three or four donkeys I had seen, as we were quitting Aibaro, trudging along in the sandy bed of the Mareb.

The country during the first day's journey was most uninteresting, hilly, and with the usual bush-jungle and occasional large trees growing in the dry beds of streams that during the rains fed the Mareb; in one of these were the remains of wells. By nightfall we reached a village, situated on a hill, where we passed the night. It belonged to the Barea tribe. The people were very friendly, and gave us milk and water. There was no water nearer than three or four miles from the village in the direction of Amedeb; and it was brought up the hill in goat-skins, and carried by the women on their backs. These people paid taxes to the Egyptian Government, and grew a good deal of *dhurra*. In appearance they much resembled their neighbours the Basé, but wore more clothing, and appeared altogether much more prosperous, which speaks well for the government. They have the reputation of being great thieves, and very troublesome people to deal with. I think the night we spent in this village was the coldest I remember passing in the Soudan; and in the morning there was a thick fog that wet one through, quite like a Scotch mist, and which did not lift until nearly nine o'clock. The people told us it occurred almost every morning at that time of year.

CHAPTER XV.

Our Journey to Amedeb. — History of Sheik Said Carcashi. — The
Bombashi.—Promises aid in recovering the Stolen Property. — Ras
Aloula. — Town of Amedeb. — Mahomet's sister. — Return to the
Mareb.

As soon as the fog cleared away we started and reached
Amedeb about three o'clock. I never traversed so bad a
road with camels, and imagine they are very rarely made
to perform the journey. We had to go over a high mountain, from which we obtained a most extensive view; to our
left were other mountains, many of them of most fantastic
shapes, and covered with loose stones and a growth of short
trees and bushes, while to our left stretched an apparently
endless plain, on which our men made out they could perceive the fringe of *dhoum*-palms that borders either bank of
Khor Baraka. The whole country was covered with what
had been *dhurra*-fields, the hills being terraced for its
cultivation, reminding me in appearance of the vines growing on the hillsides in Switzerland.

A long time before we reached Amedeb we could see it
in the plain before us. The valley in which it is situated
is surrounded on all sides by mountains, except where it
runs into the great plain, which extends east and west for
miles. This valley is very unlovely, being covered with
loose stones and having a sparse growth of small bushes.
Nevertheless villages are numerous, all being built on the
hillsides, and with the usual conical-roofed huts. We saw
plenty of cattle.

At the village where we passed the night a Basé who
had accompanied us from the Mareb left to return, being
afraid to venture into Amedeb. A son of Sheik Said

Carcashi rode with us on horseback nearly into the town, where he, too, left us and returned.

Sheik Said Carcashi was originally a Basé from the Mareb, and was captured when a boy, and sold as a slave at Massawa. There he learned to speak Arabic, as well as to read and write it. Munzinger Pacha (a Swiss, governor of that part of the Soudan and Sanheit; who was killed by the Abyssinians some years ago during an engagement between them and the Egyptians), seeing that he was possessed of some intelligence, took him to Amedeb, and made him sheik over the neighbouring people. He is, of course, hated by the independent Basé living farther south. He goes about with a small army, consisting of a handful of his followers, dressed in brilliant-coloured calico drawers and red waistcoats, and armed with government rifles. Backed by these men he squeezes taxes out of all the people he can induce to pay them. This is the man whom Sheik Kudul imagined we had brought with us into his country when he told us that, if such had been the case, he had meant to ask the Abyssinians to help him to fight us.

On arriving at the village where we had spent the night we had met our camels returning from Amedeb. They had arrived there the night before we did; and Sheik Said had detained them there, having heard that some disaster had happened to us, although he did not know what. Bad news, proverbially, travels fast; and these wild countries are no exception to the rule. They had found no *dhurra* for sale at Amedeb, but had procured some from Sheik Said; and could get only a very little cotton cloth, and that at a high price. We started them off at once for Aibaro, as we were running short of *dhurra* and had many mouths to feed.

We pitched our tents just outside the governor's house and close to an empty hut, of which we took possession for our men and luggage. We had expected to find an old friend of last year in the governor of Amedeb, as a very intelligent White Nile negro whom we had left last year in authority at Sanheit had been transferred there; but he was absent; and a Turk, a military man, was taking his place. We lost no time in going to see him, and found him very civil, and about the most energetic man I ever came across in the Soudan. The natives called him the "Bombashi," which is a Turkish expression signifying captain of a thousand soldiers. We found that the news of our trouble with the Dembelas had preceded us. Immediately on hearing of it the Bombashi had telegraphed to the Bey at Cassala, telling him of it, and asking why he had allowed us to go into that country without an escort of soldiers. He replied that we had told him we were going into the Hamran country (which belongs to the government), and that he had sent to the authorities at Jireh, where an Egyptian fort has lately been erected, telling them to look after us, but that they had sent back word that we had not been there. He said that he had sent messengers after us to Jireh and two letters.

We explained to the Bombashi that we had never told the Bey we were going to the Hamrans, as we had never intended visiting that part of the country, which had been visited by so many Englishmen that it was quite shot out. He promised to do what he could towards helping us to recover our rifles, but was not very hopeful about it. He told us that the Dembelas had only lately killed forty Beni-Amers in Khor Baraka and driven off a great number of cattle. Some of our native servants had said that Sheik Arri, who is the most powerful of the Beni-Amer chiefs on Khor Baraka, and with whom we had had a good deal to do the previous winter, was at that time on friendly terms with the Dembelas chiefs and would be very likely able and willing to help us. After hearing this, however, we made up our minds to expect no aid from that quarter. The Tigrean Abyssinians had also during the last two months stolen some thousands of cattle between Sanheit and Massawa.

The Bombashi telegraphed to Sanheit asking if they would send to Ras Aloula (who is the commander of the Abyssinian army and the chief person in the country after the king) demanding the restitution of the rifles. A reply came back very quickly, saying that they would do so. We felt sure, however, that they would never attempt such a thing. The governor of Sanheit also said in his telegram that he had telegraphed the news to the minister of the interior at Cairo. I accordingly telegraphed to Cairo asking that a telegram might be sent to England to say that we were all safe, as I feared an exaggerated account of the affair might get into the English papers. As it turned out, however, I might have saved myself this trouble and expense, for the telegram never reached its destination.

Amedeb is a wretched place; it contains a garrison of eight hundred soldiers, and boasts of four cannon and a mortar. It is the worst supplied town I met with in the Soudan, owing, no doubt, to its being off any principal caravan-route; and is a purely military post, having no trade worth mentioning. Our camel-drivers had told us how poor the bazaars were; they had only been able to get five small packets of candles to take to the camp, one of which we appropriated, having forgotten to bring any with us. We bought a few beads to take back, but they were poor and very dear; and we were also able to obtain milk and eggs. We were in great luck, too, in being able to procure camels, as during our stay a string of from two to three hundred Shukreeyeh camels arrived, bringing *dhurra* for the government. We sent a Shukreeyeh camel-driver we had brought from Aibaro to their owners, and, after a great deal of discussion, succeeded in hiring eight, with four drivers, at the rate of twelve dollars a month each— enormous wages for the country; but they were all in such fear of the Basé that they would not consent to take less.

Mahomet, before he died, had told Salee that he had a sister at Amedeb who would take charge of anything we wished to give to his wife, who lived in Khor Baraka. He said that, as he had once killed a man near Amedeb, they would not dare to go there themselves; Khor Baraka was his home, and, although we found him at Cassala, he said he had only been there a month. The Bombashi found the sister for us; and we gave her Mahomet's sword, which, I believe, was the sum total of his worldly goods, and ten dollars, which she was to give to his wife, and to tell her that if she would go to the priests at Sanheit we would look

after her and her children. A more shrivelled-up old hag
than this woman I never saw; she looked half starved and
miserably poor; and we gave her a present of money for
herself.

After a day and a half spent at Amedeb we started to
return to the rest of our party. Having proceeded about
two hours on our way we were joined by Sheik Said Carcashi. We had met him at the Bombashi's divan when
calling there the previous day, and he had been most
solicitous to return with us to the Mareb. We explained,
however, both to him and the Bombashi, that it was impossible for us to consent to his joining us, as we knew he was
anything but friends with the Basé on the Mareb, and his
going would lead to complications, to say the least of it.
He was forced to admit that they were not on the best of
terms; and I feel sure that, if we had consented to take
him, he would have backed out of it at the last moment.
This sheik had a long conversation with Suleiman, in which,
as translated by Suleiman, he expressed great surprise at
our making friends with "that beast man, Sheik Kudul."
The Basé had eyed our departure for Amedeb with considerable suspicion; and, if we had brought Sheik Said
back with us, they would at once have concluded that we
were exploring their country with a view to taxation by the
Egyptian Government.

The sheik insisted on our accompanying him to his
house, which was at the foot of the steep hill we had been
obliged to descend in going to Amedeb. He gave us some
meat, which we were, of course, obliged to eat with our
fingers, and some coffee, and also a present of honey, and
some horrid-looking cooking-butter in a dirty skin, which
we took with us. Our men made very short work of the
meat after we had tasted some of it. We spent the night
about two hours beyond the village where we had broken
the journey in going to Amedeb. The following morning,
while preparing to depart, we were visited by a number of
Basé quite as curious and as scantily clothed as their
brethren on the Mareb.

CHAPTER XVI.

Alarm of an Attack by the Basé.—Our Camp moves on.—Independ-
ence of the Basé.—Elephant-tracks—Most of the Basé leave the
Camp.—A Shot at a Lion.—Difficulty of shooting while riding
Camels.—The Arabs strike.—Abundance of Quail.—Return to
Haikota.—Departure for the Settite.—The Village of Sogada.—
Arrival at the Settite.

WE reached Aibaro in the afternoon, and found the camp
in a state of great excitement and all hands at work
strengthening the *zariba*. It appeared that Longay, who
was the son of the sheik of Koolookoo, had informed our
party that the Basé were getting dissatisfied and meditated
an attack on the camp. Longay had been with us all the
time, and was of great use to us. My attention had been
early drawn to him by George, who one day pointed him
out to me fetching wood for the cook, and said, "The
king's son makes himself most useful in bringing wood and
water." As he was a person of more importance than
most of the other Basé he was promoted to cleaning boots
and knives; and being, moreover, so serviceable, we used ·
to allow him inside the *zariba*, and his inner man was
catered for by our cook. He told us that the Basé
wanted us out of their country, and called him our slave.
My belief is that he said this to ingratiate himself further
with us; and also, it is more than probable, that the others
were jealous of our attentions to him.

The Basé had certainly done all in their power that
morning to induce the party to leave the camp; some
declaring they had just seen buffaloes in one direction, and
others that there were *tétél* in another. They would not,
I think, have attacked us when we were all together, either
by night or day; but it is quite possible that, if they had

BASÉ AT AIBARO.

succeeded in inducing a party to go out shooting, they might have endeavoured in their absence to loot the camp and make off with whatever they could lay their hands upon; and Longay further added that the Basé tribes were massing around us, preparatory to a descent on our camp. Fires in all directions gave a semblance of truth to this statement. At any rate "forewarned is forearmed," and it was just as well to neglect no precautions. Suleiman most injudiciously told some of the Basé that we had heard of the threat that had been made, but they indignantly denied it. Nothing occurred that night; but we had a watch, of course, as usual, and the next morning made a further move in the direction of Haikota.

On first arriving at Haikota we debated whether to go up the Gash or to make for the Settite, that part of it over which we wanted to shoot extending along the river eastward from the Hamran country. Sheik Achmed declared we could go in whichever direction we preferred; but we chose the Gash, as we hoped, after travelling as far as possible along its banks, to be able to go straight across country, and so reach the river. The sheik had not actually promised that we could do this, but had said he felt sure we should find some of the Basé willing to show us a way to the Settite; but, even if we had had no trouble with the Dembelas, I doubt very much if it would have been a practicable journey for camels, owing to the rugged nature of the ground, the number of hills, and the thickness of the jungle in many places through which we should have been obliged to make our way. I am sure, too, that none of the Arabs we had with us had ever made the journey, and I do not believe that any of the Basé knew the way.

The Basé are quite unlike any other African tribe I ever came across, one village having no communication or friendly relationship with another one only a few miles off, so that they are anything but a united people; and in this way one has constant delays in travelling amongst them, as it is necessary to be all the time making fresh friends as one goes along. I do not believe that the Basé dwelling on the Mareb know anything whatever of those on the Settite.

Our Haikota horsemen declared it would not be necessary to go all the way back to Haikota before crossing to the Settite, as they knew of a road which turned off about three days' journey from that place, and where we could obtain water. A very pleasant day's march took us past Koolookoo. I think this is the most picturesque part of the Gash; its bed is here narrower than usual and its course most tortuous. Immense trees in full leaf line either bank; and the undergrowth is very thick, affording excellent covert for the partridges and guinea-fowl, which are most numerous, and gave us capital sport. Where the covert is not too thick these birds run, and are very unwilling to rise. They were most useful for our commissariat department; and, although very dry eating, we were very glad to get them.

Elephants had passed quite recently in the direction of the Settite, whither they had probably gone. They frequently march through from one river to the other, and, when pursued on the Settite, very often make for the Gash, and *vice versâ*. My brothers took up the tracks and followed them for some miles. They were only a day or two old; and the whole herd, about thirty of them, at Wo Ammar had marched clean through our old *zariba*, inside which we decided to spend the night.

At this point most of our Basé left us; and none of them accompanied us more than a few miles farther. We gave Longay a good present. I feel sure that any Englishmen wishing to shoot in that country would be certain of a kind reception if they only treated the people judiciously; at the same time, of course, letting them see that they were on their guard against any possible duplicity on their part. They were soon convinced that we meant them no injury, and, when we parted, told us they would be very glad to see us again; that we had procured them meat to eat; and added that they hoped next time we came we would bring them plenty of cotton cloth.

The heat began to increase very much. We had been

BASÉ HUT AT KOOLOOKOO.

glad after dinner to draw our chairs round a blazing fire, but the evenings had become so warm now that we required no fire, and were glad to sit in our pyjamas. The early mornings were, however, still cold, and then our blankets proved most welcome.

The day we left Wo Ammar we started well ahead of the caravan, as we were anxious to see some pools of water at a rocky spot in the Gash, which we had missed in going up by cutting off a bend in the river. We were rewarded by seeing some fine *méhédehet*, which, however, made off before we could get a shot at them ; but William shot a fine buck *nellut* as he was returning from one of the pools. Late in the afternoon, on approaching the Gash, we observed a large fire, and volumes of smoke in front of us ; one of our horsemen declared it had been made by some Basé in order to drive buffaloes out of the high grass. Hardly were the words out of his mouth when we saw a great cloud of dust, towards which we rode in all haste, anxious to discover the cause of this unusual phenomenon. We soon perceived a herd of some thirty buffaloes, led by a large bull, all galloping off as hard as they could tear. We pursued them as well as we could for some distance ; but our horses were not up to much pace, and, being late in the afternoon, we could not have come up with them before darkness had set in.

On arriving in camp we found that about the worst possible place had been chosen for the tents, which had been pitched above the Gash on a piece of ground which had been lately covered with grass, and this grass having been burnt, the wind, which was very high at the time, blew the ashes about in all directions and covered everything with them. We always had our table laid for dinner outside in the open air; but on this occasion we were forced to have it moved inside a tent, as we were nearly blinded by the charred remains of the grass.

It was from this point that our Haikota horsemen had promised to turn off with us to the Settite, and we had fully expected to start the following day. Soon after our arrival, however, we felt convinced a storm was brewing, as the men were unwontedly excited, and talking a great deal among themselves. It was not very long before a deputation came to us to beg we would go another day's journey, a short one, they said, farther on before turning off; they gave as a reason for the change of route a better road and more water, and declared (which was quite true) that the majority of the camels were not in a fit state to undertake a journey over a very bad road. We decided on taking their advice, and gave the order to start the next day and encamp at the place they named, which was called Sekabah.

The following day, as Colvin and Lort Phillips were riding on ahead of the caravan on the look-out for game, they suddenly came across a lion and lioness. Lort Phillips, having had his horse taken by the Dembelas, had since been obliged to ride a camel—than which no beast can be more provoking. He jumped off as quickly as possible; but the animal set up such a fearful noise that it frightened the lions, who made off towards some high grass growing near. He had a shot at the lion at about a hundred yards, through thick bushes, and knocked him clean over as if he had been a rabbit; however, he got up again almost immediately, and, before it was possible to obtain a second shot, had disappeared into the grass. They saw his marks and some drops of blood, and followed him a short way; but were soon obliged to give it up as they lost his footprints. If either of them had been on foot and ready for a shot, they could have had one at about twenty yards.

Camels are most tiresome animals to shoot from. They will rarely allow you to mount or dismount without setting up a deafening roar, enough to scare away all the game in Africa, and are so tall that, although they afford the rider a capital view of the country, they are most conspicuous objects, and apt to frighten off any game there may be about. Still, whenever there is not much sport in prospect, I much prefer a camel to a horse as a mode of conveyance in Africa. The motion of a good camel is not tiring when once you get accustomed to it, which you very soon do; and it will travel at the rate of about five miles an hour for hours together. I am, of course, alluding only to the good ones. The *mahloofa*, or native saddle, is most comfortable; and you have the great advantage of being able to carry about with you plenty of odds and ends, in the shape of water-skins, guns, and bags. We only took camels with us on our shooting expeditions for the purpose of carrying water and luncheon, as well as to bring back any meat we might have obtained; on these occasions we invariably insisted on their keeping a long way in our rear. We were fortunate in having obtained good riding-camels; and they were better looked after than the baggage ones, as, in the first place, each of us paid a good deal of attention to his own individual camel, and we chose the best of the drivers to attend to them.

Again we were nonplussed by our tiresome Arabs, who came to us in the evening to ask us to put off our departure for the Settite, and this time declared that the only way for us to reach that river was by going first to Haikota. They gave two reasons for this: first, the reason they had given us the day before, that the road was bad; and secondly, that we should be obliged if we took that road to pass close by the village which Sheik Achmed and his men had lately attacked in revenge for their having killed some Haikota people. We were, of course, very angry and disappointed on hearing this; and then the camel-drivers all struck, and said nothing would induce them to go; the other Arabs followed suit, so that there was nothing to be done but to submit. I am quite sure that from the first none of them had the least intention of going to the Settite otherwise than by Haikota, only they did not like to say so a moment sooner than they were obliged to; and, from what we could afterwards make out, I do not believe that any single one of them had ever been that way before. Of course we had expected to find only the barest path, if even that; but it was necessary for some one to know the way on account of obtaining water, which is not very scarce between the Gash and the Settite, but some one in the party must know where it is to be found. In following the road between Cassala and the Settite, in the Hamran country, there is no water to be found till one reaches the river. I made the journey in the spring of 1878, and a more disagreeable one I never experienced. It took nearly four days; water had to be carried for the entire journey; there was not a particle of shade the whole way, and I was suffering from fever at the time.

Not far from Abiam there was a piece of ground overgrown by fine grass (which was, of course, dried up like hay) and short scrubby bushes, where, in travelling up and returning down the Gash, we found quail very numerous. We shot a good many of them, as well as partridges, which were also very plentiful. Although I have sometimes come across a quail here and there, and very occasionally two or three together, this was the first and only place in the Soudan where I ever found them plentiful. They arrive in Upper Egypt about the beginning of February; and I have found them very numerous at that time not far below the first cataract, and am at a loss to imagine where the thousands that annually visit Egypt about that time can come from; they certainly arrive from the south, and for some hundreds of miles south of the first cataract there is very little country that can afford good feeding-ground for quail. I have seen it stated that Sennar, on the Blue Nile, is the limit of their southern flight; if they go there in any numbers the country must be very different from any I have seen in the Soudan. They, doubtless, take immensely long flights without halting anywhere; which they are able to do, as proved by the great numbers that every autumn cross the Mediterranean from Europe into Africa. I believe they always make their flight by night. I have never seen them *en voyage.*

Two more long days brought us back again to Haikota, where we arrived on February 25, and pitched our tents in our old quarters close to the German animal-dealer's *zariba.* On our arrival we were delighted to find letters and newspapers, the first we had received since leaving Suez on December 7. Our latest newspapers were dated London, January 7.

Before making a fresh start we insisted on leaving behind all our Haikota horsemen, with the exception of Mahomet Salee.

We despatched a messenger to Cassala with a large budget of letters for the post, and on the same day, February 27, made a start south for the Settite. We had fully explained to the sheik where we wished to go, and had told him that we did not care to visit the Hamran country, which has of late years been so frequently shot over by Europeans as to have very little game left. He promised that we should strike the river at its junction with Khor Meheteb, a *khor* that runs into the Settite from the north. This we understood was the farthest point in that direction where European travellers had succeeded in making a camp, as it was on the borders of the Basé country, and the Hamrans and the Basé are deadly enemies. We had hoped, commencing from here, to shoot for some distance up the river, and expected to find a tract of country which, though small, had not been previously shot over.

Our first day out from Haikota we only made four hours. The country was uninteresting—the usual bush-jungle and very little game. All the grass had been eaten up by the immense herds which were in the country. Our camping-ground, however, was near some large trees, in an open space called Fahncoob—a well-known halting-place of the Arabs, and with quite a park-like appearance. There was water in a *khor* not very far off; and we shot two or three gazelles, and so were enabled to supply the camp with fresh meat. The following day, before we had started, the sheik, his brother, and nine horsemen arrived; most of the latter returned after they had had some coffee, but the rest of the party remained with us. We were informed that we were to spend the night near a Basé village called Sogada; and here it was necessary to interview the sheik before travelling any farther.

About an hour before encamping we passed a well, near which we spent the night; it was a very old one, very deep, and with an enormously wide mouth. To obtain water it was necessary to scramble down the sides of it. We were told that no one knew how long it had been made, but that it was very ancient. I should think it must have been from two to three hundred feet deep, and I am quite certain

BASÉ.

it must have been built by a far more energetic people than either the Basé or the Beni-Amers are at the present day. The inhabitants of these parts are deficient in all but the very simplest agricultural implements; spades are unknown; and when they want to dig holes for wells they do so with their hands alone.

All day long women were engaged in filling their baskets at the well, and climbing with them on their backs up to the village of Sogáda, which was a good large one, and built, as usual, on a hill. It is astonishing what a weight of water these women will carry. Little boys and girls sometimes do the water-carrying, but no men ever demean themselves by such employment.

The people of the village were at first afraid to come down to see us; but the sheik sent some of his horsemen to them, who brought back the village sheik and some of his followers to interview us. They were very like the other Basé we had seen. The sheik had married his own sister, and had several children by her. This is very common in the country, and thought nothing of. They were very curious, wanting to know what could possibly have induced us to visit them. They said no travellers had ever passed that way before. I have no doubt that such was the case; and the Haikota people confirmed them in it, declaring that no Europeans had ever been to Sogada before.

The country was very wretched, hilly, and covered with *kittar*-bushes; nevertheless a good deal of *dhurra* was grown near the village; far more than up the Mareb, where there was very little appearance of any attempt at cultivation.

Sheik Achmed left us the following day, but not before he had induced us to take three Basé horsemen from Sogada. He declared, and there seemed to be sense in his argument, that they would be able to make things easier for us with the Basé on the Settite and help us to procure a fresh supply of *dhurra*. The *dhurra* was a constant source of worry wherever we went, it being generally very scarce, and the people most unwilling to part with it even when well paid for doing so.

CHAPTER XVII.

The Road to the Settite.—The Everlasting Forest.—Sheik Achmed's Deception.—Fishing in the Settite.—The Camp moves on.—The Guides and Camel-drivers refuse to proceed.—The Return to Khor Meheteb.—Adventure with a Crocodile.—A Scare.—Encampment at Khor Meheteb.—Good Fishing.—The "*Kelb-el-bahr.*"—Capture of a *Baggar.*—A Visit from Basé of Lacatecourah. —Tracking Buffaloes.—Arab Escort sent back to Haikota.—Baboons.—Exciting Night among the Buffaloes.

THE journey from Sogada to the Settite occupied two very long and tiresome days, although we found water more than once. There was frequently no path, and the hatchets were in constant requisition to clear the way for the camels to pass; it was, moreover, often necessary to make rough steps with a pick, by which they could go up and down the banks when obliged to cross a *khor*. A more monotonous journey I never made; the country, as we approached the Settite, became less and less mountainous. For miles we traversed a thick forest of leafless trees, covered with thorns; these trees were only twelve or eighteen feet high, and grew so thickly that we could see but a very short distance in front of us.

My brother William, on the morning of the second day, ascended a small hill with Mahomet Salee, in order to fix positions for the map he was making, and Salee pointed out to him the position of Khor Meheteb and the Settite. In the afternoon he went up another hill and discovered that we were leaving Khor Meheteb a long way on our left, and bearing west in the direction of the Hamrans.

We saw at once how we were being deceived, and were naturally very angry and disappointed. On taxing Mahomet Salee with his duplicity he urged in excuse that at Sogada

the camel-drivers and servants generally had declared they
would not go farther east than Khor Meheteb, and that
Sheik Achmed had told him to take us to the Hamrans
and try and make the best of it to us. There was nothing
for it but to go on to the river as quickly as possible and
see what was to be done when we got there, and to accept
the situation as one of the inevitable drawbacks of African
travel. We did not reach the Settite until ten o'clock, all
in the worst of tempers, and having begun to fear that we
had lost our way and should be obliged to spend the night
without water.

We struck the river at a place called Geebou ; it was
broader here than we had expected to find it, and there was
a splendid pool in front of us, fully a mile long and in parts
very deep. The bank upon which we pitched the tents
was some twenty feet above the water. The country looked
exceptionally wretched. A fringe of green trees bordered
either bank of the river, beyond which the ground was bare,
with no grass, and leafless trees. We were delighted, however, to be on a real flowing river, the water of which was
very clear and full of fish ; and we determined to spend a
day where we were before deciding what was to be done
next.

The first thing next morning we launched the Berthon
boat, which had not suffered at all from its long journey.
Colvin and Lort Philips got out their fishing-tackle, and in
a short time secured two fish of four and seven pounds with
the spinning bait, and one of four pounds with a salmon-
fly ; they were clean, nice-looking fish, and we found them
very good eating. There were a good many birds about
the river, Egyptian geese, marabou storks, and various
waders, among which we noticed the sacred ibis, which we
were much interested to see ; and we were not long in
adding geese to our bill of fare.

We had brought with us a large seine fishing-net, of a
kind we had used most successfully before on the Settite ;
and in the afternoon we determined to give it a trial. We
thought we had found an excellent place for it, but unfortunately we could not walk along the bank in order to

draw it at a spot where some tamarisk-trees overhung the water and where it was very deep. We were determined, however, to have a try somewhere else, as we had got it out and had experienced considerable difficulty in getting enough men together to help us to draw it. This net was eighty yards long and three deep, with a large pocket in the middle. To be thoroughly successful with it, it was necessary to find a place tolerably free from rocks, and where it could be drawn up in shallow water. Although the Settite was flowing there were many such places, as in some parts the water was not more than a few inches deep. Our first haul, notwithstanding that it was in a most unfavourable place, was not a blank, for we secured twenty-five fish, weighing altogether eighty-six pounds, the heaviest being seven pounds.

The next day we sent Mahomet Salee off to a Hamran village called Korkee with five camels to purchase *dhurra*, having been told that plenty was to be had from the Basé living on the river farther eastward ; but, when it came to the point of fetching it, Mahomet Salee declared that none was to be got there. It was too evident that we had been grossly deceived. We also sent two of the Basé horsemen to a Basé village called Lacatecourah, east of us and back from the Settite. They declared they would summon some sheiks who would arrange for us to go farther. We did not much believe in their promises, but thought they were better away, *possibly* doing some good, than hanging about our camp doing nothing and consuming our *dhurra*.

The country swarmed with Hamrans and people from Haikota ; there was a large encampment of the latter on Khor Meheteb. Some of the Hamrans had rifles, given to them mostly by the professional animal-traders, generally Germans, who go to that country to get live animals with which to supply zoological societies and menageries. Sir Samuel Baker, who visited the country in 1861, has described the manner in which the Hamrans kill the largest animals, by hamstringing them with a single stroke of their swords. I never saw this done, and fancy, as the game has decreased, these Hamran Nimrods have decreased too.

Those we saw obtained most of their game by means of traps, some of which are very ingenious inventions. They frequently kill hippopotami by means of harpoons; and the men who procure them in this way are called *hawartis*. These animals are very scarce now in this part of the Settite; when I visited the river in 1878 they were numerous in places where they are now almost extinct. The day before we arrived one had been wounded in the pool above our encampment; but he had disappeared during the night, and had probably gone higher up the river.

As soon as we had sent the men on their various errands, we started farther up the river, and passed the place where Khor Meheteb joins the Settite; at this point we cut off a great bend in the river and crossed it at a ford, having gone about two miles across country. Here we had an altercation with our men, who wanted to stop; but we insisted on continuing the journey, and, after cutting off another great bend about four miles farther on, struck the left bank of the river and encamped.

Nothing could be more desolate than the appearance of the country at this point: it was more mountainous than lower down the river; but there was scarcely a vestige of green to be seen, and the river was narrower and its bed very rocky. In one part it forced its way between great basalt rocks for a mile or two, the water being very deep and it being impossible to get to the edge of it, as the rocks rose sheer out of the water on either side. We saw the footprints of buffaloes and hippopotami.

In spite of the desolate appearance of the country the view from the point we had chosen for our camp was decidedly picturesque. We were on a small hill a long way above the river, which we could see winding in and out, a silver streak among the black rocks, for a long way in the direction of Abyssinia.

The most conspicuous object in the distance was an immense mountain, called Bokutan, which the natives asserted was in Abyssinia. It appeared to be fifteen or twenty miles off, at least, and was table-shaped; it was

CAMP AT SETTITE, NEAR KHOR MEHETEB.

marked on a map we had with us as five thousand feet high.

In the evening we were treated to another deputation of guides and camel-drivers, now quite a common occurrence, and almost as much to be expected as the setting of the sun. They all declared that they dare go no farther, and that we were then encamped farther in an eastward direction than we ought to be. They said that there was no Basé living on the river, the Abyssinians having driven them all away into the mountains, taken their cattle, and burnt the country. The country had certainly been lately burnt, as the whole surface of the ground was covered with the ashes of grass. Between our camp and Bokutan there was a hill; and between that hill and the mountain, according to these veracious guides, there was an Abyssinian village, which they dared not approach, as the Haikota people had killed two of their sheiks. All this we were told after having been informed at Haikota that there were plenty of Basé villages along the river, the names of many of them having been given to us, and that the people were peaceably disposed, possessing flocks and herds and fields of *dhurra.* We had a long talk with the men, and could plainly see that they were not to be induced to go farther and knew nothing of the country beyond. It was most provoking; because, if we had known we could not go, we should have spent our time on the Gash without going so far south. That there were people about was evident, as we saw several large fires to the eastward. The majority were for retracing our footsteps to Khor Meheteb, which was a far pleasanter-looking place to encamp in than where we then were; and so, accordingly, though with many regrets, we moved there the next day.

I walked all the way back to Khor Meheteb, and a roasting-hot walk I found it. Arthur went part of the way with me, and we kept a sharp look-out for hippopotami; there were the fresh tracks of three having been there, but we saw none. Fish, many of them of large size, were in shoals; the water was so clear that we could see them very plainly. We kept as near the water's edge as we could, and it was a case of scrambling over the rocks almost the whole way; in many places these rose perpendicularly from the water to a height of a hundred to a hundred and fifty feet.

I had an extraordinary adventure with a crocodile during my walk which might have terminated rather unpleasantly for me. Our experience had always been that crocodiles were among the shyest animals that one meets with in Africa, the large ones more particularly so. Of course no one would ever think of going into deep water where these animals are numerous, as I believe they are anything but afraid of man when they encounter him in their native element; and one not unfrequently hears of Arabs being carried off by them when attempting to swim across rivers. We had, however, never hesitated to approach the banks of a river, even when they shelved off into deep water. On this occasion we had gone down to the river to drink at a place where the water was very deep, and I was stooping down, drinking out of the palm of my hand, when Arthur suddenly gave me a vigorous pull back. A very large crocodile with a huge head was making for me, and was within two feet of where I was standing when Arthur perceived it. As soon as I jumped back, the crocodile turned tail and made for the middle of the river. An Arab boy, who was holding our rifles while we drank, was so much astonished that he stood open-mouthed, and was so awkward that neither of us could snatch a rifle quick enough from him to get a shot before the monster sank and disappeared.

Probably, if my brother had not seen the crocodile when he did, it would have tried to knock me into the river with its tail; it had, no doubt, heard us drinking, and had popped round from behind a rock. Sir Samuel Baker says in his book, *The Nile Tributaries of Abyssinia*, that the crocodiles on the Settite are noted for their daring. This was certainly an instance of the truth of his remark.

During our walk we came across the evidence of hippopotami having been lately killed. In one place there had evidently been an encampment of Arabs, and close by a quantity of hide had been left. The place had no doubt

L

been abandoned in a great hurry, otherwise such a valuable article as hippopotamus-hide would never have been left behind; it was quite fresh, and cut in strips for the manufacture of whips. A quantity of rope, too, was lying near it, and had doubtless been used for pulling the animal on to the bank. Our men's nerves were worked up to a great pitch of excitement, and I believe they imagined all kind of dreadful things were likely to happen.

When the others joined us in the evening at the place where we had decided upon making a camp, they told us of a most amusing scare they had had just as they were engaged in striking the tents. One of our camel-drivers, an old Shukreeyeh, had come running into camp in a state of terrible excitement, declaring that he had seen a large body of Abyssinians on horseback, and armed with guns and spears, approaching us from the direction of Abyssinia. There was an immediate call to arms, and a general scurrying for rifles, cartridges, and spears. Very soon, however, it was discovered that the whole thing existed merely in the old fellow's imagination, as there was not the least sign of a human being in sight other than those belonging to our own party; and the whole thing ended in a laugh, and an excited war-dance by our natives.

We selected a lovely spot for our camp, very near the junction of Khor Meheteb with the Settite, on rising ground high above the right bank of the river, affording an extensive view, and backed by a fringe of fine trees, interlaced by a network of parasitic creepers, which gave us the much-wished-for shade; and at night when the moon shone, the boxes ranged along the bank in front of the tents presented quite the appearance of a terraced wall. Away from the river on either bank the country was wretched—miserable leafless trees, and patches of dry yellow grass, very short, and having the appearance of sandy mounds.

We remained at this camp from the 5th to the 13th of March, and had better sport there than we had expected to find. With the fish we were very successful, both with the net and rod; though we never caught any of phenomenal size, the largest being thirty-five pounds. I have little

THE SETTITE, NEAR KHOR MEHETER.

doubt, however, that they run much higher; but during neither of my visits to the Settite has it been my fortune to see any larger ones. We had several hauls with the net, one day catching sixty-eight fish, their total weight being 206½ pounds, and the largest fish seven pounds. Another day we obtained a hundred and fourteen, weighing 365½ pounds, the largest being eight and ten pounds; these were all caught in two draws. We did not use the net nearly as often as we had hoped to do when we left England, because we spent much less time on a river than we had expected. It was really hard work pulling it. We always drew it ourselves, but of course required a number of men to help. They were all fond enough of getting the fish to eat, but we always found them very loath to assist us in working the net.

The boat was of great assistance to us on these occasions in paying out the net and taking the rope across. The last part was always most exciting; the fish, finding themselves getting into shallow water, would frequently leap over the net, even when it was held three or four feet above the surface of the water. The natives then required careful looking after, and we used to scream ourselves hoarse in endeavouring to give them directions, as they would drop the net to pursue a single fish if they saw one escaping in the shallows, and so neglect looking after all the others. Sometimes a snag in the river would completely spoil what would otherwise have been a capital haul, as in freeing the net from the obstruction most of the fish would escape. By far the best fishing we obtained during the winter was at the junction of Khor Meheteb with the Settite. Here the river is dammed by huge rocks and forms a deep pool about two miles in length.

On the evening of our arrival Colvin went down to try his luck, taking with him some tackle that had already made the journey to Australia, and had not been improved by the voyage. About the first cast he had a run; but after a short struggle the fish went off, taking with it the bait, a good-sized spoon. He put on another, and another, always with the same result; and then, thinking he would

THE SETTITE.

try some we had brought from England, was more successful, and bagged a fine "*kelb-el-bahr*," weighing over ten
pounds, with a spoon-bait.   Colvin, standing on a high rock,
continued fishing most successfully, fish after fish rushing
at the novel bait almost as soon as it touched the water ;
but he was frequently startled by a loud splash and clang,
as one of the recently hooked fish that had broken his
tackle leaped out of the water and flapped its head against
the rock in futile endeavours to rid itself of the obnoxious
metal bait.

The "*kelb-el-bahr*" is a most ferocious fish, somewhat
resembling a salmon in appearance, having a movable upper
jaw and frightful teeth that fit into one another like those
of a rat-trap.   It usually lurks about where shallow water
is close to deep, on the look-out for victims who seem to
know their danger and will rarely venture into deep water.
Often when fording these shallows we have frightened a
shoal of roach-like fish down stream and into deep water.
In a minute there would be a rush and a splash, and by
the gleam of loose scales on the water it was evident that
master "kelb " had not let so good a chance escape him.
This was a most sporting fish, always fighting to the last
gasp, very much after the manner of a salmon.   One caught
in the net bit Mahoom in the ankle, causing a very painful
sore.

But it was the *baggar* (of which mention is made by Sir
Samuel Baker) that gave us most sport.   It is a true perch,
lacking only the zebra-like bands of that fish ; its scales are
as silvery as fresh-run salmon, and it has ruby eyes like
those of a white rabbit or ferret.   It loves deep, running
water ; and it was at the outlet of the above-mentioned pool
that we found them most plentiful.   They did not seem to
care much for the spoon or phantom-minnow, so we tried
to get some live bait.   This at first seemed almost impossible, as no one knew how to throw the casting-net ; and the
meshes of the big one were, of course, far too large to hold
those of a suitable size for our purpose.

Lort Phillips hit upon a plan, however, which proved
most successful.   He noticed that a species of gudgeon

frequented the large stones in the shallows, much in the manner that trout do at home; but unlike them they refused to be tickled. He got some large flat stones which he placed in the water, supporting them on smaller ones, to make a good covert into which the fish ran when frightened; he then with the help of Mahoom dropped the casting-net over the top, and all that happened to be underneath were secured. With a supply of live bait we were always sure of sport; no sooner had the float rounded the corner of a big rock in the middle of the stream than it would disappear as if it had been a stone; then came a rush, and generally a clean jump or two like that of a spring salmon.

One morning as Lort Phillips and I were going out shooting we saw Colvin at the old place, gesticulating wildly; and on going to see what was up, found he had hooked a big fish, and wanted some one to gaff it for him. After some time it came to the surface, and in one of its struggles disgorged its breakfast in the shape of a partly digested fish, weighing a pound and a half; it proved to be a magnificent *baggar* over twenty-two pounds in weight. This was the largest fish that had been caught so far; but the same evening, on our return, Lort Phillips caught one weighing twenty-four pounds. It is by far the best eating of any of the Settite fish; in fact, it would be hard to beat it anywhere for delicacy of flavour. There was another fish, a kind of silurian, of which we caught a great many; it is a very ugly, sluggish brute, and gives little or no sport; it would seize the bait, and bear straight away, taking out yards of line often without being hooked. The largest fish of this species was caught at Om Hagar and weighed thirty-five pounds. The fish we caught in the net were mostly bottom-feeders. I never saw any in such condition, their intestines being covered with fat. One species only took the fly, a kind of barbel, but its mouth was so tough that the hook never penetrated beyond the bait, and it was only by keeping a continued strain on the line that we could land them at all.

On the 7th the two Basé we had sent off to fetch some of their sheiks arrived in camp. We had despatched them the morning after our arrival on the Settite, thinking that by so doing we might be enabled to go farther up the river; they returned, bringing about twenty of their people with them, who they said came from a village called Lacate-courah, which is situated on a mountain we ought to have taken on our way from Haikota. We of course found that they could do nothing to aid us; they declared (but whether of their own accord or instigated by the men we had brought from Sheik Achmed Ageer we could not tell) that the Abyssinians had forced them to abandon their villages on the banks of the river, and had driven them into the moun-tains. We pretty well satisfied ourselves that the Basé had two villages, called Tonsār and Beergayla, situated on the Settite; but whether they were still inhabited by Basé or had been destroyed by their enemies the Abyssinians we never succeeded in discovering. They stated further that the Abyssinians had only three or four days previously captured and carried off three of their women.

They brought the sheik of Lacatecourah with them, an insignificant-looking man, to whom we made some trifling presents, with which he seemed highly delighted. On their way to our camp they had passed the night near to some water in Khor Meheteb; and while resting there a herd of elephants had come to drink about midnight, and buffaloes had visited the same pool early that morning. My brothers and Colvin started off with the intention of spending the night near the watering-place, on the chance of their return-ing; and about 3 A.M. those of us who had remained in camp heard several shots, which we hoped had been directed at the elephants. Unfortunately, however, they saw nothing of them, but returned to camp about noon, having bagged two buffaloes, a *māārif* (hippotragus Bakirii), a *tétél*, and an ariel.

They had found the pool of water about five or six miles from camp; and two of them had spent the night on the ground on the bank above the *khor*, and the other in a large baobab-tree. During the night a giraffe had come to drink, but it was before the moon was up, and they could see nothing of it. Then a herd of some twenty or thirty buffaloes made their appearance, but unfortunately there was such a poor moon that it was difficult to take a good aim; one fell dead, however; the rest made off. As soon as it was light they searched to see if there was any sign of a blood-track, as they felt sure they must have hit one or two others, and soon found evidence of a wounded beast. Salee, who was with them, tracked the animal a long way. This man was a most extraordinary tracker, and would follow wounded game for miles when there was very little blood to be seen, and that only at long intervals, and where the country was so thick and the ground so covered with fallen leaves that it was often most difficult to find the buffaloes' footprints. Frequently, too, the ground was very hard and covered with pebbles, making it extremely difficult to follow an animal's tracks, as the heaviest beast would leave so faint an impression as often to be entirely invisible to the uneducated eye. They were just on the point of giving up the chase, as the sun was at its height and they had been tracking for five hours, when they were suddenly confronted by the wounded buffalo; it turned to charge, when one of them dropped it by a lucky shot in the forehead. When first hit the ball had caught it in the hind-leg below the fetlock joint.

The *māārif* was shot by my brother Arthur, and was the first we had seen. It proved to be a small buck; and unfortunately one of the natives cut off the head so near the horns that it was spoiled as a trophy. No amount of exhortation would make them careful in this respect; and sometimes when an animal was shot one of them would be off like a deer after it, and spoil its head before you could stop him.

We found the heat was beginning to get very trying, even the nights being hot; but it was an intensely dry heat, and none of us were at all the worse for it.

On the 8th Mahomet Salee returned with *dhurra*, which he had obtained from a Hamran village. The next day we sent him back to Haikota, as well as Bayrumphy and the other Arabs given us by Sheik Achmed Ageer, for we were determined that he should make no more out of us than we could help, after the manner in which we had been served

by him. The Basé had all returned to Lacatecourah the
previous day, with the exception of the three horsemen we
had taken from Sogada ; these, we said, might either go or
stay as they pleased, and they elected to remain with us.
Very soon, however, they changed their minds, persuaded
to do so, I believe, by Mahomet Salee ; for, after settling
to remain with us, we found on returning from an afternoon's
shooting that they had all taken their departure ; the following day, nevertheless, one of them returned by himself to
our camp.

As soon as we had started them off Lort Phillips and I
went out with our rifles to a small *khor* that ran into the
opposite side of the river, and where there were some pools
of water. We found that animals often preferred drinking
at these pools away from the river to going to the river itself,
as by so doing they were less likely to be disturbed. We
did not see much game. I shot an *oterop*, and my companion a buck *nellut* with the finest pair of horns of any we
had bagged so far.

We spent some time watching a large troop of baboons.
There were nearly two hundred, and one never got tired ·
of watching them. A great many of the females carried
young ones on their backs, and a great deal of screaming
and sometimes fighting took place. It was wonderful to
see the way in which the young ones kept their seats as
their mothers, to whom they clung, were chased from rock
to rock and tree to tree by other baboons, generally not in
anger, but for pure fun and mischief. We seldom shot any
of these creatures, as none of the natives would eat them ;
we took three or four skins home, however, as they make
very handsome mats.

On our return to camp we found that my brothers and
Colvin had made another expedition up Khor Meheteb.
During the night we twice heard shots in camp, the air being
so still and clear that the report of a rifle could be heard
for a long distance ; and we began to hope it was really the
elephants this time, when at about twelve o'clock they
arrived bringing a cow buffalo. They had had a most
exciting night watching by the water, the first visitors to

arrive being a large herd of buffaloes, who, however, got their wind and galloped off without either drinking or allowing themselves to be seen ; next came two bulls, one of which they managed to send off wounded, and heard bellowing several times during the night. About daybreak a herd of about thirty made their appearance, two of which they wounded, but they got away. Having fortified themselves with a hasty breakfast, they next sallied forth to look for blood-tracks, which they soon found, and after about two hours' tracking obtained a glimpse of a wounded beast ; it was only a glimpse, however, as before any of them could fire it was off at a gallop. They lost no time in continuing the chase, and had not gone far before the infuriated buffalo charged Arthur from behind a bush, where it had stopped to hide.

Buffaloes are very cunning animals, and frequently when wounded, or perceiving themselves pursued, will retrace their steps, lie *perdu* behind some good covert, and charge the sportsman as he goes by.

My brother fired both barrels, but neither shot had the desired effect of grassing the buffalo, though both hit it ; the only result being to turn the attention of the animal to Colvin, whom it charged furiously, scarcely giving him time to raise his rifle to his shoulder, his second barrel being fired when the animal was literally at the muzzle. Colvin was sent flying in one direction, his rifle in the other, while the buffalo fell between. This was a narrow escape, too close to be pleasant ; but fortunately no harm was done ; the buffalo, though not dead, being unable to rise, as the shot had taken effect in its knee.

They then took up the track of the bull buffalo which was also wounded, and following it until they found themselves not far from the camp gave it up, as the heat was terrific, and they were rather done up after a sleepless night and a long walk in the sun with such an exciting finish. This bull, according to Salee's reading of the marks on the ground, had been attacked by no less than three lions ; they had heard the roar of two of them at night, and had seen the marks where the buffalo had turned and evidently charged his tormentors; after a time two out of these three lions had discontinued the hunt, but the third had held on a long time before also giving up. Besides these buffaloes they discovered in the morning that a giraffe had drunk at the water, but they had seen nothing of it.

CHAPTER XVIII.

A Visit from two Hamran Sheiks.—A *Shereker.*—A Second Visit from Hamran Sheiks.—Three Basé join the Camp.—They are attacked by the Hamrans.—Departure for Om Hagar.—Arrival at Om Hagar.—Capture of the First Hippopotamus.—Visit from Hamran Sheik's Son.—The Last Hippopotamus.—Marabou Storks.—Purchase of a Tortoise.—A splendid Buck *Nellut* shot.

ON the 11th two Hamran sheiks arrived in camp. They were most anxious that we should take one of their people as a guide, which we refused to do ; they told us that there was far less to shoot in their country than there had been a few years ago, and that every year the game was decreasing. We needed no one to tell us this, as it was only too evident. There was far less game on the Settite than there had been when some of us had spent a few days on the river four years previously, and even then there was nothing like as much as there had been four or five years before our first visit.

Our Hamran visitors told us that the farthest camp any European had made on the river, entering from their country, had been a few miles higher up than our last camp. They said they were friends with the Abyssinians, and that their head sheik could arrange for us to go into Wolkait by way of Cafta; that, although they were not afraid of the Abyssinians dwelling on the Settite, nevertheless they did not go very much. farther up the river for fear of the Basé. The fact was that the Haikota people would not go with us any higher up the river for fear of the Abyssinians, and that the Hamrans equally would not go for fear of the Basé, so that we were checkmated either way. I, moreover, very much doubt the ability of the

Hamran sheik to have made any arrangement for our going to Wolkait.

A great many Beni-Amers from Haikota were encamped in Khor Meheteb. They were there chiefly for the purpose of entrapping animals, their mode of doing so being the same as that practised by the Hamrans. Most of their game they obtain by means of snares, which they place on the paths made by animals on their way to drink.

They have a very ingenious invention, called *shereker*, to  prevent the noose from slipping off the leg before it has drawn tight. It is made in the following manner: two hoops are bound tightly together, and between them sharp pieces of tough wood are driven all round, their points just reaching the centre. Those intended for catching antelopes are about the size of a soup-plate; but for buffaloes, giraffes, and other large-footed game, they are made much larger.

With a supply of *sherekers*, as well as running-nooses, these latter made of twisted hide, the hunter is ready to commence operations. Having found a well-beaten track near to some watering-place he digs a hole in the middle of it, about eighteen inches deep and a little smaller in diameter than the *shereker* he intends to use. He next cuts a branch or small tree, just large enough to check the progress of the animal, but not to stop it; to this he makes fast the loose end of the noose; then he places the *shereker* over the hole, and arranges the noose over the *shereker*, brushing some loose earth over all in order to conceal the snare. Any animal stepping on the pit-fall sinks down; and, on starting back, the *shereker* remains fastened tight to its leg and prevents the noose from falling off, till it is so tightly drawn that its aid is no longer required.

The poor beast rushes off, dragging the bush after it,

which not only soon wearies it, but leaves behind a fatal
track by which to guide the hunter, who soon overtakes it;
and the spear puts a speedy termination to its sufferings.
The accompanying engraving will give a good idea of a
shereker.

Before shifting our camp from Khor Meheteb we were
favoured with a second visit from some Hamrans. A sheik
named Said, and another sheik, name unknown, made their
appearance one evening, arriving with a number of camels
from higher up the river.

Soon after their departure three Basé from Lacatecourah
made their appearance. It was dark when they arrived,
and they begged to be allowed to accompany us. We gave
them permission to do so, at the same time advising them
not to go far away from camp for fear of a hostile meeting
with any of their enemies the Hamrans.

Sheik Said and his friend returned the following morning
to pay us another visit. Very soon after their departure
we heard shouts, and perceived that some disturbance was
going on. The Hamrans had discovered that we had Basé
with us, and had pursued them with their guns, threatening
that they would shoot them; but the three Lacatecourah
men, together with the man from Sogada, ran away as fast
as their legs would carry them—the latter leaving his horse
behind with us.

The Hamrans soon gave up the chase, and went a short
way down the river; on the way they met some of our
Arabs, whom they informed that we should not go down
the river into their country, and that if we persisted in
doing so they would shoot us. We were naturally very
indignant with them for their impertinence, and very angry
at their having frightened away men who were living in our
camp with our permission; we of course laughed at their
threats, and told them we should go where we pleased.

They had a right to be annoyed at our going into their
country with Haikota people and shooting their game, as
by so doing any *baksheesh* we might distribute or wages we
might pay would go to them instead of to the Hamrans,
the inhabitants of the country; it was, however, a very

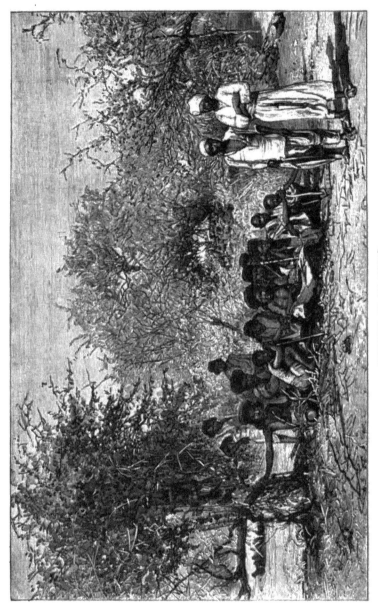

HAMRANS AT OM HAGAR.

hostile method of expostulating with us about it. Had we intended shooting in the Hamran country when we left Haikota we should of course not have taken any of Sheik Achmed Ageer's people farther than to the borders of the Hamrans, but when we left we never contemplated spending any time in their country. We took no notice of their threats, but broke up our camp and rode on. Suleiman harangued them as we passed them sitting under some trees with a number of their people and they made an apology.

The place where we encamped was called Om Gedat, or "mother of the guinea-fowl," so named from the immense number of those birds that resorted to the neighbourhood. After a night there we moved about ten miles farther down, and pitched our tents on the left bank of the river at a spot named Om Hagar, or "mother of the rock." The Arabs on the Settite are very fond of such names. A village still farther down they term Om Brega, "mother of the thorn," also a most appropriate designation, the village being situated in a wood of *kittar*-bushes.

Lort Phillips and Aylmer made the journey together to Om Hagar in the Berthon boat. This boat proved a most excellent institution, and was a great acquisition during our stay on the river. It was nine feet in length, and, being collapsible, was easily carried on one side of a camel, in which position it travelled the whole of the long journey without mishap; and, notwithstanding the great heat to which it was constantly subjected, was as sound on its arrival at the coast as on its departure for the interior. As I have already mentioned, it was extremely serviceable in shooting the net and in clearing it when foul of rocks. It moreover afforded an easy means of crossing the river, thereby saving many a weary tramp to reach the nearest ford, possibly two or three miles distant.

Before leaving for Om Gedat we engaged as guides a couple of Hamrans, who turned out fairly useful.

The appearance of the country between this point and Om Hagar considerably improved, and was, to a sportsman's eye, decidedly more promising. The hills that bordered the river, though still steep and stony, were less

M

rugged than those we were leaving behind us ; while beyond, the country opened out into a plain, interspersed with small hills on the north side of the river, and apparently boundless to the south of it. The trees, too, that fringed the river were much greener and larger than heretofore, thereby affording more covert for the game we hoped to find. Dotted about amidst grateful shade were the giant habitations of the white ants (*termites*), nowhere more numerous or of larger size than in this part of the country. Our tents were pitched on a spot high above the river, with a grassy lawn sloping down to the water, well known to Ali our cook, who had previously spent much time in the same place. He lost no time in establishing himself under a leafy bower, to which he apparently considered that he possessed a prescriptive right by virtue of old association.

On the opposite side of the river, but a little lower down, what at first appeared to be a *khor* ran for about a mile and a half to two miles parallel with the Settite, where it joined the river, forming when the water was high during the rains a large island. In its bed were several pools of water, favourite drinking-places for the game of the country, and often preferred to the main body of the stream on account of their retired situation.

We pitched our camp at Om Hagar on March 14, where we remained until the 22d, from which date we considered ourselves as more or less homeward bound. Both during our stay there and at Khor Meheteb we were very successful in shooting buffaloes and many kinds of antelope. In the present edition of my book I have omitted many descriptions of day's shooting, which in the former and larger edition I have described at length.

Not far from camp was a large *zariba* containing a great many goats and sheep. We arranged with their owners for a daily supply of milk during the rest of our stay at Om Hagar.

A few days before our departure Aylmer secured the first hippopotamus, a fair-sized bull. His first shot had apparently half-stunned it ; but several more bullets were required before life was extinct. " Hippos " were scarce in

HAMRANS DRYING HIPPOPOTAMUS MEAT.

that part of the Settite, and we did not care to shoot many; the flesh was, however, greatly appreciated by the Arabs, although we found it somewhat strong in flavour and very tough. After having gorged themselves with as much of the fresh meat as they could manage to swallow, they would cut up the remainder into strips, with which they festooned all the trees; this, when dried, was placed in skins, and afterwards cooked and eaten from time to time. The fat, when boiled down, formed a most excellent substitute for cooking-butter, which we were very glad to get, as the only butter we could obtain in the country possessed a most disgusting taste, principally owing to the fact of its being kept in badly-cured goat-skins.

Then, too, the hide is most highly prized throughout the Soudan for the purpose of making the *koorbatch*, or native whip, of which we were told one skin, if carefully divided, would make upwards of two hundred. This statement, however, must be taken *cum grano*, as we never put it to the test. The hide on the neck of a fine bull is fully an inch and a half in thickness. Altogether you cannot please your Arabs more than by shooting one of these useful animals.

The tusks are often very fine, and were at one time extensively used by dentists in the manufacture of false teeth. I believe, however, that they have been superseded by the use of some composition. They make very nice trophies, and can be made up in various ways. At home we had some made into frames for mirrors, and they looked very well.

The natives secure these animals by means of harpoons, of which Sir Samuel Baker gives a most interesting account in *The Nile Tributaries of Abyssinia*, a book that served us as a sort of guide-book, and which we found contained a most accurate and interesting description of the country.

Owing to the comparative ease with which hippopotami can be killed, they are rapidly becoming exterminated in this part of Africa. They are no longer found on the Nile farther north than the nineteenth degree of north latitude, and are nowhere plentiful north of Khartoum. Where there is cultivation on the banks of the river they do a great deal of damage. Near Berber I have seen places where every night the natives sat up to protect their crops against their depredations. Along the river they stretched a rope supported on poles, from which hung numerous bells, which they pulled vigorously whenever a " hippo " made its appearance, in order to scare the unwelcome intruder back into the river.

Agriculture in these parts is indeed no sinecure ; the husbandman has no peace night or day. All day long vast flocks of doves and small birds cause havoc amongst his crops, and necessitate perpetual vigilance. One often sees boys perched upon lofty platforms armed with slings, with which, accompanied by discordant cries, they endeavour to ward off their feathered foes.

Soon after our arrival at Om Hagar we sent a quantity of *dhurra* to a Hamran village farther down the river to be converted into flour ; with it we sent a present of a handsome burnous, a small quantity of gunpowder, and a letter to the chief sheik of the Hamran tribe of Arabs, who was at that time dwelling there. The result was that he sent his son to visit us, a very good-looking fellow, and well mannered, except for his begging propensities. He was very anxious that we should bestow some present upon him, and begged very hard for a gun and all kinds of things, and was very difficult to satisfy. He was profuse in his apologies for Said and the other Hamrans at Meheteb, and informed us that it was a fact that Said's father had been killed by the Basé, a circumstance of which we had heard before. He declared that the Hamrans were friends with the Abyssinians, and that with their permission the Hamrans hunted elephants in their country, on the stipulation that any game shot in their territory was divided with them.

On the same evening Mahomet Salee and one of our other old horsemen suddenly made their appearance with two camels that we had sent from Haikota to Cassala for some necessaries, such as bread, sugar, and candles. These camels had left Achmed Ageer's headquarters for Cassala at the same time that we left for the Settite, and had been away far longer than they ought to have been. The same evening Mahomet Salee left our camp for Om Brega to purchase *dhurra* on his own account, which he intended taking back with him to the Gash; as a peace-offering he brought us the skin of a boa-constrictor, which he said he had killed on the road between Khor Meheteb and Haikota.

The same day news was brought into camp that Colvin had killed a "hippo" three or four miles farther up the river. We despatched camels for the meat, and at the same time my brother William and I started with the photographic camera, intending to take its photograph. On arriving at the place we found a "hippo" in a large pool, rising, as is the habit of these animals, to the surface to breathe and quickly disappearing again. The Arabs declared, however, that this was another animal, and that the one Colvin had shot was lying dead at the bottom of the river, and would soon rise to the surface. We waited a long time, hoping that this would be the case; and to pass the time I fished, but with indifferent success. I saw a number of turtles, which kept coming up to the top of the water, but could not catch one, and only managed to hook a *gamoot* of seven pounds.

Colvin left the pool and went off with Aylmer. The latter shot a *mehedehet* and a very fine buck *nellut;* and in returning to camp in the evening Colvin obtained a snapshot at a leopard, which he unfortunately missed; this was the more unlucky as it was the first time any of us had had a shot at one. My brother Arthur went down to the pool where the "hippo" was, and, as there was no sign of Colvin's animal, shot our friend of the morning. Either it was the same one Colvin had fired at and not killed, or else Colvin had wounded one, which managed to keep out of our sight by remaining under the bushes which grew very thick on one bank of the river and overhung the water. At any rate we saw no signs of any other, and, in fact, saw no more hippopotami during the remainder of our stay in the country. The following morning we found my brother's "hippo" floating, and, after towing it to land, took its photograph; it proved to be an old bull, with enormous tusks which had grown through the upper lip.

It is often very difficult in shooting hippopotami to determine whether or not your shot has been successful, as, hit or miss, the animal at once sinks below the surface, to float after some two or three hours if killed; but if only

HIPPOPOTAMUS AND SALEE.

wounded, or missed, he will frequently select so well-concealed a spot for his necessary re-appearance as to baffle his pursuers. The lungs of the hippopotamus are so constructed as to enable him to remain below the surface of the water for a period of from six to ten consecutive minutes, though when undisturbed they delight in remaining with their heads entirely above water, often for a considerable length of time; but when molested they take care to show no more than the apertures of the nostrils and their eyes, and that only for a few seconds, as they quickly fill their lungs with a fresh supply of oxygen, and sink again.

The vicinity of our camp was the daily resort of numerous marabou-storks, several of which we shot for the sake of their feathers. Any one who had seen these birds in the numbers in which they occur in these parts of Africa would fully appreciate the justice and accuracy of Mr. H. Stacy Mark's admirable picture entitled " In Convocation," which attracted so much attention at the Royal Academy two or three years ago.

We purchased from some Arabs, for a trifling sum, a gigantic land-tortoise, which we had intended to have presented to the Zoological Society of London; but the fates were against us, for a journey on camel-back proved more than his constitution could bear. He weighed almost as much as a man could lift. At night we fastened him with a strong chain to a heavy provision-box, which he would frequently drag several yards in his endeavours to escape. We never could perceive that he ate or drank anything, although we tried him with everything which we thought likely to tempt his palate. Even under these adverse circumstances he nevertheless lived for some weeks, and gave no signs of failing strength until one day we found him dead. Colvin, however, succeeded in conveying to England a very diminutive specimen of what appeared to be the same species.

One day my brother William took his camera down to the *khor* to endeavour to photograph any antelopes or other animals that might come there. Both antelopes and baboons made their appearance; but, after successive attempts, he found it impossible so to arrange the camera as to be able to expose the plate without disclosing himself; accordingly he discarded the camera for the rifle, and had the good fortune to secure the finest buck *nellut* that we obtained during the expedition. The horns of this magnificent animal measured thirty-nine and a half inches in a direct line from the base to the tip, and fifty-nine inches measuring round the curves.[1]

The whole of our stay at Om Hagar was most enjoyable, and I think I cannot do better than give a few extracts from my diary of our last days there.

---

[1] Mr. F. C. Selous in his interesting book entitled *A Hunter's Wanderings in Africa*, mentions shooting a specimen of this antelope, which he designates as perhaps the handsomest species in the world. The horns of this animal measured forty-three inches from base to tip, and sixty-four measuring round the curves. It was the largest he ever came across.

CHAPTER XIX.

Extracts from Diary.—Bait set for Lions.—Mosquitoes.—Among the Buffaloes again.—Beginning of the Homeward Journey.—Journey towards Lacatecourah.—The Village of Lacatecourah.—A *Bonne-Bouche.*—Encampment at Abou Sellal.—A Native of the Basé Settite.—A Dabergoum Sheik offers to conduct us to the Basé Settite.—Basé Villages on the Settite.—Capture of a Boa-constrictor.—Arrival at Haikota.—The Beni-Amer's Raid on the Basé.—A Visit from Sheik Achmed Ageer.

"*March* 19.—William and I went out shooting together, and rode a long way on the south bank of the river. Saw one *māārif*, but miles off, and could not succeed in getting near it, and a few *tétél* and *nellut*, to which we paid no attention. I had a long shot at a *boos (Klipspringer oreotragus saltatrix)*, which I unfortunately missed. This is the only antelope, I believe, that inhabits the part of the Soudan through which we travelled that none of us ever shot. It is decidedly scarce, is larger than a gazelle, with long reddish hair, and has, for its size, big horns. Arthur saw either two or three lions, he could not say which. The first he caught a glimpse of as it vanished into some high grass, and, although he followed it, never saw it again; the second he saw almost at the same moment, but at the top of a hill about three hundred yards off; and the third he saw on returning towards camp over the same ground in the afternoon, and consequently could not be sure that it was not one of those he had seen in the morning. Owing to the thickness of the covert and the hardness of the ground it was impossible to follow them for any distance. Lions are rarely to be caught in this chance way.

"On our return to camp in the afternoon we found Arthur, who told us about the lions; and we immediately

started off again to endeavour to shoot an antelope, which
we wished to use as a bait for them. Although usually,
when we did not want them, we could obtain one or two
without much difficulty, we were on this occasion obliged
to return by nightfall without having even had one shot.
We thought that, by leaving a dead antelope near the place
where Arthur had seen the lions, one or more might visit
it during the night; in which case, on the following morning,
there would be the chance of finding one not far from the
carcass, gorged with its banquet. Aylmer had spent the
day by the water in the *khor*, and had shot a doe *māārif*
and two fine buck *nellut;* not bad, as all had heads well
worth preserving. On his arrival in camp with the spoil
we sent one of the latter to what we hoped would prove
the trysting-place of the lions.

"To-day the atmosphere has been clear again, but the
two previous days were so misty that the sun was partly in
shade. The temperature both night and day has been
much cooler, and we have had very strong gales at night,
which tried the tent-ropes.

"The mosquitoes bother us a good deal after the sun
has gone down—a plague we have not experienced before
this winter, except to a slight extent at Souakim. These
torments need hardly enter into one's calculations in undertaking a journey into these parts during the dry season;
on the few occasions that one meets with them in any
number they appear to be very local. I found them very
troublesome at Sofi, a village on the banks of the Atbara,
near its junction with the Settite, although we were encamped
very high above the river, and there was nothing to account
for their presence in that part more than in any other. This
was the place chosen by Sir Samuel Baker in which to
spend the rainy season, and he mentions their extreme
virulence in *The Nile Tributaries of Abyssinia*. Of course
it was not to be wondered at that they should be very
troublesome during the rains; but, as I found them so great
a plague there during the driest season of the year, it is
very probable that they were thicker there during the rains
than at other places.

"*March* 20.—Went very early to see if any lions had visited Aylmer's dead *nellut*, but found no signs of its having been disturbed. We are daily supplied with milk by some people who have made a large *zariba* on the north bank of the river, and have a great number of goats. The 'proprietor' came early this morning to inform us that last night a lion had had the impudence to jump over the *zariba* and carry away a goat. Colvin and I started in pursuit, hoping to be able to follow the depredator; we soon found where he had jumped over the prickly hedge, and the marks made by the wretched goat he had dragged with him. Achmet tracked him across the river and for a long distance on the other side; but we finally lost the marks of his footsteps in thick bushes, and were forced to abandon the pursuit.

"We, however, found tracks of buffalo that had drunk last night at the river, and these we followed a long way from the Settite, and finally got up to them in a '*kittar*' forest. They were all lying down tail to tail, but rose to their feet when we got to within a hundred to a hundred and thirty yards of them. We both singled out what appeared to be big ones and fired; the whole herd made off with a tremendous crash through the bushes, but none fell. We ran round and tried to cut them off as they made for the river. We could have fired again, but abstained from doing so as they would have been long shots that could have only wounded them. After following for some distance we found we had each wounded one; they lagged behind the rest of the herd, which was evidently going slowly on their account. A little farther, and the only wounded beast that left a distinct blood-track separated from the others, and we followed it for some distance, until the sun going down warned us that it was useless to go any farther that night, and we returned to camp.

"William and Lort Phillips had been out together, and had followed a herd of buffaloes which had been drinking and splashing in the river opposite our camp last night. They went a long way in the Meheteb direction, and separated, as the latter was following a bull. He could not get near it, and, having lost his reckoning, whistled, which startled the herd as William was getting near it; and the buffaloes galloped off without his obtaining the chance of a shot. Later in the day William wounded one, but not badly; and as the afternoon was too far advanced to allow of his following it he gave it up. Arthur watched the pool of water in the *khor*, and was rewarded by shooting two wart-hogs and a buck *nellut*, the latter of which he sent, as a bait for lions, to a spot where we frequently saw their marks.

"*March* 21.—Sent George out for a day's shooting; and he got a very large *tétél* and a gazelle, and wounded a *méhédehet*, which he lost. Arthur and William went to see if any lions had touched the *nellut*, but found no trace of any having done so. Lort Phillips watched 'the water,' and succeeded in shooting a small buck *nellut*. Colvin and I took up the tracks of our wounded buffalo of yesterday, and, after going for about a quarter of a mile from where we had given up the pursuit last night, we found a place where it had evidently been careering about. Achmet at once declared that it had been attacked by hyænas. Very soon we espied it quite dead. It was a large cow, which, in the thickness of the *kittar*-bushes, we had easily mistaken for a bull.

"There were the marks of several hyænas on the ground, and they had torn the poor brute's hind-quarters all to pieces. It was quite evident, from the way in which the ground was torn up by the buffalo's hoofs, that the hyænas had attacked it while alive, and that it had made a desperate struggle to defend itself before giving in. We left a camel and some men with the carcass, and started to find the herd. We had no difficulty in taking up their tracks from where we had left them yesterday, and found, too, the blood-marks of the other wounded animal; but these we soon lost again. Spent a very long hot day in the pursuit of this herd; the wind was generally wrong, and it was not until after much crawling through long grass, and dodging from tree to tree, that, late in the afternoon, we either of us succeeded in obtaining a shot; it was a long one, and the buffalo went off wounded.   Again, after a short pursuit, the setting sun obliged us to desist, and we returned to camp.

"*March* 22.—Started early after our wounded buffalo, which we had left not far from camp; its tracks were difficult to follow, and very soon crossed those of the herd. However, we were not long in finding the wounded animal, which unfortunately proved to be another cow, a very old one, with a fine head.   She had retreated into thick covert near the river, and a ball in the shoulder at fifty yards brought her to bag.   A crowd of Hamrans had followed us eager for meat; and as we had plenty in camp, and were, moreover, shifting our quarters, we gave most of it away.   One piece of hide sufficient to make a shield we exchanged for some small 'hippo's' teeth.

"This is the first day of our return homewards.   We marched to the water in Khor Meheteb, encamping near the place where we had previously sat up watching for game. Lort Phillips, who is very fond of fishing, tried the Settite for the last time on the expedition, and caught a *gamoot* weighing twenty-five pounds.   Arthur shot a small crocodile.

"We turned our backs on the river with many regrets; for, although much disappointed at being baffled in our attempt to explore farther up its course, we had, nevertheless, greatly enjoyed our stay on its banks, and had obtained better sport than we had expected in the Hamran country.

"I trust some day we shall make a regular expedition into Abyssinia from Massawa, having first obtained the necessary letters from King John authorising us to do so, and that then we shall be able to shoot along the Settite farther up the river, and perhaps travel along its banks as far as we now are on Khor Meheteb.

"It was dark before Colvin and I joined the others in our new camp, and we found them just sitting down to dinner."

We had now to go through much the same kind of journey to get back to Haikota, that we had performed to reach the Settite; but we were determined to pass through the Basé village of Lacatecourah on our return.

We reached the foot of the hill on which Lacatecourah is built at 6.45, leaving the caravan far behind. This hill, which is some four or five hundred feet high, is covered with great granite boulders; and the village is the largest we had seen of those belonging to the Basé. We saw lights from the huts above us, and after a good deal of shouting some men came down to us. The water which supplied the village was some distance farther; but as we had plenty coming on with the caravan, and the night was very dark and trees thick, we decided on remaining where we were and waiting for the camels to overtake us.

The bulk of the camels, together with Suleiman, did not make their appearance until nine o'clock the next morning, having completely lost their reckoning, as well as the apology for a path that there was; and having wandered to the back of the hill on which the village of Lacatecourah is situated, were prevented from seeing the pyrotechnic display in which we indulged the previous evening on hearing that they were lost. We found the nights away from the river much colder, and were very glad of our blankets.

In the morning we thoroughly explored the village, which was most curious. A primitive portcullis-like gate near the foot of the hill gave access to a steep path, up which we climbed; huts were built at about half-way up to the top. There seemed to be almost a greater number of women than men; and we greatly delighted many of them by presenting them with glass beads, *khol* for their eyes, and looking-glasses, while among the men we distributed a large number of knives. Some of the women's heads were remarkable objects, beads of all shapes and colours being regularly worked into the hair.

The view from the top of the hill, or rock, for it is not much more, is extensive, but by no means beautiful; a great plain covered chiefly by leafless trees does not constitute a lovely prospect. From one of the Basé we bought a baby baboon to add to our menagerie, which already consisted of two small green monkeys and a tortoise.[1] We

---

[1] We succeeded in bringing all these animals to England alive.

decided on moving the camp to some wells in a *khor*, about an hour farther on, called Abou Sellal, and remaining there for the day to allow the camels time to rest and feed. We felt we had a long journey before us to the coast, and that the camels were not in good condition, and would require great care to enable them to accomplish it. I went off with some of the party to see the place that supplied the village with water. We had sent some camels there to fetch some, but they had not returned ; and on our arrival we found they had gone on to other wells farther off, where the water was said to be better. After waiting an hour or two for them they made their appearance ; and we all went on together to the camping-ground.

As an instance of what the Basé will eat : while waiting at these wells for the camels we noticed one pare off bits of hide from his sandals, some of which he ate as they were ; but his friend, who was sitting by him engaged in the same occupation, and who was evidently a *bon-vivant*, first pounded up the pieces of sandal with a stone before consuming them !

We had always been informed by the Arabs that the Basé lived in holes in the ground, and at Lacatecourah we found what we imagined had given rise to this idea. The hill was covered with enormous boulders of granite, and these the Basé had utilised wherever possible to form roofs and one or more sides to their dwellings, so that by creeping under the rocks and filling up the apertures with a lattice-work of branches and straw they were literally living in a kind of cave.

We found our camping-ground, Abou Sellal, a rather picturesque spot, situated in a deep sandy *khor* between hills. Crowds of Basé belonging to some other village were there drawing water, and did not seem at all afraid of us.

I made great efforts, both at this village and especially at Lacatecourah, to endeavour to find out something more about the Basé villages—their names, and whether there were really any situated on the Settite above where we had been. The information I received was most contradictory, but I give it for what it is worth. In travelling in Africa one can only feel sure of what one really sees with one's own eyes; and "native report," that one reads so much about in African books of travel, must be taken very much *cum grano*.

My experience of the inhabitants of Africa I have come across is, that they will frequently lie for the mere pleasure (for to them I suppose it *is* a pleasure) of lying; and they will often do so when there is apparently nothing to be gained by it.

The moot-question of whether any Basé have permanent habitations on the Settite or not will, I believe, never be settled by us. My impression is, however, that they have villages either close to the river or at a very short distance back from it. They always build their villages on hills; and the country above Khor Meheteb is suitable for them in this respect, as there are hills on both banks of the river, generally close to it, besides hills standing back at some distance. It is not at all unlikely, however, that the Abyssinians have forced them to abandon some of their villages, as we were told had lately been the case. In answer to my numerous inquiries I was told that Toansar and Beergayla were both on the river. There is no doubt that there are such places, and that they are Basé villages. One man declared that the former was two days' journey from Lacatecourah; another, five.

There was a path running into ours, on our way from Khor Meheteb, which one authority said led into Abyssinia, and was used by the Abyssinians when they organised raids against Lacatecourah; another stated that it merely led to another Basé village now deserted, and that the inhabitants had fled to Lacatecourah on account of the too close proximity of Abyssinia being disagreeable for them.

I told Suleiman to be on the look-out for "information" about the Basé for me, and at Abou Sellal he informed me that a man had arrived on the scene from this very debatable "Basé Settite." He had a long yarn to spin, and was most communicative. His story (which in part we had heard before) was to the effect that some Sogada people had stolen five women from a Basé village called Dabergoum.

In these countries the fair, or what I should perhaps

N

term the dusky, sex are regarded as property, and are looked upon in much the same light as so many head of cattle or sheep. Dabergoum he described as on the Settite, the nearest Basé village up the river above Khor Meheteb. He told us that his father came from Haikota, but that his mother was a Sogada lady; and that he had been sent by the Egyptian Government to endeavour to extort taxes from Sogada, Lacatecourah, and two other villages. What they could possibly pay I cannot imagine, as poorer people could not easily be found. If his story were true, which I doubt, he would probably endeavour to cajole the people into paying something by promising them various advantages if they complied with his demands, and threatening them with what would happen if they did not. He said he had sent to Dabergoum to tell them that if they would send to Sogada for them, the women would be restored to their rightful lords.

We were shown a man, said to be a sheik of Dabergoum, on his way to Sogada to fetch the ladies, and who, hearing of the presents that other Basé had received from us, came to make our acquaintance, and offered if we would turn back to take us to that mystic region, the "Basé Settite." He described the shooting there as good, and said that there were ten villages between the Hamran country and Abyssinia, all of which paid taxes to King John. Some of these villages he told us were on the river, others some distance off in the mountains, but all situated on the right bank. Toansar and Beergayla were absolutely on the river. Dabergoum was four days' journey from Meheteb, but there were Abyssinians dwelling half-way between.

He gave me the following names of ten villages, which I give as nearly as I could catch the names and the order in which they come, beginning from Meheteb. The two first are off the river in the mountains. Dabergoum, Tola, Takerlumba, Beergayla, Ownseba, Usaba, Fora, Toansar, Kundigayla, Anāla. I think this information is very likely pretty correct; and it impressed me at the time as having the air of truth about it.

Only two days before our arrival at Abou Sellal some

elephants had passed, and one had been killed close to our camp; there was no mistake about it, as we saw the remains of its skeleton quite fresh.

The next day's march took us to Sogada, and we encamped on the same spot we had chosen in going south. It was a long day's journey, and some of the men lagged behind with their camels and lost themselves again. We made one halt before reaching Haikota, choosing Fahncoob again as a camping-ground.

On our way we came across the trail of a snake, which we followed, and after tracking it for some time we discovered, curled up under a *kittar*-bush, a boa-constrictor ten feet long, which we shot with a revolver. We preserved the skin. It was the only one we ever came upon, though we not unfrequently saw their marks on the ground and sometimes traced them a long way.

On March 27 we were back at Haikota again for the third time. We heard full particulars of the raid made by the people of that place on the Basé at Sarcelle; and I give them as they were given to me by some of the Beni-Amers that we had with us, and who represented themselves as being present at the time. I fully believe the main details of the story. Those who told us about it considered that they had behaved in a perfectly humane and natural manner, and never doubted for a moment but that we should think so too.

Sarcelle is a large village, and, like most Basé villages, built on a hill. As soon as the Beni-Amers made their appearance the inhabitants retreated into a cave in the mountain, which their enemies immediately surrounded. After standing a siege of four or five days, five Basé men emerged from the cave as they were getting pressed for food and water; and these men were no sooner seen than they were killed by spears. The next day four women and two men appeared; the former they kept, but killed the men. As fast as any people appeared, if men, they were killed; if women or quite young children they were made prisoners. Many died of hunger and thirst in the cave; but between one and two hundred men were put to death, while upwards

of a hundred and sixty women as well as a great number
of children were taken off. The women were apportioned
out as slaves or wives; what became of the children I did
not learn; but we saw some of the women on our return
to Haikota, and others we were told had been sent off to
other villages. The Basé women look very strong and
appear to do most of the hard work.

We reached Haikota before our caravan, and while we
were at luncheon in the *zariba* of the German, who we
found had fled, Sheik Achmed Ageer arrived to pay us a
visit. He endeavoured to appear as though nothing had
happened to displease us, but his manner was evidently
constrained. We taxed him with his duplicity, and told
him how indignant we were with him for having deceived
us. His excuses were very lame; and he tried to throw
the blame on Mahomet Salee, to whom he declared he had
given instructions to take us to Lacatecourah in the first
instance, and there arrange with the sheik to go on to
Toansar and Beergayla. He acknowledged that these were
Basé villages, and that both they and other villages were
on the Settite. His throwing the whole blame on Mahomet
Salee was of course nonsense, as the latter acted under his
orders, whatever they were, and dared not disregard them.
The probability is that he either *could* not help us to travel
farther up the Settite or *feared* to do so, but that, Arab-like,
he was anxious to meet our views and make himself as
agreeable as possible at the time.

The two following days we spent at Haikota arranging
for a start. We went out partridge shooting, but with indifferent success. When we left for the Settite there had
been plenty of grass about; but on our return we found
that for miles around it was all eaten up—every blade of
it—by the flocks and herds of the Arabs. In this those of
the Beni-Amers had been assisted by the animals of other
tribes. The sheik told us he had lately been paid six
hundred sheep as a tax by Sheik Moosa's people (the
Hadendowa sheik) for allowing their sheep to graze on his
land.

All the camel-drivers we had brought from Cassala, as

well as the boys who had charge of the horses, declined to go any farther, and wanted to go home; the only exception being En-noor,—a boy we had engaged at Cassala to help look after the horses, and Achmet, whom I have mentioned as being so good a tracker. Achmet had come with us all the way from Souakim, and had stuck to us when his companions left on our arrival at Cassala; we promised to take him with us by sea from Massawa to Souakim, as well as En-noor, if he wished to go.

Most of the camel-drivers we should have dismissed at Haikota, whether they had wished to go or not; for a more idle incompetent set of fellows it would be difficult to find.

On the 30th we moved on to Toadelook, our old quarters. From there the road turns off to Amedeb, for which place we were bound; and, having two or three days longer to wait, we thought we could not better employ our time than by waiting there. It seemed, too, to be a last and decidedly favourable opportunity for adding a lion to our bag, as the moon was full and the Arabs declared that there were plenty of these animals in the neighbourhood attracted by the immense herds of cattle there at the time.

It was long after dark before we arrived, owing to a late start; and we pitched our tents on the old spot above the river's bed.

SHEIK ACHMED AGEER AT TOADELOOK.

CHAPTER XX.

Immense Flocks and Herds.—Night Watch for Lions.—Two Panthers killed.—Two Lions bagged.—The Camp moves on.—Religion of the Basé.—Origin of various African Tribes.—First Day's Journey towards Amedeb.—A False Alarm.—Arrival at Amedeb.—Journey continued.—Khor Baraka.—Another Watch for Lions.—Thrilling Adventure with a Lion.

I NEVER saw anything like the numbers of flocks and herds that were in this part of the country. Cattle, sheep, and goats were there in thousands. We were told there were over five thousand head of cattle alone, and the number of sheep and goats must have been far greater. In a country like this the labour of watering these large flocks and herds is very great. Wells have to be dug in the bed of the *khor*, often to the depth of from ten to twenty feet, with the hands, for they possess no such implements as spades; and to prevent the soft sand from falling in they have to be lined with boughs, palm-leaves, etc. When the wells are finished a quantity of dry clay is brought from the banks; and, after being carefully kneaded and puddled, it is finally made into huge basins with raised sides, much resembling sponge-baths. These basins are, of course, made at the mouth of the wells, and filled with water. When the cattle and goats arrive, instead of rushing immediately in a body to quench their thirst, which would of course result in the trampling-down and destruction of these clay drinking-troughs, the animals are trained to approach the water in turn, no more being allowed to go at a time than can conveniently drink together. It was a most curious and interesting sight to watch; and if I had not seen it with my own eyes I should be slow to believe that these vast herds could be kept under such control. The Arab shepherds, instead of driving, "lead their flocks," and all carry the proverbial crook, which in their case is used to shake down the dry pods of the mimosa and the fruit of the *hegleek* and *nebbuk*-trees, of all of which the sheep and goats are very fond.

We heard lions roaring at night; but as it was late and we were all tired we decided to wait till the morrow before going after them. The next morning we arranged that four of us should spend the night in different places on the watch for them; and that the remaining two should pass it at a place in the mountains, called Hademdumi, where there was some water in a narrow *khor*, and where we were told we should have a very good chance. None of us had ever been there, and we drew lots who should go; the choice fell on Lort Phillips and myself.

We started off in a south-west direction, and, after going for some twelve or fourteen miles, found ourselves at our destination. The water was no more than a good-sized well dug by the Arabs in the bed of the *khor*, and filled to a level with it; and there was plenty of tall dried grass in the neighbourhood. The Beni-Amers had not yet moved there with their flocks, but intended doing so as soon as they had exhausted the grass in the neighbourhood of Toadelook.

We were disappointed at finding some Haikota people near there. They had constructed a good-sized ambush out of the leaves of the *dhoum*-palm on the bank beneath a tree, just over the water and four or five feet above it. The previous night one of them had killed, close by the water, the largest bull buffalo I think I ever saw; he had come down to drink. We were told that after the buffalo had been killed a lion had made his appearance, but had left without their having fired at him.

We were of course far more anxious to shoot a lion than a buffalo. We saw at once that, with such a smell of flesh about, there was no chance of a buffalo or a giraffe approaching the water. They had already cut the flesh of the buffalo into strips, with which the bushes were covered. After discussing some luncheon inside the hollow trunk of an immense baobab-tree I sallied forth to try and secure an antelope as bait: after a long stalk I luckily shot a large bull *tétél.* This we dragged to within about forty yards of our shelter, where we proposed passing the night. Soon after dark we ensconced ourselves inside the ambush. The moon was very brilliant, and it was most exciting work watching for the lion we hoped might appear. Our first visitors consisted of three little jackals, and we heard them barking in the bushes, very like dogs, some time before they ventured to approach the water. When they did appear we did not disturb them; but watched them as they drank at the well and tore at the carcass, barking all the while. When they had eaten and drunk their fill they took their departure; and in about ten minutes more a far larger animal made its appearance. We took it to be a leopard or a panther. Lort Phillips fired, but unluckily missed; and the animal, uttering an angry growl, scampered off into the bushes. We cursed our bad luck, and decided that next time we would both fire together. Another quarter of an hour had barely elapsed before the same animal returned. Both fired; it stood still for a second, and we feared we had missed again. Then it made for the bank, which we could hear by its cries it was not able to ascend, and it lay all night in the *khor.* We felt sure that the leopard, or whatever it might be, was mortally wounded, as we could occasionally hear it groan; and we felt confident that we should secure it in the morning. Another hour of anxious watching, and what we took for a lion made its appearance.

It is very difficult to judge of animals in the moonlight, as it has the effect of making them look nearly double their size. Our new friend roared, as we thought, just like a lion, and was answered by angry growls from the wounded animal by the bank. As soon as he got broadside to the carcass we both fired; with a roar he sprang up the side into the *dhoum*-palm bushes, without giving us the chance of another shot. There we heard him groan every now and then throughout the night. We quite thought we had shot a lion and a lioness; we felt sure the second was a lion, and that the first, which we had taken for a leopard, must be his mate.

No more beasts of the forest visited us that night; and, as soon as day dawned, we descended from our perch to see the result of the night's work. We found the first beast was a small male panther; and after first·carefully ascertaining that the "lion," as we felt sure it was, had not gone through the bushes and up the bank above them, we searched for traces of blood, which we soon found in abundance. We were not long in tracking our "lion;" which proved, to our disappointment, to be a large panther, lying quite dead in the bushes. We had both hit each panther, so we took one apiece; and, having cleaned them, we put them on a camel that we might take them to camp as they were. On our way back I left Lort Phillips to go on with the panthers, and turned off to the right, taking an Arab with me, in the hope of seeing some game. I came across the marks of several giraffes; the country looked perfect for them—plenty of covert and any number of green trees. I had a shot at a large kind of wild-cat, which I missed; and then climbed to the top of a hill to view the surrounding country in the hope of seeing game. I had no sooner reached the top than I espied a lion lying under the shade of a tree at about two or three hundred yards distance. Carefully taking its bearings, I lost no time in descending, in the hope of a shot; in this, however, I was disappointed, for I never saw it again. The animal must have seen me on the hill and made off. Unluckily, the ground was so hard and stony that its feet had left no impression; but in any case it would most likely have betaken itself to some thick covert, where I should have lost all trace of it. This was the first lion I had seen this year; for I did not get a glimpse of those I went after with Lort Phillips and Aylmer on the Settite. The only other I saw during my travels in Africa was at Furfur, on the borders of the Dembelas country; and on that occasion also none of us obtained a shot.

Before arriving in camp I heard that the others had shot two lions; and on getting there I was delighted to find the news was true. My brothers were the fortunate sportsmen, each having bagged one. All four of the party that had

remained at Toadelook had spent the night in watching ;
they had each chosen a different spot, near where they
imagined, from the tracks they found, the lions might pass
on their way to drink at the water. They had made small
zaribas under bushes, in which they sat, each with a native
holding a spare rifle. Immediately in front of the *zariba* a
sheep was tied as bait, to attract the game. Neither Aylmer
nor Colvin were fortunate enough to see any lions, though
they were roaring round them all night. My brother Arthur
posted himself near the water and William beneath a bush
in an open space, to which paths frequented by lions led in
all directions ; and he had, in fact, that very morning seen
the tracks of five passing close by the bush he selected to
sit under.

It is difficult for any one who has not had personal
experience of this kind of sport to realise adequately how
exciting it all is. Even buffalo-shooting at night is suffici◄
ently attractive ; but the excitement is tenfold increased
when the roar of the king of beasts is heard, growing louder
as he approaches the hiding-place of the watchers. Then
the rifle is grasped with firmer grip, as with beating heart
and finger on trigger the sportsman watches the trembling
sheep tugging and straining at its rope, in vain endeavour
to escape from the shadowy form and gleaming eyes, which,
though hidden as yet from the eager gaze of the hunter by
intervening bushes, are only too plainly visible to the
intended victim. An instant of intense suspense, and then
with a deep growl the lion launches himself upon his prey.
Now is the supreme moment ! a quick shot followed by a
cloud of dust often rendering a second impossible, and for
a moment it is difficult to determine how the game is going.
Is he dead or mortally wounded ? in full retreat or blindly
charging his assailant, separated from him by only a few
feet ?

During the night my brother William saw no less than
six lions, at two of which he fired ; the others made off
without giving him the chance of a shot. Of these six,
five paid him a visit at the same time, and this troop stood
under a tree too far off for him to fire in the uncertain

moonlight; suddenly one of them, with a tremendous rush and a low roar, sprang on the sheep. He fired, and knocked it over; but it recovered itself and made off for the 'bushes, where it lay groaning. Very shortly after another lion made its appearance, and stood gazing at the sheep. Feeling that he had fired too quickly before, he determined to reserve his fire until the lion should be quite close to him. Suddenly, however, with an angry growl, the beast turned sharply round and galloped off. My brother naturally felt much annoyed that he had not fired, and feared that he would not get another chance that night. Luckily, however, in a very short time the lion returned to the very same spot, about forty yards from where he was sitting, and was evidently puzzled to make out who or what he was. Raising his rifle, my brother took a steady shot at the centre of his chest. With a roar of pain the lion made off for some dwarf *dhoum*-palm bushes close by, where both he and the other which had been wounded remained all night, and from time to time could be heard groaning. In the morning, as soon as it was daylight, the other watchers, who had heard the shots in the night, came to see what had happened. They could hear one of the lions still groaning in the bushes, and surrounded him, throwing stones to induce him to rush out. They could not move him in this way; so, carefully advancing into the bushes, they found him just expiring. The bullet had entered the chest, and, having traversed the whole length of the body, was found embedded just underneath the skin in one of the flanks. The lion proved to be a very fine one, with a particularly long mane for that part of Africa, where, as a rule, their manes are rather scanty. He measured nine feet two inches in length.

They then went in search of the other lion, and found a pool of blood, where it had been lying all night. They tracked it by its blood for some miles, and caught a glimpse of it several times. It proved to be a lioness, and once they saw it under a tree in the company of two lions. Unfortunately, all three animals got into impenetrable jungle, and were never seen again, although some of us

LION AND LIONESS.

chosen the spot where my brother William had shot his lion.

BAOBAB-TREE.

Aylmer, in going to his place near the water about eight o'clock, disturbed one which had just drunk, or was going to do so; but it made off before he could get a shot.

On the 3d we resolved to start once more in a homeward direction. Old Sheik Achmed Ageer again saw us an hour or two on our journey, and then left to return to Haikota. I made frequent attempts to find out if the Basé had any religious belief, and every one I asked replied in the negative. The sheik, who was quite the most intelligent of his class I ever met in the Soudan, persisted in declaring they had none whatever; he was of course a Mahometan himself, and both read and wrote Arabic well. He said they knew nothing whatever of a God, and he gave me the following curious account of some of their customs: When he was obliged to make peace with any of their chiefs the Basé killed a black goat, and both he and the Basé sheik with whom the covenant was to be made would pluck out an eye, then cut off a hind and then a fore leg, each taking his part in the ceremony. By this they believe that if either failed in the engagement they had entered into, the defaulter would lose an eye, leg, or arm.

Another of their customs was, that if any of their number stole anything from his neighbour, the offender, accompanied by a numerous contingent from among his people, was brought to a tree growing near his village; the said tree being held, as it were, sacred. In order to prove whether the accused person had really stolen anything or not, he was required to pull a piece of bark off the tree without the aid of anything except his own fingers. If he succeeded in doing this he was acquitted and held innocent; but if not, he was condemned as proved to be guilty, and punished accordingly. As the tree invariably selected for this purpose was furnished with very tough, closely growing bark, it was usually almost impossible to disengage it with the fingers alone; and the prisoner's sentence was generally a foregone conclusion.

Although I think there is very little doubt that the Basé are without religion and have no God, they must, if the following custom told me by the sheik be true, have some belief in a future state. When a Basé man dies, his wife,

or other relations, place something he was fond of during
his life—such as the fruit of the baobab-tree, tobacco, etc.
—on his tomb.   Perhaps the wind or some human agency
makes away with the offering; they then believe that the
dead man has consumed it and perhaps shared it with other
spirits, inhabitants of neighbouring tombs.   Should these
delicacies disappear faster than the donors anticipated, the
attentive relations of the dead man will perhaps accuse the
relict of the inhabitant of a neighbouring tomb of being
lazy and inattentive in not keeping her husband properly
supplied, and so compelling his neighbour to share his
dainties with him.   I give these stories as they were told
me from notes made at the time.

I told the sheik that it seemed to me that the Basé were
the remnants of the original inhabitants of the country, and
that they were settled there before the Arabs came over
from Arabia.   He did not believe this, but adduced no
grounds either for or against my theory.   He told me there
were two brothers who emigrated from Arabia into Africa,
one called Basé, the other Nuba.   The former settled
where his descendants are now found, but he knew nothing
as to what part of the country the other brother had gone
to.   According to him, the only remnants of the original
inhabitants of any part of the Soudan that he had heard
anything of were reduced to twenty or thirty families in the
neighbourhood of Cassala.   The Hadendowas, he declared,
came from Dhalak, and other Red Sea islands; the Beni-
Amers (his tribe), Dabainas, and Shukreeyehs from the
Hejaz; and the Hallangas from Yemen.

Although he was intending to return to Haikota when
he left us, he said he would soon move some distance
farther north with his flocks and herds, in order to obtain
fresh pasturage; during the rainy season his people mostly
went to higher ground than the valley of the Gash.   During
one rainy season some years ago he stated that there was
such a heavy hailstorm near Haikota that the hail lay on the
ground nearly a foot deep for seven or eight days.   This
statement we could *hardly* swallow, though very probably
they have hail there sometimes.

Our first day's journey after leaving the Gash was about eighteen miles in the direction of Amedeb, where we encamped in the plain, away from water. The country was very much like all that part of the Soudan, very barren and hilly, but in places rather less monotonous travelling than we had usually found it to be when leaving rivers or *khors* such as the Gash. We crossed a number of picturesque rocky *khors*, on the borders of which flourished many large and fine trees in full leaf.

There was a large Basé village on our right, some miles from where we encamped for the night, and we could distinctly see the lights. The next day we arrived at Amedeb, after a long march of over thirty miles. We were up at daybreak, but could not get the camels off until 7.45; and it was 11.30 P.M. before we got dinner—a long day. The country through which we had travelled was very agreeable —far more so than we had expected to find it. The road, or track rather, was easy-going for the camels, except one steep stony bit over a high hill, and proved to be an infinitely better one for the camels than that which Lort Phillips and I had taken the first time we went to Amedeb.

All day we wound between high hills, and for a long time travelled in the bed of a *khor* called Mogoreb. I never saw a greener one. The numbers of various brightly-plumaged birds and the general appearance of the country reminded me of the Anseba valley, which we had visited the previous year and were again to pass through on our way to the coast. In this *khor* we encountered two very deep wells, situated some miles apart.

On this journey we enjoyed a Basé scare. We had gone on some distance ahead of the caravan, and suddenly came upon two Basé drawing water at a well. They were at first very much frightened at us; but we soon made friends, and riding on ahead left them. About an hour later one of our men came running after us with the alarming news that the Basé had come down in great numbers from the hills and fallen on the caravan in our rear. We, of course, all turned round, and retraced our steps at our camels' best pace; finding the whole thing, as so often

happens in these countries, a false alarm.   Before en-
countering the caravan, however, it seemed as though "the
battle" had begun.   Colvin and one of the others had got
on some distance ahead of me, when suddenly I heard a
shot, and did not know what to make of it.   I renewed
my efforts to get on as quickly as possible, and more than
once ran the chance of being knocked off my camel by the
boughs of overhanging trees.   On regaining the caravan,
the mystery of the shot was soon explained.   Colvin had
put an end to the sufferings of a camel which had been left
behind to die.

The "attack" was then explained.   The Basé, unseen
by us, had been watching our movements from the adjacent
hills, and, being unaccustomed to see so large a caravan
marching through their country, and probably never having
seen Europeans before, were very naturally frightened, and
at the same time curious to know what it all meant, and a
number of them had come down and followed after the
caravan to try and discover what was up.   The two men
we had previously met had flourished their spears at them,
shouting to them to keep back, at the same time telling
them we were friends and not Turks.   On seeing this
Gerghis and some of the other servants had thought it
necessary to point guns at them.   The Basé shouted out
for some of our people to go back and parley with them,
but this they were all afraid to do; and there certainly
would have been nothing gained by so doing, as we only
wished to travel quickly through the country, and had no
thought of stopping there.   By the time we had returned
to the caravan, all we saw of them was four men watching
us from a hill.   Soon after we met tranquil people feeding
their flocks, and a number of them drew water from a well
for our horses and goats.

Before reaching Amedeb we passed a great many large
villages belonging to the Barea tribe.   On arriving at the
town we were very glad to find newspapers and letters for
us.   Our letters, however, contained very sad news, telling
us of the death in England of the Hon. John Maxwell, who
had been one of our party in the Soudan the previous

winter. Poor fellow, he had had some thoughts of joining us on our present expedition, but had decided not to leave England again so soon, and had died of rheumatic fever.

Our latest news from England was of February 24, and it was only the second time we had had letters since leaving Suez.

In the afternoon we made a start in the direction of Sanheit, and got about four miles on our road, camping by some wells where there were plenty of *sont*-trees, abounding in doves, a number of which we shot.

The following day we made a long and very uninteresting journey of eleven and a half hours. Although we passed wells in two places, we pushed forward, encamping away from water. The Arabs objected, as usual, to our doing this, as time is no object to them, and they do not care how long they take over a journey. We went straight on past the wells, leaving a couple of camels to come on after us with a plentiful supply.

We saw no game all day, travelling in a plain where there was no grass but plenty of bushes, and crossing occasional *khors*. On both sides of us there was a range of mountains, some of them of considerable height. We passed two villages composed of mat huts, situated a long distance from any wells, and met a number of donkeys laden with water-skins, evidently carrying the daily supply.

Two more camels gave out and we presented them to some Arabs, hoping they might pick up. The work our camels had to do was not too severe, but we could not get them properly looked after. The journeys we took them were shorter, and the loads they had to carry less, than the natives would have placed on their backs; but we found it impossible to keep them in good condition.

The weather we found less hot than it had been latterly on the Gash, and the nights were cool; while in the afternoon heavy clouds would sometimes obscure the sun, rendering travelling much pleasanter. After a four hours' march we reached a place called Gargi, situated in Khor Baraka, which we had heard a great deal about as a likely place for lions. Gargi consisted of a movable village of mat huts, placed in the bed of the *khor*.

DHOUM-PALMS AT GARGI, KHOR BARAKA.

Khor Baraka is one of the largest and most important in the Soudan. It runs from the Anseba to Tokar, two days' journey from Souakim. The previous winter we had spent some time on it and some of its tributaries. It is bordered by a thick fringe of *dhoum*-palms, and in many places is very picturesque. We afterwards heard that the two officers of the " Blues " who had travelled with us from Suez to Souakim had shot a lion at that very place. One of them gave a most graphic account of their adventure in *Baily's Magazine.* They were sleeping out in the open air, which they preferred to a tent, not very long before we encamped in the same spot, and the night was very dark. After having been asleep about two hours in the sandy bed of the· *khor*, they were suddenly aroused from their slumbers by a horrible shriek and loud cries of " *Asad, asad !* " (lion). In a moment every one was in commotion, including the watchman, who had allowed all the fires but one to go out. Their first thought was that a goat or sheep had been carried off by a lion ; and they perceived the shadowy form of one walking away from the camp. One of them fired two rapid shots, the result of which was an angry roar. It soon appeared that it was not a sheep or a goat that had been carried off, but one of the natives who had been asleep near the fire. The lion had seized the poor fellow by the feet and dragged him for about four yards, and then left him, disturbed no doubt by the man's own shrieks and the shouts of his companions ; and thanks also to the plucky and determined manner in which his neighbour had held on to him. The unfortunate man had both his feet severely injured by the lion's teeth, the greater part of the sole of each being torn away, leaving the bones, however, intact. He had little faith in the European method of curing his wounds, and insisted on carrying out his own method of treatment ; this consisted in covering his wounds with wood-ashes, and placing the soles of his feet as near as possible to the fire. On examining the course taken by the lion in his peregrinations through their camp, they discovered that he had passed exactly a foot and a half from one of their beds. At daybreak they followed the tracks of the lion, and soon perceived by marks of blood that he was wounded. They followed him into a thick clump of *dhoum*-palms, where they heard him groaning. He quickly sprang out at them, receiving another bullet. He again retired into the jungle; and one of them, climbing up a palm-tree, administered the *coup de grace*.

We all, with the exception of my brothers (who gave in to the rest of the party, as they had both shot a lion) decided to lie out at night in the hope of getting a shot at a lion. We chose places a long way from each other on the banks of the *khor*, where, hidden under the shadow of the *dhoum*-palms, we could look on the sandy bed of Khor Baraka, brilliant in the moonlight, and obtain a good view of any lion that might deign to visit our tempting bait, as each of us had a sheep tied up in front of where he sat. Colvin and I saw nothing, though we remained at our posts all night and heard one or two lions roar occasionally, but they never came near us. Lort Phillips was so much bothered by hyænas, which would keep rushing at his sheep, that, after firing several shots at them, he left and went to bed. Aylmer thought he saw a lion, but it proved to be a fine panther, which he shot; not, however, before it had sprung on and killed the unfortunate sheep. He also shot a young striped hyæna, which looked different from any specimen we had shot before; it was nearly white, with very long hair.

The next day we continued our journey, and a most amusing incident took place. Gerghis, who was riding in front of the caravan, saw an elephant ahead of him, which he thought was one of a herd. As we were some distance in advance he turned back and begged George, who was in the rear, to shoot it. Some of the Arabs got most excited and danced about, waving their spears in the air. Suddenly some men ran out in great excitement from behind some bushes; and it was then discovered that the elephant over which they had been so excited was a young one that had been caught at Furfur, on the borders of the Dembelas country, and which the men had tied to a tree while enjoying a siesta. Every one of course burst out laughing, and Gerghis got greatly chaffed about it.

We made about seventeen miles before halting for the
night at Adardee in Khor Bogou. We passed wells at
three different points on the road, immense flocks and herds,
and a great many people. We travelled a long way in Khor
Bogou, which was very pretty ; in places precipitous rocks
rose to a considerable height on both banks. We saw no
game with the exception of doves, which were very numerous,
a number of which we shot for food. The mountains were
getting higher. The only thing wanting in the landscape
was more verdure ; there were scarcely any trees, though
plenty of bushes ; while we regretted, for the sake of the
camels, the almost total absence of grass. At Adardee we
came across several of our old camel-drivers of the previous
winter, and engaged one of them with his three camels to
go on with us to Massawa.

The camel question was constantly recurring, as one by
one they dropped off. It was impossible to lighten the
loads they were carrying, and we gave all the attention we
could to seeing that they were properly fed ; many of them,
however, unknown to us of course, must have been diseased
when we bought them.

CHAPTER XXI.

Perilous Ascent of Tchad-Amba.—The Church.—The Monks.—We move on again.—An Old Acquaintance.—Arrival at Sanheit.—The Town of Sanheit.—A Visit to the Church and Schools at Sanheit.— We start for Massawa.—Dra's sad Story.—The Anseba Valley.— An Attempt to make India-rubber from the *Quol-quol* Plant.—El Ain.—Bashi-Bazouks and their Prisoners.—We encamp at the Water-course Camphor.—Occasional sudden Rising of the Water in the *Khors.*

WE passed a very curious mountain named Tchad-Amba, which we left on our right. We had accomplished its ascent the year before, and were, I believe, the first white people to have done so, no Turk or Egyptian even having previously gained the summit. It is a very remarkable mountain, standing nearly alone. We spent some time at its foot, and were told by our Arabs that it was impossible to climb it except by one very difficult path known only to the Abyssinian monks dwelling on the top. We were not very ambitious of attempting its ascent, and had formed no plan for doing so, when one day an Abyssinian arrived in camp with a note from Père Picard, our missionary friend of Sanheit. He informed us in his letter that the bearer of it was one of the monks who dwelt on the top of the mountain, and that for a consideration he was willing to guide us to its summit. Père Picard added that he strongly recommended us to embrace this opportunity of seeing what former travellers had vainly attempted to accomplish.

Munzinger Pacha, a former governor of Sanheit and the surrounding country, as well as a recent Italian traveller, the Marquis Antinori, had offered considerable sums to be permitted to make the ascent, but their offers had been

invariably refused. Before six o'clock the next morning
we started, taking with us as porters an Abyssinian servant
named Butros (Peter), and four soldiers we had brought
from Sanheit. We took the soldiers in preference to our
Arab servants, as the latter were afraid to accompany us.

Our way led us up a very steep water-course, which,
at first easy enough, became more and more arduous the
farther we advanced. At length the smooth boulders of
rock, frequently piled one on the top of the other, became
so slippery that we gladly followed the example of our men,
who, having divested themselves of their sandals, were
climbing with bare feet. At last we came to an enormous
slab of rock, to surmount which was like climbing up the
roof of a house at a particularly sharp angle, and with as
dangerous a drop in case of a fall. Here one of our water-
carriers collapsed, absolutely refusing to proceed farther, as
his head would not stand it, and proposed awaiting our
return, as he felt sure that we could not get up much farther.

After climbing for another half-hour we were startled by
the fall of a large stone from above, quickly followed by
others, which made us hastily seek the shelter of an over-
hanging ledge ; where, from the shouts that greeted us from
the top of the mountain, we immediately perceived that the
fall of the rocks was not caused by accident, as we had at
first imagined, but that they were being hurled at us with
hostile intent. After a great deal of shouting on both sides,
Butros made our assailants understand that we were Christians, and wished to see their monastery.

At the commencement of hostilities our guide had
endeavoured to sneak off ; which so enraged our soldiers
that they asked our permission to shoot him on the spot,
declaring he had purposely led us into an ambuscade.
We quieted them, however, by telling him that we would
surely shoot him if he again attempted to desert us.

After a consultation as to what was to be done, we
decided on continuing the ascent. We were unwilling to
be beaten ; and moreover, owing to the formation of the
mountain, we were less exposed in advance than in retreat.
A tedious and dangerous climb brought us near the summit

—which was much farther off than we had anticipated—when we perceived an old man coming down to meet us, who told us that, seeing the tarbooshes of the soldiers, we had been taken for Turks. He then showed us the best way to reach the top, and pointed out to us how far we were from the path we should have taken.

What was nothing to this old man, who had lived on the mountain for forty years without having come down, was no joke to us; and we were sincerely glad when it was all over, and the top was reached. We found, on our arrival, a huge fig-tree and a number of conical-roofed huts. The monks received us kindly, and gave us a hut to sleep in, some dried figs about the size of hazel-nuts, and unleavened bread to eat, with very dirty-looking water to wash it down; for which, however, we were very thankful. Their daily fare consisted of figs and bread. We saw several large threshing-floors; and they grew sufficient *dhurra* for their own use.

There were eight monks, mostly aged creatures, some of whom had not been down into the valley below for over forty years. They were dressed in coarse cotton cloth, dyed yellow, with caps of the same material, and went barefooted. They took us to see their church—a round building, thatched with straw, and divided into three compartments, one inside the other; the innermost being accessible only to the high priest.

They showed us some manuscripts; one of which, evidently held in high veneration among them, we understood to be a Bible. It was placed in three covers made of skin, and had handsome silver clasps. I tried to buy some of their manuscripts, but they would not sell anything. Outside the church were three large flat stones, made to serve the purpose of bells. They were suspended by leather thongs from the bough of a tree, and, when struck by a stone, gave out a pleasant, bell-like sound.

Twelve or fourteen was the full complement of monks who lived on the top of Tchad-Amba, but eight of their number had gone on some mission to King John. We were informed that during the Abyssinian war a number of valuables were placed in the care of these monks for safe-keeping. Though they were very hospitable, I am sure they were not at all glad to see us; they told us we were the first visitors they had ever had. The night was very cold, and we were obliged to light a fire inside the hut. The next morning my brother took his rifle, and shot a small species of goat which the natives called a *sachar* (*calotragus saltatrix*). Its hair was very coarse, resembling that of a reindeer. We had never met with a specimen before; it is evidently an inhabitant of the higher mountains.

It turned out that the man whose guidance might have cost us our lives was a *mauvais sujet* who had been expelled from the monastery some years before; and, although he brazened it out, his late brethren were evidently not enraptured at seeing him again, more especially as, in offering to show us the way to the top, he had betrayed a sacred trust, having sworn never to divulge it.

The mountain is accessible only from two points. The one usually taken leads over a ridge so narrow that for more than a hundred yards the safest mode of progression is to sit straddle-legged and work one's self along, one foot hanging literally over one valley, and the other over another. It is on one of the highest points of the mountain. This road leads in the direction of Sanheit; and those monks whose heads could not stand crossing the ridge were taken round by the way we had ascended, which was a good deal farther from Abyssinian territory.

Before we started on our return the monks took us to a ledge of rock, from which we obtained a fine view of the surrounding country for many miles, our tents immediately beneath us appearing mere white specks. The monks told us they had frequently seen our tents and heard our shots, and wondered what we were doing. They started us off on our return by much the same way that we had come; but instead this time of following the ledge, as we had been obliged to do in coming up to protect ourselves against the stones thrown by them, we went a shorter and easier way, and soon reached the place where we had received their first volley of rocks. In making the ascent we had been for a great part of the way in the shade; in going down, however, towards noon, we were in the blazing sun, and hemmed in by great boulders, reflecting the terrific heat. We were obliged to take off our shoes and stockings, as in our ascent, and found clambering over the burning rocks a most painful proceeding.

To return to my narrative : Leaving Adardee, our next halt was at Ashidireh, about seventeen miles distant. Although in this country villages are by no means numerous, the Arabs have names for every well, *khor*, or hill. It is often, however, difficult to know their proper names, as it frequently happens that the different tribes have different names for one and the same thing. Ashidireh was merely a watering-place, and Adardee the name given to some wells in Khor Bogou.

On the road we met Ala-ed-Deen Pacha, an old acquaintance, who was at Massawa last year. The government of the Soudan had been lately divided into two, and the eastern part made separate from Khartoum, Berber, the White and Blue Niles, Kordofan, and Darfour. Ala-ed-Deen, as I have already mentioned, had just been made governor of Souakim, Massawa, Sanheit, Cassala, Gerdariff, Gallabat, and the intervening country. He was on his way to Amedeb, and intended visiting the various towns under his jurisdiction, making Cassala his headquarters, our old friend the Bey there having been dismissed.

Ala-ed-Deen was afterwards killed with Hicks Pacha. The Ex-Khedive Ismail told me he had a very high opinion of him; he was no doubt a man of considerable ability, and probably no worse than most other Egyptian officials. The previous winter, however, he had greatly aroused our indignation.

We had engaged camels at Sanheit for some weeks' shooting in the vicinity. On our return we found a steamer was leaving Massawa for Suez, which we could only catch by taking the same camels on to the coast. Our Shukreeyeh drivers objected, saying the road to the sea was out of their country and their camels were tired—perfectly valid excuses. We offered them half as much again as

the proper fare, but they still demurred, fearing that the
governor of Massawa would take their camels, make them
carry for the government, and probably never pay them.
On obtaining a letter from the Bey at Sanheit, asking (as
we fondly imagined) Ala-ed-Deen, who was at that time

KEREN (SANHEIT).

governor of Massawa, to let them go free, they consented
to accompany us.

On our arrival we presented the letter, which we found
merely stated that the garrison at Sanheit was in want of
salt, and he had better load up the camels with some and
return them to him.   Ala-ed-Deen, in spite of our indignant
remonstrances, seized the chief camel-drivers, put them in
prison, and sent the others out to forage for their beasts
until the salt was ready, when they were sent back with it

to Sanheit.   They came to us with tears in their eyes to
protest against this cruel conduct and beg our protection.
They further stated, but whether true or not I cannot say,
that the extra pay we had given had been taken from them.

Is it to be wondered at that these people have at last
risen against such rulers?

The next day took us into Sanheit, which we reached
on April 10.   A new road, only lately finished, had been
built over the mountain, decidedly the best piece of road-
making I have ever seen in the country, and nearly good
enough for carriages, had there been such vehicles.   It
was a broad, zigzag road, cut in places through the rock,
the work of the soldiers at Sanheit, and due entirely to the
energy of the present governor.

In the summer of 1881 the Abyssinians had come down
into the country between Ashidireh and this mountain-pass
and driven off a great many cattle, as well as killing a
number of the Sanheit people.   As usual on such occasions
the Egyptian soldiers at Sanheit remained in garrison, and
did nothing to help them.   The garrison consisted of
fifteen hundred men, all negroes from the White Nile.

Several wells had been sunk close to the road.   The air
was fresh and invigorating; and on reaching the top of the
pass, and winding in and out of the hills for a short distance,
we were delighted to look down on Sanheit in the valley
below us, surrounded by mountains, and situated over five
thousand feet above sea-level.   It is the healthiest and
coolest town in the Egyptian Soudan, and we knew it well.
We had ridden on ahead of the caravan, and went straight
to the mission-house, where we saw Père Picard.

We asked him if he had been able to do anything for
the children of poor Mahomet, our guide, of whom we had
written from Amedeb on our first arrival there.   He replied
that their family were so fanatical and afraid of the Egyptians
that they would not permit them to go to Sanheit; and consequently he could do nothing towards educating them, all
that was possible being to send them money.

Sanheit is situated in a very barren, treeless-looking
plain, in what is known as the Bogos country, and used to

be independent, until Munzinger Pacha some years ago took it for the Egyptians, and built a fort there.[1] Previous to that there had been many trees, all of which he cut down. Each family, too, had its own burying-ground inclosed in high stone walls; these he removed and used in building the present fort, and there remains scarcely a trace of these ancient sepulchres. Sanheit is usually marked on the maps as Keren, and was known by that name before the arrival of the Egyptians. It is now applied only to the part of the town built before that period, and separated from the more modern town and fort of Sanheit, which is opposite to it, by several hundred feet of arid-looking land. This arid-looking plateau, however, after the rains, which commence in June, grows a considerable quantity of tobacco; and there are several Greeks who have been established there for many years engaged in its cultivation.

We pitched our tents close to the well belonging to the mission, which was fully two hundred feet deep, and under the shadow of an immense fig-tree. By the aid of irrigation, almost anything would grow in the favourable climate of Sanheit; the soil is rich, but water scarce. The missionaries possess several gardens, in which with great success they grow potatoes, cabbages, lettuces, carrots, and other European vegetables, as well as vines and pomegranates. It is a pity they have never tried mangoes, which I am sure would flourish there, and, besides supplying fruit, would be most valuable for shade.

We went to call on the governor, and found his divan much improved in the last year; instead of a small, dirty-looking kind of barn, we were shown into a nice room furnished with plenty of comfortable chairs, and there were actually clean white muslin curtains to the windows ! The governor, a military man, and evidently very energetic, was

---

[1] By the treaty between Great Britain, Egypt, and Abyssinia, signed at Adowa on June 3, 1884, Sanheit, and the whole of the Bogos country, was to be restored to King John on September 1 of the present year ; and when the Egyptian troops shall have left the garrisons of Cassala, Amedeb, and Sanheit, the buildings in the Bogos country, stores, and munitions of war, are also to become the property of King John.

P

new to the place. He had greatly improved and strength-
ened the fort, and was commencing to build a mosque, for
which they were making red-burnt bricks instead of the
usual sun-dried ones.

We found a telegram from the English consul at Suez
to say that the next two steamers would leave Massawa on
the 6th and 30th inst. To make sure we telegraphed to
Massawa, and received an answer to say that the next boat
sailed on the 26th. Père Picard and another brother dined
with us, and afterwards a great crowd assembled to see the
magic-lantern, with which all seemed to be greatly delighted.
Although we were told that the hottest months in Sanheit
were those of March, April, and May, we found the weather
much cooler than any we had experienced for some time.
The nights were quite cold, and all day a strong cool wind
blew.

We asked to see over the church and schools—the
largest and best conducted thing of the kind in the Egyptian
Soudan—and were greatly pleased with what we saw; so
much so, that, although none of us were Roman Catholics,
we all gladly subscribed to so laudable an establishment.
It had been a good deal enlarged lately, and was altogether
far more important than we had expected. There are seven
brothers, all Lazarists; nine sisters; and also a bishop, a
Swiss, who lives usually at Sanheit, but when we were there
he was absent in Europe. They clothe, feed, and educate
seventy girls and eighty boys, all of whom live in the establishment. We were conducted over the dormitories, which
were very airy and scrupulously clean; each child had an
angareb, with the bedclothes belonging to it neatly folded
up and placed at the foot. We were shown one large
room, in which was a printing-press, where religious books
were being printed in the Amharic language (one of the
languages of Abyssinia) by one of the fathers. We were
next taken to the carpenter's shop, where cart-wheels were
being made. Everything is done by the fathers themselves.
There are two carts, drawn by bullocks, belonging to the
mission—the only wheeled conveyances I ever saw in the
Soudan.

Besides the children who live at the mission, and who are mostly from Abyssinia, they have five hundred belonging to Sanheit who attend the schools daily. It not unfrequently happens that a mother will sell her child; whenever the priests hear of such a case they go to the government authorities, who make the mother give up the money to the purchaser and hand the child over to the mission. One such child had arrived the very morning of our visit—a little boy between two and three years old ; his mother had sold him for three dollars! The priests had christened him Lorenzo.

We went inside the church—really a very good building, with a vaulted roof. A native priest, an Abyssinian I believe, was engaged in baptising some fresh converts. We were told that during an earthquake some two or three years ago a great part of the roof had fallen in, and that everything in the church had been overturned, except the image of the Virgin and Child over the high altar.

We went to see the sisters in a large airy room, opening out of a courtyard in which European flowers, such as geraniums, verbenas, and roses, were in bloom, and looked quite home-like. One of the sisters, a Swiss, possessed some medical knowledge, and with pardonable pride showed us her dispensary, well furnished with neat rows of bottles and drawers. Everything about the mission was comfortable and European looking, in great contrast to its surroundings—rooms with red-tiled floors, furnished with chairs and tables, linen-presses, a sewing-machine, etc. We saw two harmoniums; one in the church, another in a room in which one of the sisters was holding a singing-class.

Prettier children it would be difficult to find; and all looked clean, happy, and well-cared for. We heard them sing a hymn in French in praise of the Virgin, which they did very well; then they indulged us in a quaint Abyssinian dance. Sewing is a great part of the education of both boys and girls, and we saw a class in one room learning to sew.

There are three of these mission establishments in Abyssinia belonging to the same society, but they have no

sisters attached to them.   At Massawa they have, however ;
and I believe the establishment there is as large, or larger,
than that at Sanheit.   They have nothing to do with the
missions at Khartoum or Berber, which are, I believe, not
nearly so flourishing or well-managed.

The most disheartening part of the mission was, as the
fathers and sisters confessed to us, the difficulty in finding
situations for their *protégés* after they had reared and educated them.   Outcast from their own people and unable to
find employment amongst the Mussulman authorities, they
are thrown on their own resources ; which proves more
fatal to the women than to the men.

At noon, on the 11th, a start was made for Massawa.
Some of the servants belonging to Sanheit we left behind.
Gerghis, who came from the same place, and had been with
us both winters, Lort Phillips decided to take with him to
England.   He was a smart, active boy of about seventeen,
who had been brought up at the mission, where he had
learnt a little French.[1]

One of the best of our Sanheit servants, who had been
with us during both past winters, by name Dra, a most
intelligent, faithful fellow of about thirty, who could both
speak and write a little French, also left us before our
departure for the coast.   The priests told us a most horrible
story about him which we had never heard before, and
which illustrates the state of degradation in which the
people live.   It appears that a long time back his father
had stolen a cow ; the theft was traced to him, and he was
ordered to pay it back at once, but having disposed of it,
and being without money, he could not do so, and consequently, according to the law among his tribe, he was condemned to return two cows ; and this went on at a sort of
compound-interest rate (he being still unable to pay the
man back) until he owed one hundred cows.   By the law
of his tribe he then became the slave of the man from
whom he had stolen ; this slavery consisting, as far as he
was concerned, in his being obliged to follow his master

---

[1] He is still (October 1884) with Lort Phillips, and has turned out
very well.

should he go to fight against any neighbouring tribe, and in attending the ceremonies consequent on his marriage or death. The dreadful part of it, however, was, that his wife and any daughters he might have were forced to lead immoral lives; and this extended to all his female descendants; in consequence of which state of affairs no respectable woman would marry Dra. Dra's sister had married a European, and he had hoped that by so doing she would be free; but her husband dying of small-pox she was forced to become a public woman.

Dra's master was in prison when we were in Sanheit; and the priests told us that nothing could be done towards freeing Dra until his term of servitude was ended, which would be in a few weeks' time. When that event took place they said his freedom could be purchased for thirty dollars, besides two dollars which must be given to a man who would go round with some noisy instrument to the various villages about, somewhat in the manner of a town-crier, and proclaim his freedom; in addition to which a dollar each would have to be given to three witnesses. Dra did not know that all this had been told to us; and when we called him into the tent and interrogated him on the subject he became greatly excited, and evidently did not at all like our knowing about it; he, however, confessed that it was all true. We left the requisite sum with the priests to procure his freedom, with which he was greatly pleased, though they said it would take some time to accomplish. They told us that, if we spoke to the government officials about it, they would deny the existence of such a thing; as, although they would disapprove of it, they would be powerless to prevent it, because it was a purely tribal law, which with such people was of far more weight than any that the Egyptian authorities might endeavour to pass.

The first day out of Sanheit we accomplished only about eleven miles. We descended a considerable distance, Sanheit being about five thousand feet above the sea, and pitched our tents in the Anseba valley. For some distance we passed flourishing-looking gardens, where vegetables of

various kinds were growing; some of the natives having
followed the example of the mission.

Although no water flows in the Anseba in the dry season,
in many places it comes to the surface, and can always be
obtained by sinking wells to no great depth; so that irrigation becomes comparatively easy, and this was being taken
advantage.of in many places. Some three or four miles
after leaving the town we passed a fort called Sobab,
garrisoned with soldiers, and situated on the top of a hill
commanding the approach to Sanheit. The valley of the
Anseba is a most favourable ground for naturalists, many
interesting and brightly-plumaged birds being found there.
Partridges were extremely plentiful, and of two kinds—the
Francolinus Rüppelli and *F. gutturalis.* We shot a good
many of them, and they afforded excellent sport. We also
shot some beautiful trogons and large yellow pigeons,
besides doves of different kinds—the *Columba Guinea,
Turtur Senegalensis,* and *Treron Abyssinica.*

The trees were very numerous, large, and of many
different kinds; in fact, a pleasanter camping-ground it
would be difficult to find, our only regret being that we
had not more time to spend there. One tree that was
very common there had long hanging tendrils, from which
hung a pod-like fruit about two feet in length.

The journey from Sanheit to El Ain is certainly, as far
as scenery and climate are concerned, the most agreeable
I ever made in the Soudan. Our next day's journey was
as far as Calamet, twenty-three miles. After following the
course of the Anseba for five or six miles we left it, and
soon began to ascend a very steep hill, most trying for the
camels, which were rapidly decreasing in number; many
of them had died, some had been sold for an old song,
and five given to the priests.

On reaching the summit of the mountain we obtained
a most extensive view. The path down the other side was
longer and quite as steep as the one by which we had come
up. The flora differed from anything we had yet seen:
there were aloes, the castor-oil plant, cacti of many kinds,
including the *quol-quol,* and bright-coloured flowers in great

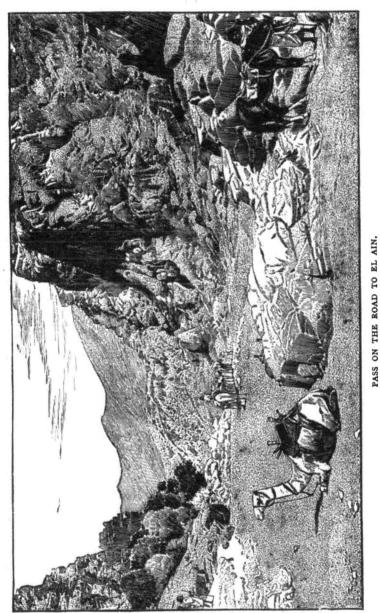

PASS ON THE ROAD TO EL AIN.

profusion. The *quol-quol* (*euphorbia Abyssinica*) contains a poisonous, white, milky juice, which is very sticky, and flows out plentifully on a sprig being wounded or broken. I believe that the Abyssinians use this juice for catching fish in the small streams, by throwing a quantity of it into the water; the fish become insensible, and float on the surface, when they are easily captured. A drop of this juice inadvertently getting into one's eye is said to be sufficient, to cause blindness; and I have heard that the milk of the *asclepia gigantea*, an extremely common desert-plant throughout the Soudan, is possessed of the same charming quality.

Some Frenchmen had lately taken it into their heads that the juice of the *quol-quol* would form a cheap substitute for India-rubber, and expected to make a large fortune by exporting it. Their expectations had been most unduly and cruelly raised by the report they had received of the first consignment sent to Europe. By some mistake their consignees had opened a case of India-rubber from Zanzibar in mistake for the *quol-quol*, and immediately wrote to them to send all they could possibly obtain at the price they had named, which was far lower than what Zanzibar India-rubber cost. On receiving this report they sent off a great quantity as quickly as they could, and had sent a great deal before a second letter reached them demanding what they meant by sending such rubbish. Then the whole mistake was cleared up, but not before the poor Frenchmen had lost largely by the transaction. In shape this tree resembles a cone reversed. It grows to a height of twenty-five to thirty feet, and bears yellow and red coloured fruit, which grow together in clusters, in much the same way as dates.

We did not see much game; but Lort Phillips shot a very fine buck *nellut*, after a stalk to the top of a hill. This species of antelope is always found in very hilly districts, but does not frequent wide open plains, like gazelle, ariel, and many other varieties of antelope. Lions are sometimes seen in this country, and used to be very common. We were also told that a panther had been lately seen near Calamet.

Another long day's march took us to El Ain. We were descending all the time; and often travelled in the wide, sandy bed of *khors.* Our road lay through a very beautiful, rocky pass, where it was difficult to believe we were in Africa; and led through a narrow gorge, barely wide enough for two camels to pass, with towering rocks on either side, the resort of the dog-faced baboon.

We passed several large burial-grounds—large, at least, to be found in such wilds—and two sheiks' tombs, which in the distance, placed as they were on prominent rocks above the path, presented quite the appearance of castles or fortresses. These Arab cemeteries are usually surrounded by a circular wall of stones, the top covered with small white pebbles, for the purpose of scaring away the wild beasts; and even the tombs are generally covered with these pebbles, which give them a decidedly neat appearance.

We lunched under an overhanging rock in the pass, where perfect shade could be enjoyed at any time of the day. It was at the junction of a narrow gorge with the main one; and here the rains had washed down quantities of *débris*, such as leaves, grass, and twigs, which, in course of time, had become fossilised in a very curious manner; the rock under which we sat being formed of these materials.

We shot no game on this day's journey; but saw several *sachars*, the kind of mountain-goat my brother had shot on Tchad-Amba. We added to our collection of birds, if not to our larder, however, by obtaining a fine secretary-bird. Two or three times during our travels we came across this singular bird, but had not been able to obtain a specimen. The Arabs call it the " Devil's horseman," from the extraordinary swiftness with which it runs. This bird lives almost entirely on reptiles, which it kills. Towards evening heavy clouds gathered, and the atmosphere appearing to be laden with moisture we expected rain; but it fortunately kept off.

The district known as El Ain, which means " the spring," is a very curious one. The Arabs give that name both to the country and the stream, which, rising to the surface in the bed of a *khor*, flows for three or four miles and then loses itself in the sand. The water is very clear, though slightly brackish. The country about, though picturesque, is unfortunately very feverish, and possesses a rainy season during what is the driest season in the adjacent country.

After passing through a very arid tract it is curious to come suddenly on the verdure of spring. Here we found the hillsides clothed in green, and everything looking fresh and flourishing. Birds were building their nests, and the great numbers of weaver-birds, whose pendant structures hung from the boughs, particularly interested us. The air was filled with the buzz of insects, among them, unhappily, mosquitoes. We found also several chameleons.

Wart-hogs (*phacochœrus œliani*) are not uncommon in this valley, my brother being lucky enough to obtain a right and left; one of those he shot had fine tusks.

After a night at El Ain we resumed our journey, fortunately escaping the rain which fell almost every day; on two former journeys we had not fared so well, getting a good wetting each time, on one occasion having three days of it. It seldom continued all day, however, usually commencing at three or four o'clock in the afternoon, when it would come down in torrents, and perhaps continue for half the night. Soon after starting we killed a small snake, which the Arabs declared to be very venomous; we had met with very few of any kind throughout our travels.

We overtook a detachment of Bashi-Bazouks in charge of a number of wretched-looking prisoners—Arabs who had been caught paying tribute to the Abyssinians. They marched in slave fashion, in single file, each with his neck in a heavy yoke made of the forked bough of a tree, and fastened together with ropes, rendering escape impossible.

We made a long march, and after ascending for a short distance from El Ain came to an immense plain, stretching away on our right to the foot of the Abyssinian mountains, while to our left we could just perceive the sea. No halt was made until after dark, when we encamped about three miles before reaching Camphor, a considerable water-course, with a deep pool, where we indulged in the rare luxury of a swim. My brother shot a *beisa* antelope (*oryx beisa*), the

first of its species we had met with; it is decidedly rare in
these parts, as we never heard of its existence in any other
part of the Soudan through which we travelled; it is
common, I believe, in South Africa. Its horns are long
and straight.

From Camphor a messenger was sent on to Massawa
with a note to the authorities there, telling them we were
on our way, and begging them to detain the steamer until
our arrival, if by chance one were just leaving port. We
crossed many *khors* between Camphor and the coast, in
some of which we found a small quantity of water in pools.
During the rains a great deal of water finds its way to the
sea from the Abyssinian mountains by these channels; and
the rise is sometimes so sudden that, without any warning,
a dry bed may be suddenly transformed into a raging torrent
perhaps ten or twelve feet deep.

The previous winter two English travellers whom we met
very nearly lost their luggage in this way. They had spent
the night encamped half way down the bank of one of these
khors, and the following morning while at breakfast they
perceived the torrent coming, and had only just time to
save their effects; in fact, they did not succeed in escaping
altogether, for some of their belongings got wet and a
number of their cooking-utensils were lost. After two or
three hours the water subsided almost as quickly as it had
risen, leaving deep pools here and there.

CHAPTER XXII.

Arrival at Massawa.—Comfortable Quarters at the "Palace."—Situation of Massawa.—Water Supply of Massawa.—The Town is guarded at Night.—Camel Sale by Auction.—The Start from Massawa.—Perilous Position of Mahoom.—Arrival at Souakim.—A Visit to Mr. Bewley.—Our Fellow-Passengers on the "Messina." Arrival at Suez.—Accounts of Abyssinian Raid in English and Egyptian Press.—Suleiman's History.—We leave Cairo for England.

ANOTHER very long march brought us to Massawa, and so, on April 15, terminated our wanderings by land. It was after dark when we arrived, having made a caravan journey of over thirteen hours. We had intended making two easy days of it; but the messenger we had sent forward the previous day met us early in the afternoon to tell us that an Italian boat of the Rubattino Company would leave the next morning, and that, if we wished to catch it, we must hurry on. This was luck, and of course we did not hesitate to take advantage of it. On the way Aylmer's servant shot a fine buck ariel, and my brother wounded a gazelle in the shoulder, but not badly. His fox-terrier, Tartar, after a long and exciting chase caught it, and so at the last moment retrieved his character, as we had come to look upon him as a useless kind of dog; he stood the heat and journey well, and soon learned to bark if tired, when he would be placed on the back of one of the baggage-camels. We saw a large troop of baboons, which are not often observed so near the coast.

On arriving at Massawa the first thing we did was to call on the governor, who was very civil, and gave us rooms in what Suleiman called the "palace." We were amused to learn from the latter that he had tacked on to a telegram we told him to send to the governor of Massawa from

Sanheit, " Have palace ready for us ;" and his instructions had happily been carried out to the letter. It was the most comfortable place imaginable for such a climate, and proved to be far more so than our quarters at Souakim had been ; and, being built on a small island, was, comparatively speaking, cool. It consisted of a very large square house ; the living rooms were all on the first floor, the ground-floor being given up to offices, storerooms, the kitchen, etc. To reach our apartments we had to ascend a broad double flight of steps, at the top of which a massively-carved wooden door gave access to a lofty-domed hall, out of which opened four large rooms ; the only furnished one was kept as a sort of divan, and the other three were given up to our use. A broad verandah, upon which three doors opened, ran all round the house, except over the front steps. We placed our dining-table in the centre of the hall, and there in hot weather by opening all the doors, " the four winds of heaven" could be enjoyed. Massawa, like Souakim, is built on an island, which is completely covered with houses, and is joined to another island by a causeway about two hundred yards long, on which are the barracks, the governor's residence, and a number of small houses; to this again is joined another, on which the palace stands, but no other building. To reach the mainland it is necessary to pass the barracks and follow a very long causeway for fully three-quarters of a mile.

There is no water in Massawa, and pipes are laid on from the mainland as far as the barracks ; and from there into the town may be seen a constant stream of donkeys going to and fro with the necessary supply. It is slightly brackish, but excellent water for drinking purposes is brought into the town from a distance of four or five miles.

Massawa has the reputation of being about the hottest place on earth. I have been there several times, and on each occasion was singularly fortunate in not experiencing anything phenomenal. There was generally a strong sea-breeze and a good deal of cloudy weather ; still I have no doubt that at times, and for long together, the heat becomes all but unbearable.

At sunset the gate leading into the town was closed and guarded by soldiers, and no one admitted without a permit. The causeway to the mainland was also guarded at the other end. These precautions, we were told, were taken for fear of the Abyssinians, who, having no port of their own, were naturally very anxious to possess Massawa. Let us hope there is a brighter future in store for Abyssinia. During Admiral Hewett's mission to that country last summer, the treaty, signed at Adowa, June 3, 1884, between Great Britain, Egypt, and Abyssinia, granted free transit through Massawa to and from Abyssinia for all goods, including arms and ammunition, under British protection. The anchorage is fairly good, and the country about very mountainous and picturesque. A few Europeans live there, engaged in trade; and a number of Banians from India, who make their living out of the pearl-fisheries off the coast and the adjacent islands, Dhalak especially being famed for them.

We have had no consul at Massawa since the time of the Abyssinian war; and it is much to be regretted that we have had no representatives in the Soudan, as they could have done more towards suppressing the slave-trade than any one else.

The number and variety of fish at Massawa is something extraordinary, and many are of great beauty. Numbers of large fish are to be seen jumping in the harbour and in the shallow water near the causeway; among them the beautiful zebra-fish, a small species striped yellow and black, others brightest blue, and some with black bands across the back; while that curious creature the beckoning-crab is quite common in the wet sand near the edge of the water and in marshy places; it is bright yellow and blue, with one long claw, with which it always appears to be beckoning; hence its name. We found them very difficult to catch, as they all had holes in the sand, down which they promptly retreated on our approach.

We all bathed in the sea before breakfast—a proceeding which seemed greatly to astonish the natives. We, of course, avoided the deep water for fear of sharks; but, all the same, were informed by residents that we had done a most dangerous thing from a sanitary point of view, and one man explained that the extreme saltness of the water made bathing hurtful! A real danger, however, most certainly existed in the presence of vast numbers of a kind of sea-urchin, which lived at the bottom of the water, and were of a most formidable variety. They were very large, and furnished with very long, sharp spikes, which broke off on being touched, leaving their points embedded in the flesh. I think they were poisonous, for Lort Phillips got some in his hand, and suffered agonies in consequence, the painful effects of which did not wear off for some time.

We sold by auction our *hygeens* and the camel which Shereef the waiter always rode with the luncheon when on the march: and they of course fetched very low prices, as buyers knew we were leaving and must dispose of them. Lort Phillips' fetched the highest price—forty-five and a half dollars, having cost eighty. It was a female and a wonderfully easy-goer; in fact, I never saw a better. My beautiful animal only brought twenty-four; he cost me forty at Cassala, and was in as good condition when I sold him as when bought. We were, of course, able to look after our own riding-camels to a considerable extent ourselves, and, moreover, told off those men we considered the most careful to take charge of them. I was very loath to part with mine; and, had I been intending to return to the country the following winter, I should have endeavoured to make some arrangement to have kept him for me. He was fast and easy, though not so much so as Lort Phillips', which would go seven or eight miles an hour and be comfortable to ride at that pace. My animal made scarcely any noise when I wanted to mount or dismount—a rare virtue in camels; a slight jerk at the rope which did duty as bridle, and he would go off at a trot; he never had a sore back; and his coat was wonderfully clean, not covered with ticks as most camels are.

We had lost numbers of our camels, had given away a good many, and for those that remained on our arrival at Massawa we were offered such low prices that we gave

most of them away to the more deserving of our drivers
and servants. We had nine goats; these, too, were distributed in the same way; the boy who looked after them
was so lazy that he did not come in for them as he had
expected to do. The year before we had given them to
the man who had had charge of them, and he sold them
and purchased a camel with the proceeds; the boy had
heard of this and entirely reckoned his chickens before
they were hatched, as he had to take his departure without
any present.

We had promised our Arabs the present of a bullock on
which to feast themselves on their arrival at Massawa, and
had entrusted Suleiman to purchase one for their benefit;
but on inquiring if he had done so, he said "No," adding,
"People only bring hen cow, he no good, he make plenty
shild!"

Our steamer, the "Messina," put off her departure until
the morning of the 17th, when we all embarked about 8.30.
The arrangements for getting on board were rather primitive,
our servants and the steerage-passengers having to reach the
steamer by swarming up a rope. Soon after we had got
under way it was discovered that "Molly" (Mahoom) was
missing. The ship was searched in vain; when some one
happening to look over the side of the vessel discovered
poor "Molly," in the last stage of exhaustion and terror,
hanging on to the end of the rope like grim death. Assistance was at hand, and he was soon placed in safety. It
appeared that he was the last of the servants to come on
board, and having caught hold of the rope the shore-boat
rowed away, leaving him clinging to it. Climbing was not
one of his accomplishments. An Italian sailor who witnessed his predicament hauled away at the rope in a feeble
sort of way, but, finding "Molly's" weight rather too much
for him, quietly let go and gave it up for a bad job, leaving
him hanging over the vessel's side, a tempting bait for the
voracious sharks.

There were two other steamers in port at the time—the
"Khartoum," a gunboat, and a small Egyptian vessel. The
latter was about to start for Belool, a place a little to the

north of Assab Bay (the new Italian colony), where there
was to be an inquiry into the massacre about a year before
of seventeen Italians in that country; and I believe the
Italian consul was going about it himself.

Besides the servants we had brought with us from Egypt,
we were taking Achmet and the cook-boy as far as Souakim,
and we make up altogether a large party; the only first-
class passenger besides ourselves was a Frenchman, M.
Michel, for several years the head custom-house officer at
Massawa, who had just been dismissed and his place filled
by a native. Mr. Brewster, who held the same post at
Souakim, had already gone; his position too being filled
by an Egyptian. I imagine the government will find the
revenue from these places considerably decreased in consequence. During the passage to Souakim we caught
seven fish by hanging out lines from the stern, the hooks
being simply dressed with white rag. Three varieties were
caught, among them some small tunny and a fish very like
a pike.

The next afternoon, at half-past five, we arrived in
Souakim, just at the right time, as, had we been a little later,
we should have been obliged to spend the night outside the
harbour, as it is impossible to enter after dark. We landed
the same evening, and paid Mr. Bewley a long visit. We
heard that the officers of the "Blues," with whom we had
travelled in going down the Red Sea, had gone to Suez in
the last trip of the "Messina." We also heard that English
consuls had been appointed to Souakim and Khartoum; and
none too soon, if what we heard were true—that hundreds
of slaves were still being shipped from the neighbourhood
of the town to Arabia.

M. Elsen, the Belgian gentleman, had returned from the
interior, and sailed for Europe. He had been very unfortunate in being ill most of the time he was in Africa, and,
although he had collected a great many antelope-heads,
they had mostly been destroyed, owing to their not being
properly prepared. He had got no lions or elephants, but
had shot one buffalo.

Arriving on the afternoon of the 18th, we did not get

off again until the morning of the 22d, at nine o'clock ; our
time, however, was very pleasantly spent, partly in fishing,
though with no great success.   We had a great deal of
cargo to take on board, and· they were very slow about it ;
but we were told the reason was that they would have to
wait some days at Suez for a boat from Italy before going
south again, and so we were only too glad to take things
easily.   A great deal of the cargo consisted of ivory from
the White Nile, and the rest was chiefly gum.   The ·
" Cosseir " arrived while we were waiting here, one of the
Khedivial post-boats that had been newly done up, and was
bound for Massawa, Hodeida, Aden, Zeilla, Tajurra, and
Berbera.   These last three ports have lately been added to
these steamers' ports of call, as they are now under the
Cairo government; and I trust the country from these
points will soon be opened up.   A small steamer, belonging
to some merchants at Aden, has also lately commenced
trading with these places, which are in the Soumali country.
A second steamer came into Souakim while we were there
—the " Kassin Kerim," for cattle, a filthy-looking vessel,
flying the Turkish flag.   We little thought when leaving
Souakim how soon the place would be alive with British
soldiers.   How utterly useless the slaughter of so many of
our old friends the Hadendowa Arabs has been, and the
loss, too, of our own brave soldiers !

We took several first-class passengers from Souakim,
among others two Americans whom we had met at Shepherd's Hotel before leaving Cairo.   They had been sent
out by the " Freedman's Aid Society" of New York, I believe, to endeavour to find out suitable places for establishing schools and stations for this society on the White Nile
and at Khartoum.   It is proposed to send out educated
negroes from America, both ordained and laymen ; the idea
being that they will be more suited to the climate, and
have more influence over their black brethren than white
people possibly could have.   These American gentlemen
had travelled to Khartoum *viâ* the Nile and Korosko
Desert, and had been up the White Nile in one of the
government steamers as far as the Sobat River, seven

hundred miles south from the junction of the Blue and White Niles. Their scheme has the sanction and approval of the Khedive, who had promised before they left Cairo to aid them in the undertaking.

Then, too, we had as passenger the French consul from Khartoum, going home on leave of absence. He was taking with him a perfect menagerie of animals and birds, most of which he intended presenting to the Jardin des Plantes in Paris. His collection comprised two large *aboo geders* (literally, father of strength)—the same species of land-tortoise we had endeavoured to take home, and of which we did succeed in bringing one diminutive specimen, some parrots of various kinds, ducks and geese from the White Nile, and a beautiful black-and-white monkey of a kind that had never previously been brought to Europe.

Another of our first-class passengers was an Egyptian official, a far better educated man than one usually meets in such out-of-the-way places. He spoke French fluently, and was reading Sainte-Beuve and Lamartine on the voyage. We were delayed in starting by some cattle we had to take on board, over a hundred, all from Khor Baraka, where they are very cheap; some of them, having got loose at night, took a walk "aft," much to the inconvenience of those passengers who were sleeping on deck.

Leaving Souakim, as I have already said, on the morning of the 22d, after a very pleasant and not disagreeably warm voyage we reached Suez on the 26th, early enough to break-fast at the hotel. We were very glad to find a good budget of letters waiting for us. By them we learned that our friends in England had been considerably alarmed about us. Both the telegrams I sent from Amedeb had gone wrong: instead of being sent on from Cairo to the address in London which I had left at the former place, they were sent by mistake to my address in London, and my house-keeper returned them with my other letters; one I received at Massawa, the other at Suez.

Meantime all kinds of nonsense had been put in both the Egyptian and English newspapers; in the latter we were reported to have been robbed of camels, baggage, and everything in the Atbara Mountains—wherever they might be—and described as making the best of our way to the coast on foot. Not exactly dressed in newspapers, but something very like it. These veracious statements did not appear in the English papers until the end of March; and it was on February 17 that I telegraphed to Cairo to say we were all well. Our deplorable condition had even been made the subject of a question in the House of Commons. We felt quite important at having so much interest taken in our welfare, and lost no time in telegraphing to our friends to say we were in a highly prosperous state and on our way home.

We left Gerghis and Mahoom at Suez to go to England in a direct steamer, *viâ* the canal. Suleiman, who had been with us for two winters in the Soudan, and had proved a most excellent, trustworthy fellow, my brothers and I resolved to take to England for the summer; and, as we required his services at Cairo, we took him on there with us.

The story of his life is an interesting one, and evinces far more pluck, combined with a keen desire for acquiring knowledge, than one generally meets with among Egyptians. He was born near Wady Halfah, at the Second Cataract; and at the age of ten years was sent to his uncle, a baker by trade, at Alexandria. He remained there some time; but his uncle ill-treated him, and he ran away to Cairo, where he took several situations as a domestic servant. Here he conceived a strong desire to learn to read and write; so, having saved enough money out of his wages to purchase a native apparatus for making tea, having a small grate underneath it to burn charcoal—the Arabic name of which I forget—and a sufficient quantity of the requisite articles, such as cups, tea, sugar, and fuel, he left service, hired a little garret, and became a regular attendant at one of the native schools.

As soon as his lessons were over he would rush off to his room, fetch his teapot, and go the round of the carriage-stands in the European quarter, crying, " *Tchai ! tchai !*" ("Tea ! tea !"), and so generally earned more than enough to cover the day's expenses. His relations in Cairo were at a loss to imagine how he maintained himself; for they knew he had left service and spent his days in school. His great delight was to go to an uncle who was a grocer, living in the native quarter, to buy provisions, and listen to the inquiries as to how he lived, and where he got money enough to pay for his lodging and education; but he kept his secret, and never ventured into that quarter to sell his tea.

At length some of his schoolfellows, meeting him on his evening rounds, told their master, who was so struck with the boy's perseverance that he gave him permission to bring his teapot into school with him; where, in addition to what he sold in the streets, the boys bought from him; and some of them, being sons of well-to-do people, would pay him a trifle more than what he asked outside. After leaving school he entered the service of Sir Samuel and Lady Baker, and went with them up the White Nile to the lakes, on the expedition described in "*Ismailia.*" On their return Sir Samuel obtained a place for him in the late Khedive's private dispensary; and, on his abdication, Suleiman followed him to Naples, where he remained for some time in the same employ.

At length, being, to use his own expression, "gusted" with the people in Naples, and, as a Mahometan, living in constant dread of eating pig's flesh in some form or other in his food, he returned to Cairo, and again entered into service. His master, an Englishman, was just leaving Egypt, and, having no further need for his services, recommended him to us; and we took him to the Soudan.

We spent two days at Suez before going to Cairo, where we separated on 3d May, Colvin and Aylmer going to Suez, *en route* for Bombay, and the rest of us returning to England. Before separating, Aylmer agreed to meet us the last week of the following December in the city of Mexico. We all, except my brother Arthur, who remained in England, met there, and only a week later than the date named.

Although anxious to get to England we were all very sorry to break up our pleasant party; and all look forward to another winter in the Soudan at no very distant date,

CHAPTER XXIII.

Berber.—Native Entertainments.—The Bazaars.—Visit to the School.
—Fine Breed of Donkeys.—Population.—Start for Wady Halfah.
—Pacha Gordon's Shelters.—Wells of Abou Kereet.—Pyramids of
Nourri.—Ruins of Gebel Barkal.—A Sheik's Hospitality.—Voyage
to Debbeh.—Plague of Midges.—Journey to Dongola by River.—
Across the Desert from Merowi to Dongola.—Visits to the Mudir.
—The Third Cataract. — Temple at Tolib. — Meet Caravan of
Manchester Goods. — Cataracts of Dal and Tangour. — Wady
Halfah.—Return to Cairo.

I ARRIVED for the first time at Berber on December 4,
1877. Accompanied by my brother William ; a friend, Alfred
Sutton, and a doctor. We had taken a dahabeah up the
Nile as far as Korosko, and had left that place on November
15, taking, as is usual, the same camels the whole distance.
We had crossed the formidable Nubian desert from Korosko
to Abou Hamed (a stretch of nearly 240 miles, with only
one well on the entire route), without any difficulty. From
Abou Hamed to Berber, a distance of 143 miles, we had
for the most part followed the course of the river, and a
very pleasant journey it was. Having made several previous
voyages up the Nile as far as the Second Cataract, and
being well acquainted with the birds found in those latitudes, we were greatly interested in a species new to us, and
here met with for the first time. Before reaching Berber
we had, moreover, come across gazelles and hippopotami,
although we had only shot the former.

The night before we arrived at Berber, our caravan,
which preceded us, had been stopped at a place called
the Khor, a village about five miles from Berber, by Sheik
Achmet Khalifa, and our servants were informed that we were
to be his guests for the night. He had refused our cook

wood wherewith to make a fire for our dinner, saying he wished to entertain us himself. He met us some short time after the arrival of the caravan, and took us into his house, which was large and well appointed. He was a fine-looking old man, apparently about sixty-five years of age. After telling off a number of slaves for our use he left us to our own devices. The entertainment was most sumptuous, as, in addition to an exceedingly well-cooked dinner, we were provided with English china, and even knives, forks, and spoons; our host, however, did not favour us with his presence. We remained his guests only one night, and then started for Berber. About half-way Hamed Khalifa, Achmet's brother, met us, attended by numerous slaves and the *élite* of Berber. It seems, as far as I can gather from the newspapers, to be uncertain whether this man has been hostile to the Egyptian Government or not during the present crisis. General Gordon, who was at that time governor-general of the Soudan, had telegraphed to him to pay us every attention; we certainly found him a most amiable, intelligent man, and no one could have done more for us; from our experience he was justly noted for his hospitality to European travellers.

After passing many villages we reached Berber, and went straight to Hamed Khalifa's house. We entered a large courtyard, at the end of which grew an immense *lebbak* tree, of the same species as those that shade the road leading from the bridge over the Nile at Cairo to the pyramids. On ascending a flight of steps we found ourselves in a verandah, sixty-three feet long, fifteen wide, and about eighteen high, with a roof which formed a good protection against the sun. The whole house was built of mud, or rather sun-dried bricks, the roof supported by rafters. Off this verandah were several rooms, with large windows furnished with green shutters; the largest of these rooms was thirty feet by twenty-four, and very lofty. An enormous gilt mirror was hung at one end (how they ever transported it there was a mystery), the rest of the furniture consisted of divans, tables, and even a large iron bedstead. I have never been to Khartoum, but certainly in no other part of the Soudan in which I have travelled have I met with so civilised a native dwelling. Some verses from the Koran framed were hung on the walls, and also a large piece of paper with the following words very neatly written in large letters : " *O quoi de plus beau que la douceur et la vertue de notre juste Roi Gordon Pascha.*" A bracket for books, and some Persian rugs on the floor, completed the furniture of this apartment. Very soon after our arrival a most elaborate meal was served us, to which, after the extensive breakfast we had been entertained with, we found it difficult to do justice.

Khalifa's house is outside the town, on one side is a large garden with numerous palms, orange, lemon, and pomegranite trees, affording a most agreeable shade. Berber, in fact, abounds in these pleasant gardens. The largest belonged at that time to Halleem Bey, who entertained Sir Samuel and Lady Baker during their first visit to that town in 1861. We spent a week at Berber before leaving for a journey along the banks of the Atbara, and which we continued up to the Abyssinian frontier ; on our return in the middle of March we were again the guests of Hamed Khalifa, who for another week was most hospitable, and aided us in procuring camels for our journey.

As a rule, the climate was not unpleasantly hot during our stay, owing to the strong north wind which blew nearly every day (one day in March, however, we had the thermometer up to 99° in the shade), but the dust-storms were frequent and most disagreeable, and we were considerably bothered by midges. So strong was the north wind that (on our return to Berber in March) we went some little distance up the river in a dahabeah under bare poles.

The town of Berber is built of mud like the other towns in the Soudan. I should say it was larger than Assouan ; the bazaars are certainly more extensive, and better supplied. One of the merchants, who was selling cotton goods, had visited Manchester several times, and spoke a little English. There were three Greek shops of the kind usually met with in the Soudan, supplied with bad spirits, pickles, sardines, and such things ; in one we actually found Eley's central fire cartridge cases, and English gunpowder, as well as shot. Iron manacles and collars for slaves were also exposed for sale. A Greek offered to sell us a boy, saying he had bought him cheap, but pointing out that as he had been well-fed for some time, and had had the small-pox (the evidence of which he bore on his face), he expected a good profit. As we walked through the bazaars, a tall black woman rushed at Thomas Ferranti, our Maltese servant, and embraced him with great effusion; he explained that she had once been his slave, and he had married her to a native of Berber. This Maltese had travelled a great deal in the Soudan, having as General Gordon's servant accompanied him on many of his journeys; he had also been to Darfour with some American officers sent there by the Khedive. Among other objects of merchandise exposed for sale were balls of mutton-fat, each weighing almost half a pound, of a frothy appearance, caused by their having been chewed by the women. One of these balls serves as a single dressing for the hair, and is used by both men and women for this purpose. All the Bishareen Arabs, and many, though not all, of the Ababdah, smear their hair with fat. We had travelled from Korosko to Berber entirely with the Ababdah tribe. The bazaars swarmed with both Bishareen and Ababdah Arabs. Although the territory of the latter is to the north of that of the Bishareen, both tribes wander a great deal in each other's country.

During our first visit to Berber we came across a number of Europeans; Gessi (who was afterwards made governor of the Bahr el Gazal, and has since died) was there with an Italian, Dr. Matteucci, also dead. We had left them at Korosko and they arrived soon after we did. A dahabeah took them on to Khartoum which, with a strong north wind, they reached in three days; we also met a Swede from the University of Upsala, engaged in making a study of the Bishareen language; several Italian Roman Catholic missionaries; and lastly, the French Consul of Khartoum, a very garrulous German. He told us he had been in the country since 1853, only visiting Europe at long intervals, and that he had resided at Gondokoro long before Sir Samuel Baker's arrival. He was then at Berber, in consequence of the death of a woman known as the Sitt Miriam, an Abyssinian, and the widow of a Frenchman named Lafargue. She had made the French Consul her executor, and her house at Berber, which was very large, and was described to us as "like a palace," was to be sold to Hamed Khalifa. Madame Lafargue, we were told, had long kept what was neither more nor less than a slave-breeding establishment, consisting of about eighty black women. She died, leaving a large property, considering the resources of the country in which she had lived, but we did not hear the amount; and had a son thirty-one years of age, who was an idiot, and so was his boy a child of eight; we saw them, and pitiable objects they were. The Consul was sending them to a lunatic asylum in France.

We visited the school, and were told that a large proportion of the boys had been slaves who had been captured from the slave traders, and it was intended to make soldiers of them. The "shipping" at Berber was not very extensive, all we saw consisted of open boats or *nuggurs,* and one shabby-looking dahabeah. The Nile bank was strewn with goods of various kinds, cotton cloth, gum, and the tusks of some two hundred elephants. Ivory is a monopoly of the government which, we were told, paid £30 for a *Rantar* (about 100 lbs.), and sold it for £37; and in consequence of this monopoly the trade was decreasing, there being great difficulty in inducing the natives to hunt the elephants. Formerly there was a great deal of cruelty used in obtaining ivory; slaves were used as barter, and much was procured for a mere song from natives ignorant of its value. The bank of the river was thronged with negroes, most of them from the White Nile, women washing their clothes, nearly naked, fat and flourishing-looking, very ugly, and with bosoms fantastically tattooed. They kept up such a chattering and laughing all the time that it was like Babel broken loose!

I never saw finer donkeys than the Berber breed. Most of them are black and have a wonderfully glossy coat; they are very high at the shoulders, most comfortable to ride, and, at the same time, quick in their paces; they were very cheap, too, costing only from ten to twenty dollars apiece.

The governor informed us that the population of the
town of Berber amounted to 4000 ; but that of the district
or mudirieh to 200,000.   This comprised the whole of the
country, extending from Abou Hamed to the cataract below
Shendy, the Red Sea coast (Souakim included), and territory between.   A great deal of the traffic of Berber goes
by way of Abou Hamed to Korosko on the Nile : from
30,000 to 40,000 camels passed annually, and the chief
sheik of the Khalifa family took a tax of one dollar on each
camel.   In return for this tax he was responsible for the
safety of all goods in transit   We frequently, during our
journey across the desert, came across camel-loads of gum,
Manchester cloth, etc., which their owners had been obliged
to leave behind in consequence of the camels giving out on
the journey, and they left their property behind feeling
quite sure that it would not be touched.

After a week's stay at Berber, on our return from
Cassala, and much vexatious delay in procuring camels, we
started for Wady Halfah.   Our route lay across the desert
until we reached the Nile, opposite the village of Merowi,
a distance of 150 miles,[1] and from that point we were to
follow the course of the river partly by boat and partly by
camels to Wady Halfah.

Since leaving Berber for the south our party had increased, my brother Arthur with two friends — R. M.
Courage and A. S. Dalglish—having travelled from Suez
to Souakim by sea, and joined us on the Atbara.

Our journey from Berber to Wady Halfah is, perhaps,
best described by giving extracts from my diary, as from
these it is easy to understand the distances covered from
day to day.   Since the expedition for the relief of Gordon
was decided upon, this part of the Soudan has acquired a
special interest, for through the greater of it our troops will
have to pass.

March 19, 1878.—We crossed the Nile in boats from

---

[1] I carefully timed the number of hours that it took our baggage-
camels to perform this journey, and found it to be exactly sixty, which,
allowing the ordinary rate of travelling by caravan to be 2½ miles an
hour, makes the distance exactly 150 miles.

Berber, and at 3.30 P.M. started on our desert journey, halting for the night at seven by some wells, the water of which was muddy but not bad to drink, although there was very little of it. Our way lay over an undulating plain with low hillocks to right and left of our route, and plenty of dried grass and mimosa trees.

March 20.—A fearfully hot day, 106° in the shade—the wind was like the blast of a furnace from blowing over so much rock and gravelly ground scorched by the sun. Some of the camels were so bad we felt sure they would never live to reach Merowi, so we left four behind with five camel-loads of luggage, and had them changed for eight others, in case we should lose any on the way. The new camels caught us up about midnight. Each morning we endeavoured to get off before daybreak ahead of the caravan and spend the hottest part of the day under shelters that Gordon had erected on the road as a protection against the sun. They were the greatest blessing to the traveller in these regions, being built of dried grass with mat roofs. Some of our men were, however, so unappreciative that we had to expostulate on account of their dismantling them for firewood. In one of these huts we rested and allowed the caravan to overtake and get well ahead of us, each day catching it up at about dinner-time; we did not find them "beds of roses," however, as they swarmed with camel ticks; what these creatures can find to live on in the sand is a mystery. We frequently found numbers of them in absolutely desert spots. We had seven water barrels and twelve girbahs for ourselves, besides twelve for our men; notwithstanding the fact that we were more than two days from water one of the camel-drivers actually cut a girbah with a knife when he wanted a drink, to save himself the trouble of untying it. There was good vegetation and many gazelle tracks, although we saw nothing of the animals themselves. Passed a range of hills composed of blocks of syenite, on our left, called by the Arabs the Blue Mountains. We occasionally came across camels feeding quite alone, sometimes only two or three together, at others forty or fifty. We were told their owners drove them off to feed a long way in the desert, and that after three or four days they would return of their own accord to water. Made a march of ten hours.

March 21.—We again did ten hours; the general aspect of the country much the same as what we had passed. An undulating plain with a few low hillocks, and a range of hills some 500 or 600 feet high on the horizon. From ten to three we rested in one of the shelters, the thermometer 104° in the shade, and during the hot blasts of wind it reached 110°. Came across the telegraph-wires on the line from Abou Hamed to Merowi; all the posts were of iron and must have cost an immense sum of money to put up. Many of them were surrounded with branches of prickly mimosa, for the purpose, I imagine, of keeping the camels off. We met scarcely any people, and there was evidently very little traffic. Our riding-camels were good, and we easily travelled in six hours a distance it took the caravan ten to accomplish.

March 22.—This day's journey was through a country fully as monotonous as the one we had already traversed —more desolate, if possible, for there was scarcely a shrub, and very little grass. We carried *dhurra* for our riding-camels, but they were so thirsty they refused to eat. This was the fault of the men who had charge of them, for they had allowed them to drink too frequently before starting from the Nile, and so made it more difficult for them to go without water for any length of time. Saw two gazelles, the first seen since leaving Berber. I came across a man who would no doubt have died of thirst had I not found him; he was so much exhausted he could not speak, and could scarcely swallow. Our guide wished to go off with some barrels and four camels to a spring in the hills to fetch water; but we would not allow him to do so, as we had enough for everybody, and we thought he might never come back. Passed some hills on our right about 1500 feet high. Marched ten hours and three quarters.

March 23.—The next day three hours and a quarter brought us to the wells of Abou Kereet, and very glad we were to reach water, and be able to indulge in a bath, after our excessively hot journey. The going for the camels

before reaching the wells was very bad for some miles—a
plain covered with large stones, which hurt their feet. The
wells at Abou Kereet are deep ; they are situated in a water-
course about a hundred yards wide, running from west to
east. The water seemed good, but the supply was becoming
exhausted. We saw eight gazelles, and shot one. Some
Arabs at the well sold us a sheep and milk. There was
one *dhoum*-palm, a sickly-looking specimen, near the water,
and plenty of mimosas. We had travelled thirty-four hours
from the last wells, or about eighty-five miles.

March 24.—After our rest at Abou Kereet we were quite
ready for another long day, and got nine hours and a quarter
out of our camels. After going half-way we passed the brackish
wells of Sania ; also others in a water-course, where grew
plenty of *dhoums* and mimosas. Country more hilly and
vegetation more plentiful and varied, although it was by no
means a garden of Eden. An Arab came to complain
that a soldier (the Mudir of Berber had asked our permission to travel with us) had stolen and killed one of his
sheep. We rated the delinquent well for his conduct, took
the sheep ourselves, and paid its owner handsomely for his
loss. The soldier saw nothing wrong in what he had done,
and it was impossible to make him understand our feelings
about it. He was an Albanian, and calmly said that all soldiers
when travelling helped themselves in the same way ; that they
were very badly paid, and often got no pay at all for a long
time together. We met the Mudir of Dongola with a large
following going to Berber ; he said he had been only seventeen or eighteen days on the road from Wady Halfah.

March 25.—The next day the country got worse again,
scarcely a tree, but a few low hills to our right and left.
Saw twenty gazelles, and imagined we espied ostriches.
Marched ten hours and a quarter.

March 26.—A farther march of three hours took us to the
Nile, the last part of the ground being very uneven, and
rocky and volcanic in character, presenting much the same
appearance as a great part of the desert bordering the Nile
in Upper Egypt and Lower Nubia. What a relief to reach
the river again, and know we had no more long desert journeys

in prospect! The course of the Nile here was much obstructed
by rocks and rocky islands, and was decidedly picturesque ;
much like parts of the Nile between Abou Hamed and Berber,
but not nearly so green.   We rode on along its banks to a
village called Nourri, and lunched among some date-palms
near the pyramids.   The Arabs who inhabit this region
belong to the Shaggeeh tribe, and are considered a very
brave and warlike race; the banks of the river are extensively cultivated, and there are many villages.   We saw
fields of millet and ripe barley; cotton was also grown;
"sakias" were very numerous on both banks of the river;
and palm trees grew in abundance.   In fact there was
more cultivation, and the palm groves were more extensive,
than at any point between Assouan and the Second Cataract.

The pyramids of Nourri are not very interesting, they
are situated in a slightly elevated part of the desert, about
two miles from the river.   There are said to be traces of
fifteen, of which very few are in any kind of preservation.
They are not ornamented with hieroglyphics, and are so
much dilapidated that almost all the original outline is lost.
They are said to be as old as any ruins in the Nile valley,
if they are not the oldest in existence ; but there are no
inscriptions remaining to prove the truth of this assertion.
From Nourri the rocky character of the country changed
entirely, and gave place to deep sand.   The river was
unusually low for the time of year ; it was, however, quite
navigable even for large boats—no rocks or even sandbanks
to obstruct its course.

We spent the night close by a village called Aboo
Dhoum, exactly opposite Merowi ; the country is quite flat,
no hills in sight except Gebel Barkal on the west bank of
the river.   Although this hill only rises 350 feet above
the plain, it is very picturesque, indeed imposing, in
appearance, with a flat surface somewhat resembling that
of the Acropolis of Athens.   Our caravan had made a
march of ten hours.

The following day we crossed the river in a boat to
the village of Merowi opposite, and the chief man of the
district, called by the Turkish appellation *Katschef,* procured

us donkeys on which we rode three and a half miles to the ruins of Gebel Barkal. This was the only official I heard spoken of as *Katschef* in the Soudan. The ruins consisted of a temple with three chambers cut in the rock : we entered them, but found no very interesting inscriptions. Close by was an almost perfect column, but one of no great height. The hill from which its material was taken was of sandstone, and this accounted for its extremely dilapidated state. The remains of a second temple were half-buried in the ground, and we noticed a large block of blue granite covered with hieroglyphics. There were, too, a number of small pyramids in a very tumbledown condition. Altogether we were greatly disappointed with what we saw, having been led to expect more extensive and remarkable remains. The antiquities below the Second Cataract, with which we are well acquainted, are on the whole far more interesting than those at Nourri.

We returned through the palm groves by the river. On our way an old sheik insisted on our accompanying him to his house. We accepted his invitation, and found his residence, though not palatial, very clean and comfortable. Outside was a courtyard in which flourished a magnificent tree. He regaled us with milk and dates, and was most anxious we should taste the native "bousa" or beer, which we declined with thanks. He was full of Gordon, who, he told us, was greatly beloved by all the people, and added that he had remitted them their taxes owing to the un- usually bad Nile.

We noticed many small square-shaped buildings of mud near the villages ; these are used by the Arabs as places for prayer, and are kept exclusively for that purpose.

The following day, March 29, we started for Debbeh, in three flat-bottomed boats. There were no boats with sails on that part of the Nile, as the river flows from north to south, and the prevailing wind being north, boats returning from Debbeh to Merowi have to be towed from the bank against both wind and current. Consequently very few boats navigate that portion of the river, and those that do are small flat-bottomed ones, which can be towed with comparative ease. As we were anxious to spend no more time on the journey than was necessary, the doctor offered to cross the desert from Merowi to Dongola alone, and to get camels ready to take us on to Wady Halfah from that place.

We managed to make ourselves fairly comfortable ; as, by rigging up part of our tents on our own boat we made a very good awning, and by partly filling the stern of the servants' boat with sand we constructed a kitchen, and were able to have hot meals when we pleased without stopping the boats.

We were off at noon, and rested for the night at 6.30 by a sandbank near the village of Baheet. Passed numbers of small villages, and endless sakias, which were worked day and night with a never-ceasing groan. We saw an enormous turtle and a number of crocodiles, but not many water-birds, which are infinitely more numerous on the Lower than the Upper Nile. We shot a few Egyptian geese, however, and saw numbers of scissor-billed terns, and the great bee-eater, which latter bird was evidently migrating, as it arrives in Lower Egypt about April.

Our " crew " consisted of two bright intelligent boys, aged respectively twelve and fourteen. The former belonged to the Shaggeeh tribe, the latter was of White Nile origin, and informed us that although originally a slave he was now free ; we delighted them on our arrival at Debbeh by presenting them with some old shirts, in which they instantly arrayed themselves. We simply floated with the current : the navigation merely consisted in keeping the boats as much as possible in the swiftest part of the stream, and in poling them off the sandbanks, which occasionally impeded our progress.

The second night we moored opposite a village called Hertän, where there are the remains of a Saracenic castle, picturesquely situated at a considerable elevation above the Nile.

Close to the water's edge we came across the skull and bones of a child ; they were close to an ambush that had evidently been built by the Arabs so as to enable them to

R

shoot crocodiles. We saw numbers of these reptiles, but being very shy we did not succeed in shooting many of them.

The country was flat, with the exception of some hills near the river on the east bank, which only extended, for a mile or two. As we approached Debbeh the culti-vated land decreased, and bright almost orange-coloured sand frequently fringed the banks.

We were greatly tormented by midges, the most horrible pest imaginable. From sunrise to sunset, when they happily went to sleep, they attacked us in swarms, and bit voraciously. Before leaving Cairo we had been warned to provide our-selves with veils, and very thankful we were we had done so. Despite the heat we tied our heads up in them, and our faces and hair soon became of a bright green colour, from the dye that came off the veils, and we did not entirely get rid of it until long after we reached Cairo. We were informed that the midges were sometimes so bad that the natives, when gathering their crops, were obliged to fasten lighted fire-brands to their heads to keep off these venomous insects. Certainly no insect pests I ever came across were half so bad as these midges, and they seemed to plague the natives quite as much as they did us.

Until we reached Debbeh we only saw one boat, and that was being tracked up stream, with the exception of ferry boats that plied between villages on opposite banks of the Nile.

On April 1, at 7 P.M., we reached Debbeh, where we were to change into larger boats.

Debbeh, the last village of the Shaggeeh tribe, is a small place, and the point of departure of the caravans for Kor-dofan and Darfour; there is also a road to Khartoum across the Bahionela desert. We found an immense quantity of merchandise scattered on the bank, chiefly gum and cotton cloth. There were fourteen large sailing boats, *nuggurs*, as they are called, of the rudest build, but being very deep they were capable of carrying large cargoes. We selected two of the smaller ones for our journey to Dongola, for which we paid 300 tarif piastres, or a little over £3. We told their owners we wished them sent about a quarter of a mile lower down the river, where the boats we had arrived in were moored. The promptness in executing our orders was wonderful—in less than an hour the boats we had left were side by side with those we had just arrived in.

We did not like the large boats so well as the smaller ones; they were half-decked, and we felt the heat much more than in the others, in which we got all the air. Unlike the boats that navigate the Lower Nile the big sail is never taken down, nor is it lowered in descending the river. They occasionally tried tacking, an operation I never saw attempted except by the smallest craft on the Lower Nile. I cannot say, however, that we made any great progress in that way.

Although the country from Merowi to Debbeh, and that between Abou Hamed and Berber, is in the same latitude, its general aspect is very different. In the former there is far more cultivated land; wheat, barley, and extensive groves of date-palms flourish; while in the latter the crops consist chiefly of millet, and here and there fields of *dhurra*, and *dhoum* take the place of date palms. The stretch of river from Abou Hamed to Berber is, however, far more picturesque. The *dhoums* are festooned with green creepers, bearing scarlet flowers; numbers of sweet-scented mimosas, laden with yellow blossoms, overhang the water; and the course of the Nile is intercepted by numbers of rocky islands: some of these are covered with grass, others with acacia trees festooned with creeping plants, while others again are cultivated. Altogether the scenery is far more tropical than that of any part of the Nile with which I am acquainted. Between Merowi and Debbeh, however, except where the date-palm fringes the river, all this luxuriant vegetation is exchanged for a few wretched-looking mimosas and scrubby tamarisk bushes.

April 2.—Off by 10 A.M. and stopped for the night at an island a little to the south of Old Dongola. The wind was fitful and from the west; but we managed to make fair way, and at one time were going at the rate of five or six miles an hour. The midges bothered us terribly all day. Numbers of sakias on both banks, and a good deal of cultivation, although the desert frequently approached the river. Old Dongola is a miserable half-deserted place, almost entirely in ruins, situated on a hill on the east bank of the Nile, but picturesque in its decay.

April 3.—Did not make much way; the wind, which was from the north, came in short gusts. Our crew consisted of only two Arabs, one of them being a very old man, who was continually complaining that he had a snake in his stomach that ate all his victuals. Our only mode of progression was floating with the current, which, as the river was low, was very slow work. The sailors could not row, as the boats were not provided with oars, and tacking was almost useless. Stopped for the night anchored to a sandbank near a village called Becker. Saw very few crocodiles, and scarcely any birds. The midges gave us no peace, and in spite of veils (which were getting worn out) got into one's nose, mouth, eyes, and ears.

April 4.—Owing to the strong head-wind only made ten miles. Country perfectly flat and most uninteresting; the wretched mimosa trees that frequently lined the banks of the river were almost leafless; but there was plenty of cultivation and numerous sakias. By four o'clock the wind was blowing so hard from the north that, finding we were being carried up stream, we were obliged to moor to an island called Comi. A perfect hurricane blew all night, the strongest wind we had experienced all the winter.

April 5.—The wind continued so strong all day that we were unable to move, though we made several unsuccessful attempts. The skeleton of a woman was found on a sandbank; the front teeth of the lower jaw had been extracted. This is the custom with the women of some of the White Nile tribes; they consider it adds to their personal attractions.

April 6.—During the morning the gale prevented our moving, but late in the afternoon somewhat abated, and we managed to make about five miles.

April 7.—Got off at daybreak, when the wind lulled slightly, but after making a mile or two had to " come to," between Dumbo and Handak, until nearly sunset, when we again started, and got a little below Handak; the men then declared there were dangerous rocks, and they could go no farther before daylight. Handak is the largest village between Debbeh and Dongola; a great part of it, however, is now in ruins. Formerly, all this country was far more thickly inhabited than it now is, as numerous remains of towns and villages testify.

April 8.—Still the north wind continued to blow violently. We resorted to tracking along the bank by means of a rope; also tried tacking, but made little progress in that way. By sunset we were three miles south of a village called Ordee. Country flat and monotonous; numerous sand-banks, but scarcely a bird to be seen. We amused our-selves in an india-rubber canoe we had brought from England, which sailed very well with the strong north wind. We insisted on going at night, which our men so far had always objected to doing, but we were determined to try. Between 8 P.M. and 6 the next morning we only made five miles. Nearly every night the wind was so strong that it would have been impossible to have accom-plished so short a distance as this.

April 9.—Less wind, but still from the north; we alternately drifted with the current, tracked, and tacked. Spent the night opposite an old ruined fort or castle called Hellat el Manoo.

April 10.—Reached Dongola at 5.30 P.M. This town is called by the Arabs Ordee, and is marked in some maps New Dongola, to distinguish it from the ruined town of the same name.

As I have already mentioned, the doctor had gone across the desert from Merowi to Dongola, by the east bank of the Nile, in order to try and save time by getting camels ready for us. On the morning of our arrival we sent a note to him saying we were coming; he came to meet us, and at two o'clock we took him on board.

Very few undertake the journey from Merowi to Dongola across the desert, the only published account I know of being in a book entitled *Khartoum and the Niles*, by George Melly, written in 1851. Then there were actually two English ladies in the party. The author describes the journey as hazardous, and as requiring four long days for its accomplishment. He was told that ninety guides had perished on the road, and although he considered the number exaggerated, he adds that "the difficulties and uncertainties of the path were sufficient to account for a very considerable loss of life." The ladies who accompanied him, his mother and sister, were the first European ladies who had ever reached Khartoum.

The following is what I wrote down at the time from an account given me by our doctor of his desert journey. Although essentially "dry" reading, it may prove interesting at the present time :—

There is scarcely any path the whole way ; the doctor had a compass and a map ; the Arabs steered by the sun during the day and by the stars at night. For the first two hours on leaving Merowi there was no path at all, for the next two an apology for one could be made out at intervals of 200 or 300 hundred yards. This first four hours' travelling was over a desert of ravines consisting of gravel and sand. The traveller then enters on a great plain of rolling, bright, almost orange-coloured sand. For the first two or three miles an occasional stunted mimosa is seen ; beyond that distance not a vestige of any living thing, until some wells are reached, three and a quarter hours before arriving at Dongola. Far away to the left, and about eleven hours' journey from Merowi, are three serrated peaks, called Abou Syal, a conical hill named El Midreh, and on the right two others called Abou Koran. Thirty-two miles after leaving Merowi, a stony district is entered which lasts for two and a half hours' travelling, after which the route passes through great sand drifts, most trying in windy weather. Another five hours and some ridges of low hills are reached which must be traversed, and another three hours brings the traveller to the wady, in which the wells are situated, and where there are plenty of mimosas on which the camels can feed, but at the wells themselves there are only a few *dhoum* and date palms. The wells are marked by an almost perpendicular hillock about forty feet in height. A farther march of three and a quarter hours completes the desert journey, and the town of Dongola, partly hidden by its palms, and rising over the right bank of the Nile, suggests at least a shelter from the sun. Throughout the whole journey, which occupied thirty-seven hours and three-quarters, a distance of about ninety-five miles, there is no path that can be depended on. The heat was terrific, one day the thermometer registering 114° in the shade of a small tent. The sand was so heavy it was impossible for a riding-camel to trot, and one of the baggage animals died on the road. The doctor came across the skeleton of a man and camel lying together; they had perished side by side. The guide informed him that some years before an Englishman and his guide had both lost their way and never been heard of since; and on one occasion he had overtaken some Arabs reduced to such extremities from want of water that they had been compelled to kill a camel and slake their thirst with the water out of its stomach.

Dongola is situated some little distance from the river, and is hidden by trees. We found the Mudir sitting in a courtyard, near one of the inevitable Greek shops; he was an old Turk, who looked eighty, had been forty-three years in Egyptian employ. Notwithstanding his long service in the country he spoke Arabic with considerable difficulty.

There was a great deal of small-pox in the town ; it had been very bad indeed, and had carried off a great many people, but was on the decrease when we arrived.

At Dongola we met Colonel Mason, an American officer in the Khedive's employ, who was on his way to Cairo from the Albert Nyanza, and had been surveying the whole course of the Nile from the Second Cataract, with a view to seeing what could be done towards rendering the cataracts more navigable. His opinion was that it would be an enormously expensive undertaking to dam the Nile at the cataracts or to blast the rocks as had been proposed.[1]

We arranged to pay six dollars apiece for camels to Wady Halfah, a distance of over 200 miles. The

---

[1] Colonel Mason, now Mason Pacha, at present governor of Massawa.

bazaars of Dongola we found unattractive. The government buildings are large and built round a courtyard
containing some fine trees. We paid several visits to the
old Mudir; on one occasion the Mudirieh was full of people
who had come to pay their taxes, some of them did not
bring sufficient, and were promptly bastinadoed. Morning .
and evening crowds of black slaves, both men and women,
might be seen filling their water-jars at the river; many of
them had heavy iron shackles on their ankles, which were
fastened together with chains. I saw women, shackled
in this way, shuffling along with heavy water-jars on their
heads, and not able to move more than a few inches each
shuffle.

As the camels were not ready on April 11, we started
off in the boat we had arrived in, leaving the luggage to
follow. Large boats, even in April, *can* go as far as just
below the Third Cataract; but we decided on taking to
camels as soon as they overtook us. We started at two
o'clock, and about 9.30 moored the boat on the east bank,
just above some rocks seven or eight miles to the north
of Dongola. During our voyage from Merowi we frequently tried fishing, and were rewarded by occasionally catching a "gamoot," an uncanny-looking monster,
barely eatable, and an old Atbara acquaintance. I do
not think "Tommy Atkins" will do much good with the
fishing-lines that are part of his outfit on the present
campaign.

April 12.—We were off at daybreak, and the camels
overtook us about ten o'clock, having been four hours on
the march from Dongola. We at once began to shift the
luggage from the boat, but it was four o'clock before we
finished loading the camels and were able to start. At
seven we halted for the night near a village called Binné,
opposite the island of Argo, a large and fertile spot with
numerous palm-trees. Numbers of these trees flourished
on the banks of the river. The province of Dongola, we
were told, was the best paying one in the Soudàn, all the
country south to Merowi being in the Mudiriat. We
decided on travelling by the west bank, for, although

Colonel Mason told us it was better to go by the east, our drivers objected, and we were disposed to grudge the loss of time that would take place were we to ferry the camels across. Colonel Mason therefore travelled by the east bank alone, for his camels were already on that side of the river, and it was therefore the simpler one for him to choose.

Our camel-drivers were a very wild-looking set, most of them belonging to the Kababisch tribe. They wore their hair in long broad plaits, resembling in that respect the Dabainas, with whom we had travelled along part of the Settite. In addition to the Kababisch Arabs there were others from the Mahass district,—a tract of country we were to pass before reaching Wady Halfah.

April 13.—Marched eleven and a half hours, halting for the night about three miles beyond what is marked in the maps as the Third Cataract, and although we were encamped fully half a mile from the Nile we could hear the roar of the cataract. In the morning we visited it, and found that rocks had formed a weir almost across the river, which at that season of the year appeared quite impassable for boats. The Nile was, however, unusually low even for the month of April. We kept near the river the greater part of the day, where there were plenty of palms and cultivated land, and the journey therefore was a very pleasant one. Both in this and in the Merowi district a great deal of irrigation is done by sinking wells, from which water is obtained by *sakias ;* these wells are frequently a considerable distance from the river. The day was cloudy, but very close and hot. From Hannek, the Third Cataract, the character of the country changed from a wide sandy plain, fringed with cultivated land, to a very sterile and rocky track.

April 14.—After a seven hours' journey we reached what the Arabs term the Hash mel·Akabah, where we spent the night at a place called Fakir Bruti, previous to crossing a long stretch of desert in order to cut off a bend of the Nile. The whole country through which we passed was barren and wretched in the extreme ; the few villages we passed were very small, and some of them quite deserted. Just before reaching our camping-ground we were rewarded by a really pretty view of the river, which was very broad, and somewhat resembled a lake dotted with rocky islands, on which grew palm and *sont* trees ; and a background of mountains, purple and red in the setting sun, completed the picture.

We passed several ruined buildings of considerable extent, built of sunburnt bricks, which formerly had been the residence of sheiks or meks who ruled over the country before it fell into the hands of the Egyptians. Far more of this country must at one time have been under cultivation ; but the abominable Egyptian system of taxation, especially that of taxing every *sakia* and *shadoof*, has discouraged the inhabitants from endeavouring to make the most of their resources.

April 15.—This part of the country is called the district of Mahass. After a long journey across the desert, of eleven hours and three-quarters' good marching, we again struck the river at a village called Kage. All day the north wind blew violently, but as the desert was fortunately stony, it did not annoy us much. The desert was hilly, with plains two or three miles broad between the belts of hills, and the rock was evidently volcanic.

The river at Kage is very wide ; there are a few palms, but very little cultivation is to be seen. Although there were a good many rocks in the river's bed it still looked navigable.

April 16.—A ten and a half hours' journey brought us to a village called Hamied, opposite Say Island, a large island with plenty of palm-trees and some cultivated land. The north wind was very strong and the dust terrible. With the exception of two "akabas," of about an hour each, the road followed the course of the river.

We passed two temples, Tolib and Sukkoot ; the former is well worth seeing, and is an example of the purest Egyptian architecture. It is situated on the edge of the desert, about a quarter of a mile from the river. There are eight entire columns standing, and the remains of another ; the sculptures are, however, in bad preservation, and the whole temple is surrounded by its own ruins. It is altogether the finest temple south of the Second Cataract, although, being Egyptian, it is not, in an antiquarian point of view, as interesting as the purely Ethiopian remains at Merowi.

Wherever the receding river gave a chance for a crop, the natives had planted beans, often in almost ridiculously small patches. On arriving at our camping-ground for the night our drivers allowed their camels to graze on the crops, and there was a great disturbance in consequence. We were much annoyed, and paid liberally for the damage done, giving the money to the sheik of the village, with instructions to divide it as he thought best. He probably kept it himself, but we could do no more, and the poor people seemed satisfied. We passed more ruins of fortresses, evidently belonging to a more prosperous past.

April 17.—Met the first caravan seen since quitting Dongola ; it consisted of ninety camels carrying Manchester goods. Cairo merchants frequently hire a string of say 100 camels by the year ; if any die, or become unfit for work, their owners supply others in their place. The same camels will often go all the way from Wady Halfah to Kordofan.

This was a very trying day for the camels. The desert, extending to the water's edge, consisted of great billows of shifting sand, deeper and far worse going than anything we had previously experienced. Twice we found our path covered by almost perpendicular banks of sand fully forty feet high, which necessitated our going round them, and making a path for ourselves. The north wind constantly blows in these regions, and the sand is always shifting, and forming huge orange-coloured drifts, rendering travelling very tedious work. We made a march of nine hours and three-quarters, and in the whole distance scarcely saw a palm or anything green, although we were continually near the river. There were no villages, or signs of inhabitants, excepting two or three minute patches of beans, where the receding river had left a little soil. We spent the night at a place called Selib ; the Arabs have names for every rock, hill, or resting-place..

April 18.—Made a long march of thirteen hours, most of it through very heavy sand. After two and a half hours' journey away from the river we joined it again at the Cataract of Dal, a most picturesque spot. Both banks of the Nile were bounded by a range of volcanic rocks— peaks piled in endless confusion. At the most formidable part of the Cataract there was a half-circle of rocks, extending from 150 to 200 yards, over which the water boiled, and where it appeared as though one could wade across the Nile. The whole scene was wild and desolate in the extreme; numbers of rocky islands, some of them uplifting themselves fully 100 feet from the river's bed. Scarcely an inhabitant, an occasional palm or *sont* tree, and the wrecks of two boats that had gone on the rocks in attempting to pass the Cataract. A complete picture of desolation, but nevertheless one with an indescribable charm about it.

After leaving Dal we struck again into the desert, away from the river, to cut off another of the numerous bends it makes in its course. It was even worse travelling than on the day before; the whole way was over hillocks of rolling sand, and our progress was of the slowest. Sometimes the hills we had to traverse were so steep we preferred to dismount and lead our camels. It was 9.15 before we reached our camp, a tiny village called Okme, close to the river. Our camels began to give out—one had died in crossing the last *akabah*, and several others were useless. The poor brutes got scarcely anything to eat in the miserable country we were travelling through.

April 19.—Rested our jaded beasts until after mid-day, and then only travelled for four hours and fifty minutes, camping by the Cataract of Tangour, the whole way through heavy sand.

It is absurd to talk of Hannek as the Third Cataract, the whole river between it and Wady Halfah being a succession of cataracts—I am afraid to say how many. As I have already remarked, the Nile, during the spring of 1878, was exceptionally low, and I am certain that not even small rowing-boats could have descended it. In fact, we *frequently* wondered how at any time large boats could be made to pass some of the cataracts. Between the cataracts of Dal and Tangour is another (the name of which I have forgotten), with a finer fall than any of the others.

We met a number of caravans, most of them consisting of from forty to eighty camels, carrying gum from Kordofan.

April 20.—All of our party, except Courage and myself, started with the caravan across another desert *akabah*. In seven hours and twenty minutes they struck the Nile again, which they followed until they reached the village of Semneh, an eleven hours' march altogether.

Courage and I, being weary of these long desert tramps, decided on following as much as possible the course of the Nile, although we knew that by doing so we should have to travel considerably farther. We did not, however, bargain on losing our way, and not reaching camp until 1.30 A.M.!

We followed the river for some time, plunging through and climbing over great sand drifts, until we reached a small village on an island that could be reached at low Nile by walking over some rocks. There was very little cultivation, no *sakias*, and but few palms. We passed two cataracts. We procured a boy from the village to act as guide. He proved worse than useless, as the path, though very rocky, was for the greater part of the way plainly marked, and the only time that a difficulty occurred he led us wrong and then decamped, leaving us in a complete *impasse*, to find our own way out as best we could. It was now dark, so we were obliged to wait until the moon had risen, then, retracing our steps, fortunately soon found the right road. We arrived in camp very hungry and tired, having gone without dinner, and in addition been obliged to walk a great part of the journey leading our camels, which had become thoroughly done up from the roughness of the ground.

At Semneh there is another cataract, and on either bank a small temple of the time of the 3d Thothmes. They did not look particularly interesting, and, being so near the end of the camel part of our journey, we grudged the time it would have taken to explore them, so passed on without a visit.

April 21.—Our camels were giving out one by one from hard travelling and insufficient food; and hearing that from Saras, on the opposite bank a little farther on, we might finish our journey to Wady Halfah in the train, we started ahead of the caravan to see if the news were true, and if so to endeavour to find a boat to take our luggage across the Nile. The nearer we approached Wady Halfah the worse the travelling became. After four to five hours of crawling over the most fearful desert imaginable, and being obliged to lead our camels the greater part of the way, we arrived opposite Saras. On an island in the river was a very picturesque castle; we regretted that none of us were able to sketch. We saw a gazelle for the first time since our arrival at Merowi; the previous day we saw an immense number of their tracks, the only time since leaving Dongola we had seen them in any quantities. Colonel Mason had reached Saras the morning we arrived at the opposite bank, and sent us a note to say the train was hourly expected! It sounded too good news to be true. We had ridden since leaving Korosko on November 15 nearly 2000 miles on camels, and it seemed quite absurd to finish in the train! My brothers crossed the river in the only "boat" the neighbourhood possessed. This primitive "craft" merely consisted of five logs lashed together, which two boys, regardless of crocodiles, swimming behind, pushed forward. After remaining all night at the railway station my brothers sent us a note to say that the train was delayed in consequence of a bridge having broken down, but that we had better cross the river early in the morning.

April 22.—We sent our bags, bedding, and some stores over in our india-rubber canoe, after which we crossed on the raft. Obtained no more news of the train. The railway station was built of brick, and was wonderfully neat, with waiting-rooms, etc., furnished with wooden doors and green-painted window-shutters. Colonel Mason said the estimate for the railway from Wady Halfah to Shendy was £4,000,000; that in 1877 they had spent £90,000, and the two previous years £300,000 each year upon it. How they managed to spend such large sums with such poor results I cannot say. The whole thing, however, was done in true Egyptian style, unnecessarily large sums being spent on plant—stations, with waiting-rooms and everything complete, being evidently considered of more importance than the permanent way itself. The distance the rails were laid was 53½ kilometres, and another 50 was prepared and ready to be laid. It was proposed that trains should cross the river at Kohie, either by means of a bridge or by a ferry, as is frequently done in America. The line would then follow the west bank to somewhere near Debbeh; thence across the Bahioudah desert to Shendy on the Nile —the intended terminus of the railway. My brother Arthur and Courage set off on donkeys, intending to see how long it would probably take to repair the bridge that had given way. They were told that it was only an hour and a half's ride off, and that Mr. Gooding (the English engineer of the line, who lived at Wady Halfah) was there. Starting at 10 A.M. they reached the bridge at 2.20. Gooding was not there; the Arabs informed them that "Inshallah," the line would be in order for traffic in two or three days' time. Having got so far on their way to Wady Halfah they decided on going the whole distance, and sent a note informing us of their intention.

April 23.—Our last day's camel journey! Tired of waiting for the train we re-crossed the river, and leaving the caravan to follow started for Wady Halfah. The entire journey was through the desert, and some little distance from the river; a great part of our path lay over firm and gravelly ground, but there were occasionally patches of shifting sand, one of which we were over an hour in passing. On the opposite bank of the river there is little or no deep sand, and the road is no doubt much less fatiguing for the camels.

During the middle of the day we halted near the river, sitting under the shade of a dismantled sakia, where there were two or three huts and an apology for cultivation. The shade was so tempting we remained too long, got overtaken by the darkness, and lost our way, reaching camp about ten o'clock. Our camels had marched thirteen hours, and our tents were pitched opposite the village of Wady Halfah (which is on the other bank). Nine of our camels had died since leaving Dongola, and two were unable to carry loads.

A great deal of luggage was strewn about the bank. One merchant had been waiting ten months for camels to take his goods to Dongola. Gooding, who was acting as "wakeel" of Wady Halfah, as well as engineer of the railway, informed us that 6000 camels passed annually to and from Dongola. It is a very severe journey for camels, owing to the heavy sand, and in this respect is far more formidable than the desert from Korosko to Abou Hamed. On the latter road, however, there is only one well, whereas on the Dongola route there is water the whole way.

My brother Arthur and Courage were with Gooding at Ancash, a village about five miles below Wady Halfah, where the workshops of the railway were situated. They were built of burnt brick, and contained a steam hammer and five engines. At the time of our visit the railway works were silent, and we felt sure that everything would soon be given up and the engines left to rust. We were informed that coal at Wady Halfah cost 65s. a ton.

April 24.—A tremendously strong north wind blew all day. Wady Halfah is well known for the frequency and violence of the north wind, which often blows much stronger there than farther down the river. It was too strong to permit of our making a start down the river.

My brother and Courage arrived at Gooding's quarters at 11 P.M. thoroughly tired out; they had been obliged to walk nearly all the way, as their donkeys were in such bad condition that they were unable to carry them.

April 25.—We left Wady Halfah bound for Cairo in a comfortable dahabeah, reaching Philœ, above the First Cataract, on May 5. There we changed into another dahabeah lying below the cataract at Assouan, and dropped down the river to Siout. At Kantara, a little below Assouan, and opposite a village marked Koobanieh in Keith Johnston's Map of Egypt, the channel left by the receding Nile was extremely narrow, and only three feet six inches to four feet deep. In spite of all precautions we stuck fast for twenty-four hours in getting through. We saw many natives actually *fording the Nile*, with luggage on their heads. It is to be hoped that in the event of our troops returning from the Soudan about the same time of year the Nile will not be so low, or the delays in reaching Cairo will be endless.

Owing to our constantly sticking in sandbanks from the lowness of the river and the strong north wind, it was May 31 before we arrived at Siout, where we gladly took the train to Cairo. The dahabeah did not reach Cairo until eighteen days later.

In this last chapter I have purposely given many details that I should have thought superfluous were it not for the present interest attaching to the expedition up the Nile for the relief of Gordon, and I am not without hope that there may be some who will be interested in a somewhat lengthy description of the country that our army must pass through, —a country that has not been often described, and one that is so much the subject of discussion at the present time.

[As I send this second edition of my book to press, we are all, with the exception of my brother Arthur and the doctor, starting for Berberah. Thence we propose to enter the Soumali country, and there spend the winter exploring parts hitherto unknown to Europeans.]

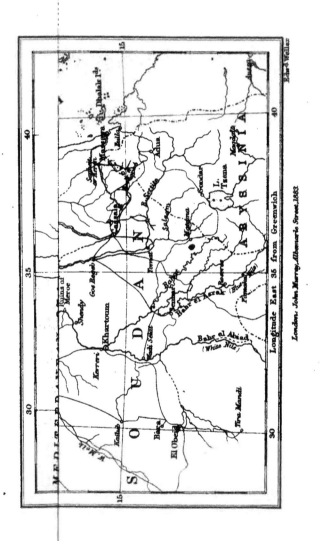

London: John Murray, Albemarle Street, 1883.

Longitude East 35 from Greenwich

INDEX.

A

Abiam, good sport near, 135.

Aboo Dhoum, village, 239.

Abou Gumba, the, 60.

Abou Hamed, 12, 230, 243.

Abou Kereety, wells of, 237.

Abou Sellal, 176.

Abyssinia, difficulty of getting into, 144.

  treaty with, 222, 209.

Abyssinian chief, visit from an, 66.

Abyssinians, a hundred armed, 108.

  contemplated expedition against, 113.

  Dembelas tribe, 109.

Achmed Ageer, Sheik, 62, 194.

  sends four horsemen as interpreters, 63.

  accompanies the caravan, 67.

  takes his leave, 69.

  rejoins the party, 73.

  returns to his people, 74.

  again turns up, 180, 193.

Achmed Effendi, the palace of, 13.

Achmet, a servant, 181, 225.

Achmet, Mahomet, xxiii.

Adowa, Treaty of, 209.

Adventure with a buffalo, 75.

Adventure with a lion, 68, 199.

"Agra," the British-India steamer, 2.

Aibaro, 127.

Ain, El, a halt at, 217.

Akabah brings alarm of the Abyssinians, 106.

Ala-ed-Deen Pacha, supreme governor, 13, 15, 206.

  frees the prisoners, 15.

Ali Reza Pacha, 13, 14.

Ali the cook, 6, 39, 97, 115.

Amān, signification of, 91, 113.

Amedeb, 125.

  the town of, 125.

American travellers, two, 226.

"Angareb," an, 35.

Animal-catcher, the German, 60.

Anseba Valley, the, 213.

Anselmier, Swiss servant, 5.

Antelope—

  Beisa, 218.

  Boos, 170.

  Dik-dik, 71.

  Mora, 78.

Antinori, the Marquis, 112.

Ants, destructive white, 50, 162.

Arabi, rebellion of, xxii.

  Trial and sentence, xxiii.

Arabia, slaves shipped to, 225.

Arabica gazella, 24.

Arabs, action of the loyal, xxvi.

Arabs, encampment, an, 145.

  solemn covenants of, 91.

Ariel, herds of, 41.

  shot, 56.

Ashidireh, 206.

Atbara River, the, 47, 232.

Attman, Galani, Sheik, 17.

Avenging jackal, the, 37.

B

Baboons, 58, 154.

Baby crocodiles, 73.

Baggar-fish, capture of a, 151.

Baheet, a Nile village, 241.

Baker Pacha, xxvii.

Baker, Sir Samuel, 79, 141, 145, 164, 171.

Baobab-tree, the, 57, 79.
Baraka, Khor, 22, 229.
Barea tribe, the, 121.
Basé country, the, 1, 79, 84, 175.
 a scare, 195.
 customs, 193.
 natives first seen, 79.
 people, the, 1, 79, 82-88, 89-92, 95, 130.
 superstitions, 194.
 suspect the, 115, 127.
 village first seen, 80.
 visit from a sheik, 101.
Bashi-Bazouks and their prisoners, 218.
Beads, fondness of the natives for, 89.
Bedouin prisoners, the, 13, 14.
Beer, made from *dhurra*, 90.
Beisa antelope shot, 218.
Belgian doctor, the, 37.
"Bellus," a camel, 19.
Berber, xxi, 12, 230-235.
Berthon boat, usefulness of the, 140, 161.
Birds, scarcity of, 28.
 bright plumaged, 41, 195, 214.
Blue Mountains, the, 236.
Boa-constrictor shot, 179.
Bogos country, the, 5, 208.
Bogou, Khor, picturesqueness of, 201.
Bokutan, Mount, 142.
Bombashi, governor of Amedeb, 124.
Bonne-bouche, a, 176.
Both barrels at once, 99.
Brewster, Mr., 9.
British-India steamer, the "Agra," 2.
Budget of letters from home, a, 135, 227.
Buffalo-hunting, 75, 93, 98, 103, 106, 132, 155, 172, 174.

C

Cairo, 1, 2, 229.
 route from Wady Halfah to, 256.
Camels, 19, 24, 28, 29, 47, 119, 133, 201, 223, 236.
Camel-drivers, 16, 23, 144, 181.
Camel sheik demands *baksheesh*, 22.

Camel saddle, a good, 134.
Camp, first, 21.
 deaths in, 45, 118.
Camphor, the watercourse, 218.
Capsules, claret, as jewellery, 92.
Caravans, slave, 12.
 merchant, 44.
Caravan, the, 24.
Carcashi, Sheik Said, 123.
Cargo, a large, of ivory, 226.
Cassala, the town of, xxi, 1, 51.
Ceremony of making peace, 91, 113.
Cholera, the, 2, 7.
Church, the, on Mount Tchad-Amba, 204.
Climate, 37, 95, 97, 144, 153, 197, 214, 221,
Col. Gordon, 6, 14.
Compensation, nine thousand dollars, 14.
Consul, appointed to Khartoum, 225.
 appointed to Souakim, 225.
Consul's, the French, collection of animals, 227.
Cook, Ali the, 6, 39, 97, 115.
Country, the, 27, 80, 92, 237-38, 243, 249.
Cows, 22.
Crocodiles, 73, 145.
 adventure with, 145.

D

Dal, Cataract of, 252.
Dama, gazella, 24.
Daoud, Suleiman, 5, 228.
Darfour, xxiii, 12.
Daro Mai, a visit from Sheik of, 91.
Days, heat of, 29, 97, 132, 190.
Debbeh, a small village on the Nile, 12, 240, 242.
Dembelas villages, a visit to some, 18, 116.
 the, 18, 109-113.
Desert, vegetation in the, 21.
Devil's horseman, the, 217.
Dews, heavy, 68, 97, 120.
Dhoum-palms, 28, 30, 44, 56.
 baskets, 90.
Dhurra, staple article of food, 15.
 beer made from, 90.

Diary, extracts from, 170-174, 235-257.
Dik-dik antelope, 71.
Doctor, the, 3, 32, 35, 43, 45.
Dongola, province of, xxi.
  Mudir of, 238, 247.
  (Ordee), town of, 245.
Donkeys, Berber breed of, 234.
Dorcas, Gazella, 41.
Doves, several varieties of, 41, 214.
Dra's sad story, 212.
Dufferin, Lord, xxxiii.

E

Effendi Achmed, palace of, 9.
Egyptian Government, the, 12.
  officials, 9, 227.
  Soudan, the, 1.
  tents, 21.
El Ain, 217.
El Belad, a visit from the Sheik, 62.
Elephants, 58, 59, 130.
Ellegua, the sand-storm at, 29.
Elsen, M., 225.
English consuls, appointment of, 222.
En-noor, the servant, 181.
Equatorial lakes, the, 5.
Everlasting forest, the, 139.
Explorations, Capt. Gascoigne's, 112.

F

Fahncoob, halt, at, 136, 179.
Felkin, Dr., 6.
Fillik, headquarters of the Haden-dowa tribe, 40.
Fish, a haul of, 148, 151.
  abundance of, 18, 151, 222.
  capture of a *baggar*, 151.
Fishing, good, 148.
Flocks, large, 183.
Forest, everlasting, the, 139.
Fox-terrier "Tartar," the, 6, 7, 220.
Freedman's Aid Society, the, 226.

G

Galani, Attman, Sheik, 17.

Gallabat, xxii, 13.
Game, 72.
Gargi, the village of, 197.
Gascoigne's, Capt., explorations, 112.
Gash, the *khor* on which Cassala is built, xxi, 40, 43, 56, 68.
Gazella Arabica, 24.
  Dama, 24.
  Dorcas, 41.
Gazelles, three shot, 36.
Gebel Barkal, 239, 240.
Gedariff, 13, 50.
George, the English servant, 6, 173.
Gerghis, Mr. Lort Phillips's servant, 200, 228.
German animal-catcher, the, 60.
Giraffes, 80, 97.
Giraffe-stalking, 87.
Gordon, Col., 10, 11, 14, 231, 236.
Government, Egyptian, the, 12.
  agent, Wakeel, the, 11.
  of the Soudan, division of the, 12, 206.
Governor of Cassala, the, 44.
  dinner with the, 51.
  gives military escort, 54.
Graham, General, xxviii.
Grass, dearth of, 22, 78.
  eaten up, 180.
Greek shops, 15, 232.
Greeks, omnipresence of, 15.
Green paroquets, seen for the first time, 37.
Grooms, the, give warning, 181.
Gudgeon, contrivance for catching, 150.
Guffer, the disease among camels, 119.
Guides, duplicity of the, 139, 253.
Guide, the, a *mauvais sujet*, 205.
Guinea-fowl, 40, 41, 67, 78.
Gumba, Abou, the, 30.
Gum, large cargo of, 226.

H

Hadaiweb, halt at, 36.
Hadendowa tribe, headquarters of the, 40.
Hadendumi, two of the party start for, 184.
Haikota, the village of, 60, 135, 180.

Halfah, Wady, route to, 12.
Hamed Abou, 12, 230, 243.
Hamran country, the, 13, 140, 165.
Handak, Nile village, 245.
Hawartis, the, 142.
Heat, intensity of, 29, 38, 97, 132, 190.
Hegleek-trees, rich in potash, 78.
Herds, immense number of, 183.
Hicks, General, xxv, 206.
Hippopotami, 142.
Hippopotamus, the first shot, 162.
   the last, 166.
Holloway's pills, popularity of, 117.
Home, letters from, 135, 227.
Homeward journey, beginning of the, 174.
Horseman, the Devil's, 217.
Hôtel du Soudan, 16.
Household gods, hidden for fear of enemies, 86.
Hush-money, 11.
Hyæna, a new species killed, 200.

I

Illuminations in honour of the new governor, 13.
India-rubber made from the *quol-quol* plant, 216.
India, saloon passengers bound for, 7.
Ismail, Khedive, xxii, 206.
Ivory, a large cargo of, 226.

J

Jackal, the avenging, 37.
Jackals, three appear, 185.
James, W., shoots a splendid buck *nellut*, 168.
Jeddah, arrival of pilgrims at, 7.
Jewellery, claret capsules as, 92.
Journey, a long and tiresome, 139.
Jules, Swiss servant, 5.
   illness of, 29, 30, 31, 32, 35, 43.
   death of, 45.
   funeral of, 45.
   his grave, 50.
Jungle, road-making through the, 75.

K

Kage, village of, 250.
Kelb-el-bahr, capture of a, 150.
Khalifa, Sheik Achmet, 230.
   Hamed, 231.
Khartoum, English consul appointed to, 225.
Khartoum, xxi, xxix, xxxi, xxxiv.
Khedive Ismail, xxii.
   Mahommed Tewfik, xxiii, xxvii.
Khor Baraka, 15, 199.
   Belag, 35.
   Langeb, 29.
   Omri, 36.
   Rassay, 37.
   Wandi, 31.
Khors, 22, 28, 37, 38, 76.
Koolookoo, at the village of, 82.
Kordofan, xxi, xxiii.
Kudul, Sheik, 101, 113, 115.

L

Lacatecourah, village of, 174-175.
Lakes, the equatorial, 5.
Leopard, shot at a, 166.
Letters from home, 135, 227.
Lions, 68, 133, 135, 155, 186-191, 199.
   two shot, 187.
London, arrival of pilgrims in, 8.
Longay, 84, 91, 127, 129, 130.

M

Ma Ambasah, Khor, 98, 102, 111.
Määrif shot, 152, 171.
Magic-lantern, the, 65, 92, 210.
Mahomed, the servant, speared, 110.
   death of, 118.
Mahomet, Salee, 139, 141, 154, 165.
Mahommed Tewfik, xxiii, xxvii.
Mahoom, negro from the White Nile, 6, 32, 224.
   Christmas plum-pudding, 32.
Mai-Daro, visit from Sheik, 91.
Maieedah, signification of, 90.
Malet, Sir Edward, consul-general, 17.
Mareb, the, 92, 95.
Mason, Col., 247.
Massawa, the town of, 220-224.

Mauvais sujet, a, 205.
Mecca, pilgrimage to, 7, 30.
Medicine-man, the, held in awe, 117.
Méhédehet, or water-buck, shot, 94,
　173, 166.
Mehemet Ali, Pacha, xxi.
Meheteb Khor, 136, 179.
Merowi, Nile village, 239, 243.
　to Dongola, desert route, 246.
Midges, pest of, 242-243.
Mimosa, a fresh variety of the, 74.
Monastery, a mountain, 204.
Monks of Mount Tchad-Amba, 204.
Mora, seen for the first time, 78.
Mosconas and his son, 49.
Mosquitoes prove troublesome, 171.
Mother, a, sells her son for three
　dollars, 211.
Mountain, ascent of the Tchad-Amba,
　202-204.
Mount Bokutan, 142.
Munzinger Pacha, 202, 209.

N

Naouri, the village of, 47.
Nebbuk-bushes (*rhamnus lotus*), 27.
Negroes as schoolmasters, 226.
Nellut shot, 69, 166, 168.
News, budget of, from the Settite,
　177.
Nights, temperature of the, 97, 190.
Night-watch, an exciting, for buffa-
　loes, 155.
Night-watches in hopes of a shot,
　70.
Nile, numerous cataracts on the, 252.
Nile, the, route to Soudan, 12.
Nourri, Nile village, 239.
　pyramids of, 239.

O

Omelette à l'autriche, 70.
Om Brega, "mother of the thorn,"
　161.
Om Gedat, "mother of the guinea-
　fowl," 161.
Om Hagar, "mother of the rock,"
　161.
Ostrich, exciting chase after an, 95.

P

Pacha Ala-ed-Deen, supreme gover-
　nor, 15, 206.
　frees prisoners, 15.
Pacha, Ali Reza, 13, 14.
Palace of Achmed Effendi, 13.
Palms, *dhoum*, 28, 30, 44, 56.
Panther killed, 186, 200.
Paroquets, green, first appearance of,
　37.
Partridges, good sport among the,
　59, 74, 130, 214.
Party of travellers, a, leave Cairo for
　the Egyptian Soudan, 1.
Peace, ceremony of making, 91, 108,
　113.
Père Picard, 44, 204, 208.
Pilgrimage to Mecca, 7, 30.
Pilgrims, Persian, a party of, 7.
　Takrooris, a band of, joins the
　caravan, 30.
Pills, popularity of, among the natives,
　117.
Political aspect of the Soudan, xix-
　xxxiv.
Potash, *hegleek*-trees rich in, 78.
Press, alarming account in the Eng-
　lish and Egyptian, 227.
Provisions taken from England, 19.

Q

Quails appear, 60, 74.
　abundance of, 80, 135.
Quol-quol plant, attempt to make
　India-rubber from, 216.

R

Raid, horrible account of a, 179.
Railway, a, five miles long, 12.
Rains, coast, 9, 20.
Ras Aloula, 124.
Reefs, dangerous, 11.
Rhamnus lotus, nebbuk-bushes, 27.
River Atbara, the, 3, 47.
Road-making through the jungle, 75.
Rose-breasted shrike shot, 28.

Routes to Wady Halfah, 235.
to Dongola, 246.
from Wady Halfah to Cairo, 256.

S

Said Carcashi, Sheik, 123, 126.
Salee, a tracker, 45, 106, 153, 155.
Mahomed, 114, 139, 141, 180.
Sand-grouse shooting, 18, 34, 58, 70.
Sand-tempest, effects of a, 29, 30, 31.
Sanheit, 206, 208-209.
often called Keren, 45, 207.
Roman Catholic church and schools at, 210-212.
Savage, African, fondness for medicine, 117.
Say Island, 250.
Scare, a, 195.
Scenery, monotony of the, 27, 121, 142.
Schools, good management of, at Sanheit, 210.
Scorpions, 39.
Secretary-bird shot, 217.
Seine fishing-net, success of the, 141, 148.
Sellal, Abou, the camp moves to, 176.
Senaar, xxi.
Settite, the, 140.
budget of news from the, 177.
fishing in the, 140, 148-151.
the travellers bid adieu to the, 174.
Sheiks, a visit from two Hamran, 157.
offer to take the travellers to the Basé Settite, 178.
try to shoot the Basé, 159.
Shendy, xxi.
Shereef, the staid and stately waiter, 5.
Shereker, the, 158.
Shrike, rose-breasted, shot, 28.
Siterabb, 26.
Slave-trade, the, 11, 222, 234.
caravans, 12.
Snake, venomous, killed, 179.
"Snodgrass," a camel, 19.
Sogada, village of, 136, 179.
Souakim, port on the Red Sea, 2, 9, 12.

Souakim, curious washing-bill at, 16.
derivation of the word, 18.
English consuls appointed to, 222.
party of Bedouins come to, 13.
routes from, to Cassala, 22.
Soudan, the, 9-11, 206.
abandonment, xxvi.
ancient history, xx.
boundaries, xix.
British interposition, xxiii.
Egyptian possessions in, xxii.
insurrection, xxvii.
political aspects of the, xix-xxxiv.
prospective resources, xxxi-xxxiv.
rebellion, xxiii.
rebels defeated, xxviii.
signification, xix.
subjugation by Egypt, xxi.
various races in, xix.
Soumali country, three new ports added to the ports of call, 226.
Sport at Abiam, 135.
Steamers, various, 2.
Stewart, Col., xxvii, xxx.
Stork, the Marabou, 49, 140.
Suez, arrival at, 1, 227.
Sukkoot, temple at, 250.
Suleiman, history of, 5, 228.
Surprise, a, 107.
Swiss servants, two, 5.

T

Takrooris, the, 30.
Tamai, battle of, xxviii.
Tamarind-trees, seen for the first time, 73.
Tamarisk-trees, favourite food of the camel, 30.
"Tartar," a fox-terrier, 6-7, 220.
Tchad-Amba mountain, ascent of, 202.
Telegrams sent to England, fate of the, 125, 228.
Temperature, change of, 67, 97, 120.
Tétel found for the first time, 68.
abundance of, 78.
shot, 69, 185.
Tewfik, Bey, xxvii.
Ticks, black, 74.

Toadelook, halt at, 68-69, 181.
Toadwan, halt at, 72.
Tokar, nearest village to Souakim, 15.
Tolib, temple at, 250.
Tomatoes, discovery of wild, 97.
Tortoise, purchase of a big, 168.
Tracker, Salee, a, 45, 106, 153, 155.
Tracks of hippopotami, 142.
Trappers, Beni-Amer, 158.
Travellers nearly lose their way, 28.
Travellers encamp up the Settite, 142.
a scarcity of, on the road, 44.
Tribe, the Barea, 121.

U

Uganda, 6.

V

Valley, the Anseba, 213.
Vegetation, scantiness of, 38.
Village, a deserted, 36.
of Gargi, 197.
Villages, visit to some Dembelas, 18, 112.
Koolookoo, 82, 84, 130.
Lacatecourah, 174-175.
Naouri, 47.
Nourri, 239.
paying taxes to King John, 112.
Sogada, 136, 179.

Virgins, story of the seven, 18.
Vultures, 111.

W

Wady Halfah, routes to, 12, 235.
arrival at, 256.
route from, to Cairo by river, 256.
Wakeel, the government agent, 9.
Walkait minstrel, 68.
Wandi, Christmas Day at, 32.
Wart-hog, the, 101, 173, 218.
Watch, the night, 70.
Water-buck, *Méhédehet*, shot, 94.
Watercourse, Camphor, 218-219.
Water, digging for, 68, 72, 74, 183.
White ants, 50, 162.
Wild tomatoes, discovery of, 97.
Wo Ammar, halt at, 78.
Wolseley, Lord, xxx-xxxi.
Woman, the old, who had been robbed, 26.

Z

Zariba, a, 54, 107.
Zebechr conquers Darfour, xxii.
Zem-Zem, sacred waters of, 8.
Zoological societies, collections for, 53.

THE END.

Printed by R. & R. CLARK, *Edinburgh.*

uy

MR. MURRAY'S LIST.

HANDBOOK—EGYPT: THE COURSE OF THE NILE THROUGH EGYPT AND NUBIA, ALEXANDRA, CAIRO, THE PYRAMIDS, AND THEBES, THE SUEZ CANAL, THE PENINSULA OF SINAI, THE OASES, THE FYOOM, &c. In Two Parts. Maps and Plans. Post 8vo. 15s.

HANDBOOK—MEDITERRANEAN: FORMING A COMPLETE GUIDE TO ITS PRINCIPAL ISLANDS, CITIES, SEAPORTS, HARBOURS, &c., FOR TRAVELLERS AND YACHTSMEN. *Second Edition, Revised.* With 50 Maps and Plans. Post 8vo. 20s.

HANDBOOK—ALGERIA AND TUNIS: ALGIERS, CONSTANTINE, ORAN, THE ATLAS RANGE, &c. Maps and Plans. Post 8vo. 10s.

With Maps, complete in 4 vols., Post 8vo.

MURRAY'S HANDBOOKS FOR TRAVELLERS AND RESIDENTS IN BRITISH INDIA. By E. B. EASTWICK, C.B., F.R.S., F.S.A.

I.—BOMBAY—POONAH, BEEJAPOOR, KOLAPOOR, GOA, JUBULPOOR, INDORE, SURAT, BARODA, AHMEDABAD, SOMNAUTH, KURRACHEE, MOUNT ABOO, &c. Map. 15s.

II.—MADRAS—TRICHINOPOLI, MADURA, TINNEVELLY, TUTICORIN, BANGALORE, MYSORE, THE NILGIRIS, WYNAAD, OOTACAMUND, CALICUT, HYDERABAD, AJANTA, ELURA CAVES, &c. Map. 15s.

III.—BENGAL—CALCUTTA, ORISSA, BRITISH BURMAH, RANGOON, MOULMEIN, MANDALAY, DARJILING, DACCA, PATNA, GAYA, BENARES, N.-W. PROVINCES, ALLAHABAD, CAWNPORE, LUCKNOW, AGRA, GWALIOR, NAINI TAL, DELHI, KHATMANDU, &c. Map. 20s.

IV.—THE PANJAB—AMRAOTI, INDORE, AJMIR, JAYPUR, ROHTAK, SAHARANPUR, AMBALA, LODIANA, LAHORE, KULU, SIMLA, SIALKOT, PESHAWAR, RAWUL PINDI, ATTOCK, KARACHI, SIBI, &c. Maps. 15s.

PROFESSOR E. H. PALMER'S LIFE AND ACHIEVEMENTS: FROM HIS BIRTH TO HIS MURDER BY THE ARABS OF THE DESERT, 1882. By WALTER BESANT, M.A. Fourth Edition. With Portrait. Crown 8vo. 12s.

THE RIVER OF GOLDEN SAND: A NARRATIVE OF A JOURNEY THROUGH CHINA TO BURMAH. By the late Captain GILL. *An Abridged Edition*, by E. COLBORNE BABER. With MEMOIR and Introductory Essay by Colonel H. YULE, C.B. With Portrait, Map, and Illustrations. Post 8vo. 7s. 6d.

SIR RICHARD TEMPLE'S WORKS ON INDIA:—

I. ORIENTAL EXPERIENCE. With Woodcuts and Maps. 8vo. 16s.

II. INDIA IN 1880. Third Edition. 8vo. 16s.

III. MEN AND EVENTS OF MY TIME IN INDIA. 8vo. 16s.

JOHN MURRAY, ALBEMARLE STREET.

ALBEMARLE STREET, LONDON,
October, 1884.

MR. MURRAY'S
GENERAL LIST OF WORKS.

ALBERT MEMORIAL. A Descriptive and Illustrated Account of the National Monument erected to the PRINCE ;CONSORT at Kensington. Illustrated by Engravings of its Architecture, Decorations, Sculptured Groups, Statues, Mosaics, Metalwork, &c. With Descriptive Text. By DOYNE C. BELL. With 24 Plates. Folio. 12*l*. 12*s*.

———————— HANDBOOK TO. Post 8vo. 1*s*.; or Illustrated Edition, 2*s*. 6*d*.

———— (PRINCE) SPEECHES AND ADDRESSES. Fcap. 8vo. 1*s*.

ABBOTT (REV. J.). Memoirs of a Church of England Missionary in the North American-Colonies. Post 8vo. 2*s*.

ABERCROMBIE (JOHN). Enquiries concerning the Intellectual Powers and the Investigation of Truth. Fcap. 8vo. 3*s*. 6*d*.

ACLAND (REV. CHARLES). Popular Account of the Manners and Customs of India. Post 8vo. 2*s*.

ADMIRALTY PUBLICATIONS; Issued by direction of the Lords Commissioners of the Admiralty:—

CHALLENGER EXPEDITION, 1873—1876: Report of the Scientific Results of. ZOOLOGY. Vol. I. 37*s*. 6*d*. Vol. II. 50*s*. Vol. III. 50*s*. Vol. IV. 50*s*. Vol. V. 50*s*. Vol. VI. 42*s*. Vol. VII. 30*s*. Vol. VIII. 40*s*.

A MANUAL OF SCIENTIFIC ENQUIRY, for the Use of Travellers. Edited by R. MAIN, M.A. Woodcuts. Post 8vo. 3*s*. 6*d*.

GREENWICH ASTRONOMICAL OBSERVATIONS, 1837 to 1880. Royal 4to. 20*s*. each.

GREENWICH ASTRONOMICAL RESULTS, 1847 to 1881. 4to. 3*s*. each.

MAGNETICAL AND METEOROLOGICAL OBSERVATIONS, 1841 to 1847. Royal 4to. 20*s*. each.

MAGNETICAL AND METEOROLOGICAL RESULTS, 1848 to 1881. 4to; 3*s*. each.

APPENDICES TO OBSERVATIONS.
1837. Logarithms of Sines and Cosines in Time. 3*s*.
1842. Catalogue of 1439 Stars, from Observations made in 1836, 1841. 4*s*.
1845. Longitude of Valentia (Chronometrical). 3*s*.
1847. I. Description of Altazimuth. 3*s*.
    III. Description of Photographic Apparatus. 2*s*.
1851. Maskelyne's Ledger of Stars. 3*s*.
1852. I. Description of the Transit Circle. 3*s*.
1853. Bessel's Refraction Tables. 3*s*.
1854. I. Description of the Reflex Zenith Tube. 3*s*.
    II. Six Years' Catalogue of Stars from Observations. 1848 to 1853. 4*s*.
1860. Reduction of Deep Thermometer Observations. 2*s*.
1862. II. Plan of Ground and Buildings of Royal Observatory, Greenwich. 3*s*.
    III. Longitude of Valentia (Galvanic). 2*s*.
1864. I. Moon's Semi-diameter, from Occultations. 2*s*.
    II. Reductions of Planetary Observations. 1831 to 1835. 2*s*.
1868. I. Corrections of Elements of Jupiter and Saturn. 2*s*.
    II. Second Seven Years' Catalogue of 2760 Stars. 1861-7. 4*s*.
    III. Description of the Great Equatorial. 3*s*.
1871. Description of Water Telescope. 3*s*.
1873. Regulations of the Royal Observatory. 2*s*.
1876. II. Nine Years' Catalogue of 2283 Stars. 1868-76. 6*s*.
1879. Description of Greenwich Time Signal System. 2*s*.

B

ADMIRALTY PUBLICATIONS—*continued.*

Cape of Good Hope Observations (Star Ledgers). 1856 to 1863. 2s.
—————————————————— 1856. 5s.
—————————————————— Astronomical Results. 1857 to 1858. 5s.
Cape Catalogue, 1834 to 1840, reduced to Epoch 1840. 7s. 6d.
————————— of 1159 Stars, 1856 to 1861, reduced to the Epoch 1860. 3s.
—————————, 12,441 Stars for Epoch 1880. 31s. 6d.
Cape of Good Hope Astronomical Results. 1859 to 1860. 5s.
—————————————————————— 1871 to 1873. 5s.
—————————————————————— 1874 to 1876. 5s. each.
Report on Teneriffe Astronomical Experiment. 1856. 5s.
Observations on the Transit of Venus, 1874. 20s.
Paramatta Catalogue of 7385 Stars. 1822 to 1826. 4s.
REDUCTION OF THE OBSERVATIONS OF PLANETS. 1750 to 1830. Royal 4to. 20s. each.
—————————————————— LUNAR OBSERVATIONS. 1750 to 1830. 2 Vols. Royal 4to. 20s. each.
—————————————————— 1831 to 1851. 4to. 10s. each.
ARCTIC PAPERS. 18s. 6d.
BERNOULLI'S SEXCENTENARY TABLE. 1779. 4to. 5s.
BESSEL'S AUXILIARY TABLES FOR HIS METHOD OF CLEARING LUNAR DISTANCES. 8vo. 2s.
ENCKE'S BERLINER JAHRBUCH, for 1830. *Berlin*, 1828. 8vo. 9s.
HANNYNGTON'S HAVERSINES. 21s.
HANSEN'S TABLES DE LA LUNE. 4to. 20s.
LAX'S TABLES FOR FINDING THE LATITUDE AND LONGITUDE. 1821. 8vo. 10s
LUNAR OBSERVATIONS at GREENWICH. 1783 to 1819. Compared with the Tables, 1821. 4to. 7s. 6d.
MACLEAR ON LACAILLE'S ARC OF MERIDIAN. 2 Vols. 20s. each.
MAYER'S DISTANCES of the MOON'S CENTRE from the PLANETS. 1822, 3s.; 1823, 4s. 6d. 1824 to 1835. 8vo. 4s. each.
MAYER'S TABULÆ MOTUUM SOLIS ET LUNÆ. 1770. 5s.
————————— ASTRONOMICAL OBSERVATIONS MADE AT GÖTTINGEN, from 1756 to 1761. 1826. Folio. 7s. 6d.
NAUTICAL ALMANACS, from 1767 to 1887. 2s. 6d. each.
————————— SELECTIONS FROM, up to 1812. 8vo. 5s. 1834-54. 5s.
————————— SUPPLEMENTS, 1828 to 1833, 1837 and 1838. . each.
————————— TABLE requisite to be used with the N.A. 1781. 8vo. 5s.
SABINE'S PENDULUM EXPERIMENTS to DETERMINE THE FIGURE OF THE EARTH. 1825. 4to. 40s.
SHEPHERD'S TABLES for CORRECTING LUNAR DISTANCES. 1772. Royal 4to. 21s.
————————— TABLES, GENERAL, of the MOON'S DISTANCE from the SUN, and 10 STARS. 1787. Folio. 5s. 6d.
TAYLOR'S SEXAGESIMAL TABLE. 1780. 4to. 15s.
————————— TABLES OF LOGARITHMS. 4to. 60s.
TIARK'S ASTRONOMICAL OBSERVATIONS for the LONGITUDE of MADEIRA. 1822. 4to. 5s.
————————— CHRONOMETRICAL OBSERVATIONS for DIFFERENCES of LONGITUDE between DOVER, PORTSMOUTH, and FALMOUTH. 1823. 4to. 5s.
VENUS and JUPITER: OBSERVATIONS of, compared with the TABLES. *London*, 1822. 4to. 2s.
WALES AND BAYLY'S ASTRONOMICAL OBSERVATIONS. 1777. 4to. 21s.
————————— REDUCTION OF ASTRONOMICAL OBSERVATIONS MADE IN THE SOUTHERN HEMISPHERE. 1764—1771. 1788. 4to. 10s. 6d.
ÆSOP'S FABLES. A New Version. By REV. THOMAS JAMES. With 100 Woodcuts, by TENNIEL and WOLFF. Post 8vo. 2s. 6d.

AGRICULTURAL (ROYAL) JOURNAL. (*Published half-yearly.*)

ALICE; GRAND DUCHESS OF HESSE, PRINCESS OF GREAT
BRITAIN AND IRELAND. Biographical Sketch and Letters, Edited by
H.R.H. Princess Christian. With portraits. Crown 8vo. 12s.

AMBER-WITCH (THE). A most interesting Trial for Witchcraft. Translated by LADY DUFF GORDON. Post 8vo. 2s.

AMERICA. [See NADAILLAC.]

APOCRYPHA: With a Commentary Explanatory and Critical,
by various Writers. Edited by the REV. HENRY WACE, D.D.
2 vols. Medium 8vo. [*In the Press.*]

ARISTOTLE. [See GROTE, HATCH.]

ARMY LIST (THE). *Published Monthly by Authority.*

———— (THE QUARTERLY OFFICIAL). Royal 8vo. 15s.

ARTHUR'S (LITTLE) History of England. By LADY CALLCOTT.
New Edition, continued to 1878. With 36 Woodcuts. Fcap. 8vo. 1s. 6d.

————HISTORY OF FRANCE, from the earliest times to the
Fall of the Second Empire. With woodcuts. Fcp. 8vo.

AUSTIN (JOHN). LECTURES ON GENERAL JURISPRUDENCE; or, the
Philosophy of Positive Law. Edited by ROBERT CAMPBELL. 2 Vols.
8vo. 32s.

———— STUDENT'S EDITION, compiled from the above work,
by ROBERT CAMPBELL. Post 8vo. 12s.

———— Analysis of. By GORDON CAMPBELL. Post 8vo. 6s.

BABER (E. C.) Travels in W. China. Maps. Royal 8vo. 5s.

BARCLAY (BISHOP). Extracts from the Talmud, illustrating
the Teaching of the Bible. With an Introduction. Post 8vo. 14s.

BARKLEY (H. C.). Five Years among the Bulgarians and Turks
between the Danube and the Black Sea. Post 8vo. 10s. 6d.

———— Bulgaria Before the War; during a Seven Years'
Experience of European Turkey and its Inhabitants. Post 8vo. 10s. 6d.

———— My Boyhood: a True Story. Illustrations. Post
8vo. 6s.

BARROW (JOHN). Life, Exploits, and Voyages of Sir Francis
Drake. Post 8vo. 2s.

BARRY (EDW. M.), R.A. Lectures on Architecture. Edited,
with Memoir, by Canon Barry. Portrait and Illustrations. 8vo. 16s.

BATES (H. W.). Records of a Naturalist on the Amazons during
Eleven Years' Adventure and Travel. Illustrations. Post 8vo. 7s. 6d.

BAX (CAPT.). Russian Tartary, Eastern Siberia, China, Japan,
&c. Illustrations. Crown 8vo. 12s.

BECKETT (SIR EDMUND). "Should the Revised New Testament be Authorised?" Post 8vo. 6s.

BELL (SIR CHAS.). Familiar Letters. Portrait. Post 8vo. 12s.

———— (DOYNE C.). Notices of the Historic Persons buried in
the Chapel of St. Peter ad Vincula, in the Tower of London. Illustrations. Crown 8vo. 14s.

BENSON (ARCHBISHOP). The Cathedral; its necessary place in
the Life and Work of the Church. Post 8vo. 6s

BERTRAM (JAS. G.). Harvest of the Sea: an Account of British
Food Fishes, including Fisheries and Fisher Folk. Illustrations.
Post 8vo. 9s.

BESANT (WALTER). The Life and Achievements of Professor E.
H. Palmer, from his Birth to his Murder by the Arabs of the Desert,
1882. With Portrait. Crown 8vo. 12s.

B 2

BIBLE COMMENTARY. THE OLD TESTAMENT. EXPLANATORY and CRITICAL. With a REVISION of the TRANSLATION. By BISHOPS and CLERGY of the ANGLICAN CHURCH. Edited by F. C. COOK, M.A., Canon of Exeter. 6 VOLS. Medium 8vo. 6l. 15s.

Vol. I. 30s.	GENESIS, EXODUS, LEVITICUS, NUMBERS, DEUTERONOMY.
Vols. II. and III. 36s.	JOSHUA, JUDGES, RUTH, SAMUEL, KINGS, CHRONICLES, EZRA, NEHEMIAH, ESTHER.
Vol. IV. 24s.	JOB, PSALMS, PROVERBS, ECCLESIASTES, SONG OF SOLOMON.
Vol. V. 20s.	ISAIAH, JEREMIAH.
Vol. VI. 25s.	EZEKIEL, DANIEL, MINOR PROPHETS.

THE NEW TESTAMENT. 4 VOLS. Medium 8vo. 4l. 14s.

Vol. I. 18s.	INTRODUCTION, ST. MATTHEW, ST. MARK, ST. LUKE.
Vol. II. 20s.	ST. JOHN. ACTS OF THE APOSTLES.
Vol. III. 28s.	ROMANS, CORINTHIANS, GALATIANS, PHILIPPIANS, EPHESIANS, COLOSSIANS, THESSALONIANS, PASTORAL EPISTLES, PHILEMON.
Vol. IV. 28s.	HEBREWS, SS. JAMES, PETER, JOHN, JUDE, AND THE REVELATION.

———— THE STUDENT'S EDITION. Abridged and Edited by PROFESSOR J. M. FULLER, M.A., Crown 8vo. 7s. 6d. each Volume.
THE OLD TESTAMENT. 4 Vols.
THE NEW TESTAMENT. 2 vols.

BIGG-WITHER (T. P.). Pioneering in South Brazil; Three Years of Forest and Prairie Life in the Province of Parana. Map and Illustrations. 2 vols. Crown 8vo. 24s.

BIRD (ISABELLA). Hawaiian Archipelago; or Six Months among the Palm Groves, Coral Reefs, and Volcanoes of the Sandwich Islands. Illustrations. Crown 8vo. 7s. 6d.

———— Lady's Life in the Rocky Mountains. Illustrations. Post 8vo. 7s. 6d.

———— The Golden Chersonese and the Way Thither. With Map and Illustrations. Post 8vo. 14s.

BISSET (SIR JOHN). Sport and War in South Africa from 1834 to 1867, with a Narrative of the Duke of Edinburgh's Visit. Illustrations. Crown 8vo. 14s.

BLUNT (LADY ANNE). The Bedouins of the Euphrates Valley. With some account of the Arabs and their Horses. Illustrations. 2 Vols. Crown 8vo. 24s.

———— A Pilgrimage to Nejd, the Cradle of the Arab Race, and a Visit to the Court of the Arab Emir. Illustrations. 2 Vols. Post 8vo. 24s.

BLUNT (REV. J. J.). Undesigned Coincidences in the Writings of the Old and New Testaments, an Argument of their Veracity. Post 8vo. 6s.

———— History of the Christian Church in the First Three Centuries. Post 8vo. 6s.

———— The Parish Priest; His Duties, Acquirements, and Obligations. Post 8vo. 6s.

———— University Sermons. Post 8vo. 6s.

BOOK OF COMMON PRAYER. Illustrated with Coloured Borders, Initial Letters, and Woodcuts. 8vo. 18s.

BORROW (GEORGE). The Bible in Spain; Post 8vo. 5s.

———— Gypsies of Spain; their Manners and Customs. Portrait. Post 8vo. 5s.

———— Lavengro; The Scholar—The Gypsy—and the Priest. Post 8vo. 5s.

BORROW (George). Romany Rye. Post 8vo. 5s.
———— Wild Wales: its People, Language, and Scenery. Post 8vo. 5s.
———— Romano Lavo-Lil; Word-Book of the Romany, or English Gypsy Language. Post 8vo. 10s. 6d.

BOSWELL'S Life of Samuel Johnson, LL.D. Including the Tour to the Hebrides. Edited by Mr. Croker. *Seventh Edition.* Portraits. 1 vol. Medium 8vo. 12s.

BRADLEY (Dean). Arthur Penrhyn Stanley; Biographical Lectures. Crown 8vo. 3s. 6d.

BREWER (Rev. J. S.). The Reign of Henry VIII.; from his Accession till the Death of Wolsey. Reviewed and Illustrated from Original Documents. Edited by James Gairdner, of the Record Office. With portrait. 2 vols. 8vo. 30s.

BRIDGES (Mrs. F. D.). A Lady's Travels in Japan, Thibet, Yarkand, Kashmir, Java, the Straits of Malacca, Vancouver's Island,&c. With Map and Illustrations from Sketches by the Author. Crown 8vo. 15s.

BRITISH ASSOCIATION REPORTS. 8vo.

York and Oxford, 1831-32, 13s. 6d.	Leeds, 1858, 20s.
Cambridge, 1833, 12s.	Aberdeen, 1859, 15s.
Edinburgh, 1834, 15s.	Oxford, 1860, 25s.
Dublin, 1835, 13s. 6d.	Manchester, 1861, 15s.
Bristol, 1836, 12s.	Cambridge, 1862, 20s.
Liverpool, 1837, 16s. 6d.	Newcastle, 1863, 25s.
Newcastle, 1838, 15s.	Bath, 1864, 18s.
Birmingham, 1839, 13s. 6d.	Birmingham, 1865, 25s.
Glasgow, 1840, 15s.	Nottingham, 1866, 24s.
Plymouth, 1841, 13s. 6d.	Dundee, 1867, 26s.
Manchester, 1842, 10s. 6d.	Norwich, 1868, 25s.
Cork, 1843, 12s.	Exeter, 1869, 22s.
York, 1844, 20s.	Liverpool, 1870, 18s.
Cambridge, 1845, 12s.	Edinburgh, 1871, 16s.
Southampton, 1846, 15s.	Brighton, 1872, 24s.
Oxford, 1847, 18s.	Bradford, 1873, 25s.
Swansea, 1848, 9s.	Belfast, 1874, 25s.
Birmingham, 1849, 10s.	Bristol, 1875, 25s.
Edinburgh, 1850, 15s.	Glasgow, 1876, 25s.
Ipswich, 1851, 16s. 6d.	Plymouth, 1877, 24s.
Belfast, 1852, 15s.	Dublin, 1878, 24s.
Hull, 1853, 10s. 6d.	Sheffield, 1879, 24s.
Liverpool, 1854, 18s.	Swansea, 1880, 24s.
Glasgow, 1855, 15s.	York, 1881, 24s.
Cheltenham, 1856, 18s.	Southampton, 1882, 24s.
Dublin, 1857, 15s.	Southport, 1883, 24s.

BROCKLEHURST (T. U.). Mexico To-day: A country with a Great Future. With a Glance at the Prehistoric Remains and Antiquities of the Montezumas. Plates and Woodcuts. Medium 8vo. 21s.

BRUGSCH (Professor). A History of Egypt, under the Pharaohs. Derived entirely from Monuments, with a Memoir on the Exodus of the Israelites. Maps. 2 vols. 8vo. 32s.

BUNBURY (E. H.). A History of Ancient Geography, among the Greeks and Romans, from the Earliest Ages till the Fall of the Roman Empire. Maps. 2 Vols. 8vo. 21s.

BURBIDGE (F. W.). The Gardens of the Sun: or A Naturalist's Journal in Borneo and the Sulu Archipelago. Illustrations. Cr. 8vo. 14s.

BURCKHARDT'S Cicerone; or Art Guide to Painting in Italy. New Edition, revised by J. A. Crowe. Post 8vo. 6s.

BURGES (Sir James Bland) Bart. Selections from his Letters and Papers, as Under-Secretary of State for Foreign Affairs. With Notices of his Life. Edited by James Hutton. 8vo.

BURGON (J. W.), Dean of Chichester. The Revision Revised :
(1.) The New Greek Text; (2.) The New English Version; (3.) Westcott and Hort's Textual Theory. 8vo. 14s.

BURN (Col.). Dictionary of Naval and Military Technical
Terms, English and French—French and English. Crown 8vo. 15s.

BUTTMANN'S LEXILOGUS; a Critical Examination of the
Meaning of numerous Greek Words, chiefly in Homer and Hesiod.
By Rev. J. R. Fishlake. 8vo. 12s.

BUXTON (Charles). Memoirs of Sir Thomas Fowell Buxton,
Bart. Portrait. 8vo. 16s. Popular Edition. Fcap. 8vo. 5s.

——————— Notes of Thought. With a Biographical Notice by
Rev. J. Llewellyn Davies, M.A. Second Edition. Post 8vo. 5s.

——————— (Sydney C.). A Handbook to the Political Questions
of the Day; with the Arguments on Either Side. Fourth Edition,
revised and enlarged. 8vo. 6s.

BYLES (Sir John). Foundations of Religion in the Mind and
Heart of Man. Post 8vo. 6s.

BYRON'S (Lord) LIFE AND WORKS :—

Life, Letters, and Journals. By Thomas Moore. Cabinet
Edition. Plates. 6 Vols. Fcap. 8vo. 18s.; or One Volume, Portraits.
Royal 8vo., 7s. 6d.

Life and Poetical Works. Popular Edition. Portraits.
2 vols. Royal 8vo. 15s.

Poetical Works. Library Edition. Portrait. 6 Vols. 8vo. 45s.

Poetical Works. Cabinet Edition. Plates. 10 Vols. 12mo. 30s.

Poetical Works. Pocket Ed. 8 Vols. 16mo. In a case. 21s.

Poetical Works. Popular Edition. Plates. Royal 8vo. 7s. 6d.

Poetical Works. Pearl Edition. Crown 8vo. 2s. 6d. Cloth
Boards. 3s. 6d.

Childe Harold. With 80 Engravings. Crown 8vo. 12s.

Childe Harold. 16mo. 2s. 6d.

Childe Harold. Vignettes. 16mo. 1s.

Childe Harold. Portrait. 16mo. 6d.

Tales and Poems. 16mo. 2s. 6d.

Miscellaneous. 2 Vols. 16mo. 5s.

Dramas and Plays. 2 Vols. 16mo. 5s.

Don Juan and Beppo. 2 Vols. 16mo. 5s.

Beauties. Poetry and Prose. Portrait. Fcap. 8vo. 3s. 6d.

CAMPBELL (Lord). Life : Based on his Autobiography, with
selections from Journals, and Correspondence. Edited by Mrs. Hard-
castle. Portrait. 2 Vols. 8vo. 30s.

——————— Lord Chancellors and Keepers of the Great
Seal of England. From the Earliest Times to the Death of Lord Eldon
in 1838. 10 Vols. Crown 8vo. 6s. each.

——————— Chief Justices of England. From the Norman
Conquest to the Death of Lord Tenterden. 4 Vols. Crown 8vo. 6s. each.

——————— (Thos.) Essay on English Poetry. With Short
Lives of the British Poets. Post 8vo. 3s. 6d.

CAREY (Life of). See George Smith.

CARLISLE (Bishop of). Walks in the Regions of Science and
Faith—a Series of Essays. Contents :—Connection between Mechanics
and Geometry; Unity of Nature : a Speculation; God and Nature;
Philosophy of Crayfishes; Man's Place in Nature; Law, Physical and
Moral; Analogies and Contrasts between Human and Divine Science;
Natural Theology; Pessimism; Evolution and Evolution; Charles
Darwin. Crown 8vo. 7s. 6d.

CARNARVON (LORD). Portugal, Gallicia, and the Basque Provinces. Post 8vo. 3s. 6d.
———————The Agamemnon : Translated from Æschylus. 8m. 8vo. 6s.

CARNOTA (CONDE DA). The Life and Eventful Career of F.M. the Duke of Saldanha; Soldier and Statesman. 2 Vols. 8vo. 32s.

CARTWRIGHT (W. C.). The Jesuits: their Constitution and Teaching. An Historical Sketch. 8vo. 9s.]

CAVALCASELLE'S WORKS. [See CROWE.]

CESNOLA (GEN.). Cyprus; its Ancient Cities, Tombs, and Temples. With 400 Illustrations. Medium 8vo. 50s.

CHAMBERS (G, F.). A Practical and Conversational Pocket Dictionary of the English, French, and German Languages. Designed for Travellers and Students generally. Small 8vo. 6s.

CHILD-CHAPLIN (Dr.). Benedicite; or, Song of the Three Children; being Illustrations of the Power, Beneficence, and Design manifested by the Creator in his Works. Post 8vo. 6s.

CHISHOLM (Mrs.). Perils of the Polar Seas; True Stories of Arctic Discovery and Adventure. Illustrations. Post 8vo. 6s.

CHURTON (ARCHDEACON). Poetical Remains. Post 8vo. 7s. 6d.

CLASSIC PREACHERS OF THE ENGLISH CHURCH. Lectures delivered at St. James'. 2 Vols. Post 8vo. 7s. 6d. each.

CLIVE'S (LORD) Life. By REV. G. R. GLEIG. Post 8vo. 3s. 6d.

CLODE (C. M.). Military Forces of the Crown; their Administration and Government. 2 Vols. 8vo. 21s. each.
——— Administration of Justice under Military and Martial Law, as applicable to the Army, Navy, and Auxiliary Forces. 8vo. 12s.

COLEBROOKE (SIR EDWARD, BART.). Life of the Hon. Mountstuart Elphinstone. With Selections from his Correspondence and Papers. With Portrait and Plans. 2 vols. 8vo. 26s.

COLERIDGE'S (S. TAYLOR) Table-Talk. Portrait. 12mo. 3s. 6d.

COLES (JOHN). Summer Travelling in Iceland. Being the Narrative of Two Journeys Across the Island by Unfrequented Routes. With a Chapter on Askja. By E. DELMAR MORGAN, F.R.G.S. With Map and Illustrations. 18s.

COLLINS (J. CHURTON). BOLINGBROKE: an Historical Study. Three Essays reprinted from the *Quarterly Review*, to which is added an Essay on Voltaire in England. Crown 8vo.

COLONIAL LIBRARY. [See Home and Colonial Library.]

COMPANIONS FOR THE DEVOUT LIFE. Lectures on wellknown Devotional Works. Crown 8vo. 6s.

COOK (Canon F. C.). The Revised Version of the Three First Gospels, considered in its Bearings upon the Record of Our Lord's Words and Incidents in His Life. 8vo. 9s.
——— The Origins of Language and Religion. Considered in Five Essays. 8vo. 15s.

COOKE (E. W.). Leaves from my Sketch-Book. With Descriptive Text. 50 Plates. 2 Vols. Small folio. 31s. 6d. each.
——— (W. H.). Collections towards the History and Antiquities of the County of Hereford. In continuation of Duncumb's History, and forming the Third Volume of that Work. Illustrations. 4to. £2 12s. 6d.

COOKERY (MODERN DOMESTIC). Founded on Principles of Economy and Practical Knowledge, and Adapted for Private Families. By a Lady. Woodcuts. Fcap. 8vo. 5s.

CRABBE (Rev. George). Life & Poetical Works. Illustrations. Royal 8vo. 7s.

CRAIK (Henry). Life of Jonathan Swift. Portrait. 8vo. 18s.

CRIPPS (Wilfred). Old English Plate : Ecclesiastical, Decorative, and Domestic, its Makers and Marks. With a Complete Table of Date Letters, &c. New Edition. With 70 Illustrations. Medium 8vo. 16s. *₊* Tables of the Date Letters and Marks sold separately. 5s.

———— Old French Plate; With Paris Date Letters, and Other Marks. With Illustrations. 8vo. 8s. 6d.

CROKER (Rt. Hon. J. W.). Correspondence and Diaries, comprising Letters, Memoranda, and Journals relating to the chief Political and Social Events of the first half of the present century. Edited by Louis J. Jennings. With Portrait. 3 vols. 8vo.

———— Progressive Geography for Children. 18mo. 1s. 6d.

———— Boswell's Life of Johnson. Including the Tour to the Hebrides. *Seventh Edition.* Portraits. 8vo. 12s.

———— Historical Essay on the Guillotine. Fcap. 8vo. 1s.

CROWE and CAVALCASELLE. Lives of the Early Flemish Painters. Woodcuts. Post 8vo, 7s. 6d.; or Large Paper 8vo, 15s.

———— History of Painting in North Italy, from 14th to 16th Century. With Illustrations. 2 Vols. 8vo. 42s.

———— Life and Times of Titian, with some Account of his Family, chiefly from new and unpublished records. With Portrait and Illustrations. 2 vols. 8vo. 21s.

———— Raphael ; His Life and Works, with Particular Reference to recently discovered Records, and an exhaustive Study of Extant Drawings and Pictures. Vol. I. 8vo. 15s. Vol. II. (*in the press.*)

CUMMING (R. Gordon). Five Years of a Hunter's Life in the Far Interior of South Africa. Woodcuts. Post 8vo. 6s.

CURRIE (C. L.) An Argument for the Divinity of Jesus Christ. Translated from the French of the Abbé Em. Bougaud. Post 8vo. 6s.

CURTIUS' (Professor) Student's Greek Grammar, for the Upper Forms. Edited by Dr. Wm. Smith. Post 8vo. 6s.

————Elucidations of the above Grammar. Translated by Evelyn Abbot. Post 8vo. 7s. 6d.

———— Smaller Greek Grammar for the Middle and Lower Forms. Abridged from the larger work. 12mo. 3s. 6d.

———— Accidence of the Greek Language. Extracted from the above work. 12mo. 2s. 6d.

———— Principles of Greek Etymology. Translated by A. S. Wilkins, M.A., and E. B. England, M.A. 2 vols. 8vo.

———— The Greek Verb, its Structure and Development. Translated by A. S. Wilkins, and E. B. England. 8vo. 12s.

CURZON (Hon. Robert). Visits to the Monasteries of the Levant. Illustrations. Post 8vo. 7s. 6d.

CUST (General). Warriors of the 17th Century—Civil Wars of France and England. 2 Vols. 6s. Commanders of Fleets and Armies. 2 Vols. 18s.

———— —— Annals of the Wars—18th & 19th Century. With Maps. 9 Vols. Post 8vo. 5s. each.

DAVY (Sir Humphry). Consolations in Travel; or, Last Days of a Philosopher. Woodcuts. Fcap. 8vo. 3s. 6d.

———— Salmonia; or, Days of Fly Fishing. Woodcuts. Fcap. 8vo. 3s. 6d.

DARWIN'S (CHARLES) WORKS :—

JOURNAL OF A NATURALIST DURING A VOYAGE ROUND THE WORLD. Crown 8vo. 9s.

ORIGIN OF SPECIES BY MEANS OF NATURAL SELECTION ; or, the Preservation of Favoured Races in the Struggle for Life. Woodcuts. Crown 8vo. 7s. 6d.

VARIATION OF ANIMALS AND PLANTS UNDER DOMESTICATION. Woodcuts. 2 Vols. Crown 8vo. 18s.

DESCENT OF MAN, AND SELECTION IN RELATION TO SEX. Woodcuts. Crown 8vo. 9s.

EXPRESSIONS OF THE EMOTIONS IN MAN AND ANIMALS. With Illustrations. Crown 8vo. 12s.

VARIOUS CONTRIVANCES BY WHICH ORCHIDS ARE FERTILIZED BY INSECTS. Woodcuts. Crown 8vo. 9s.

MOVEMENTS AND HABITS OF CLIMBING PLANTS. Woodcuts. Crown 8vo. 6s.

INSECTIVOROUS PLANTS. Woodcuts. Crown 8vo. 14s.

EFFECTS OF CROSS AND SELF-FERTILIZATION IN THE VEGETABLE KINGDOM. Crown 8vo. 12s.

DIFFERENT FORMS OF FLOWERS ON PLANTS OF THE SAME SPECIES. Crown 8vo. 10s. 6d.

POWER OF MOVEMENT IN PLANTS. Woodcuts. Cr. 8vo. 15s.

THE FORMATION OF VEGETABLE MOULD THROUGH THE ACTION OF WORMS. With Illustrations. Post 8vo. 9s.

LIFE OF ERASMUS DARWIN. With a Study of his Works by ERNEST KRAUSE. Portrait. Crown 8vo. 7s. 6d.

FACTS AND ARGUMENTS FOR DARWIN. By FRITZ MULLER. Translated by W. S. DALLAS. Woodcuts. Post 8vo. 6s.

DE COSSON (E. A.). The Cradle of the Blue Nile; a Journey through Abyssinia and Soudan. Map and Illustrations. 2 vols. Post 8vo. 21s.

DENNIS (GEORGE). The Cities and Cemeteries of Etruria. A new Edition. With 20 Plans and 200 Illustrations. 2 vols. Medium 8vo. 21s.

DERBY (EARL OF). Iliad of Homer rendered into English Blank Verse. With Portrait. 2 Vols. Post 8vo. 10s.

DERRY (BISHOP OF). Witness of the Psalms to Christ and Christianity. The Bampton Lectures for 1876. 8vo. 14s.

DEUTSCH (EMANUEL). Talmud, Islam, The Targums and other Literary Remains. With a brief Memoir. 8vo. 12s.

DILKE (SIR C. W.). Papers from the Writings of the late CHARLES DILKE. 2 Vols. 8vo. 24s.

DOG-BREAKING. [See HUTCHINSON.]

DOUGLAS'S (SIR HOWARD) Theory and Practice of Gunnery. Plates. 8vo. 21s.

DRAKE'S (SIR FRANCIS) Life, Voyages, and Exploits, by Sea and Land. By JOHN BARROW. Post 8vo. 2s.

DRINKWATER (JOHN). History of the Siege of Gibraltar, 1779-1783. With a Description of that Garrison. Post 8vo. 2s.

DU CHAILLU (PAUL B.). Land of the Midnight Sun; Journeys through Northern Scandinavia, with Descriptions of the Inner Life of the People. Illustrations. 2 Vols. 8vo. 36s.

———— Journey to Ashango Land; and Further Penetration into Equatorial Africa. Illustrations. 8vo. 21s.

DUFFERIN (LORD). Letters from High Latitudes; a Yacht voyage to Iceland, Jan Mayen, and Spitzbergen. Woodcuts. Post 8vo. 7s. 6d.

———— Speeches and Addresses, Political and Literary, delivered in the House of Lords, in Canada, and elsewhere. 8vo. 12s.

DUNCAN (Col.) History of the Royal Artillery. Compiled from the Original Records. Portraits. 2 Vols. 8vo. 18s.
———— English in Spain; or, The Story of the War of Succession, 1834-1840. With Illustrations. 8vo. 16s.

DÜRER (Albert); his Life and Work. By Dr. Thausing. Translated from the German. Edited by F. A. Eaton, M.A. With Portrait and Illustrations. 2 vols. Medium 8vo. 42s.

EASTLAKE (Sir Charles). Contributions to the Literature of the Fine Arts. With Memoir of the Author by Lady Eastlake. 2 Vols. 8vo. 24s.

EDWARDS (W. H.). Voyage up the River Amazon, including a Visit to Para. Post 8vo. 2s.

ELDON'S (Lord) Public and Private Life, with Selections from his Diaries, &c. By Horace Twiss. Portrait. 2 Vols. Post 8vo. 21s.

ELGIN (Lord). Letters and Journals. Edited by Theodore Walrond. With Preface by Dean Stanley. 8vo. 14s.

ELLESMERE (Lord). Two Sieges of Vienna by the Turks. Translated from the German. Post 8vo. 2s.

ELLIS (W.). Madagascar Revisited. The Persecutions and Heroic Sufferings of the Native Christians. Illustrations. 8vo. 16s.
———— Memoir. By His Son. Portrait. 8vo. 10s. 6d.
———— (Robinson) Poems and Fragments of Catullus. 16mo. 5s.

ELPHINSTONE (Hon. M.). History of India—the Hindoo and Mahomedan Periods. Edited by Professor Cowell. Map. 8vo. 18s.
———— Life of. [See Colebrooke.]
———————— (H. W.). Patterns and instructions for ornamental Turning. With 70 Illustrations. Small 4to. 15s.

ELTON (Capt.) and H. B. COTTERILL. Adventures and Discoveries Among the Lakes and Mountains of Eastern and Central Africa. With Map and Illustrations. 8vo. 21s.

ENGLAND. [See Arthur—Brewer—Croker—Hume—Markham —Smith—and Stanhope.]

ESSAYS ON CATHEDRALS. Edited, with an Introduction. By Dean Howson. 8vo. 12s.

FELTOE (Rev. J. Lett). Memorials of John Flint South, twice President of the Royal College of Surgeons and Surgeon to St. Thomas's Hospital (1841-63). With Portrait. Crown 8vo. 7s. 6d.

FERGUSSON (James). History of Architecture in all Countries from the Earliest Times. With 1,600 Illustrations. 4 Vols. Medium 8vo.
     Vols. I. & II. Ancient and Mediæval. 63s.
     III. Indian & Eastern. 42s. IV. Modern. 31s. 6d.
———— Rude Stone Monuments in all Countries; their Age and Uses. With 230 Illustrations. Medium 8vo. 24s.
———— Holy Sepulchre and the Temple at Jerusalem. Woodcuts. 8vo. 7s. 6d.
———————— Temples of the Jews and other buildings in the Haram Area at Jerusalem. With Illustrations. 4to. 42s.
———— The Parthenon. An Essay on the construction of Greek and Roman Temples, with especial reference to the mode in which light was introduced into their interiors. 8vo. 21s.

FLEMING (Professor). Student's Manual of Moral Philosophy. With Quotations and References. Post 8vo. 7s. 6d.

FLOWER GARDEN. By Rev. Thos. James. Fcap. 8vo. 1s.

FORBES (Capt.). British Burma and its People; Native Manners, Customs, and Religion. Crown 8vo. 10s. 6d.

FORD (Richard). Gatherings from Spain. Post 8vo. 3s. 6d.

FORSTER (John). The Early Life of Jonathan Swift. 1667-1711. With Portrait. 8vo. 15s.

FORSYTH (WILLIAM). Hortensius; an Historical Essay on the Office and Duties of an Advocate. Illustrations. 8vo. 7s. 6d.

———————— Novels and Novelists of the 18th Century, in Illustration of the Manners and Morals of the Age. Post 8vo. 10s. 6d.

FRANCE (HISTORY OF). [See MARKHAM —SMITH —STUDENTS'— TOCQUEVILLE.]

FRENCH IN ALGIERS; The Soldier of the Foreign Legion— and the Prisoners of Abd-el-Kadir. Translated by Lady DUFF GORDON. Post 8vo. 2s.

FRERE (SIR BARTLE). Indian Missions. Small 8vo. 2s. 6d.

———————— Missionary Labour in Eastern Africa. Crown 8vo. 5s.

———————— Bengal Famine. How it will be Met and How to Prevent Future Famines in India. With Maps. Crown 8vo. 5s.

———————— (MARY). Old Deccan Days, or Hindoo Fairy Legends current in Southern India, with Introduction by Sir BARTLE FRERE. With 50 Illustrations. Post 8vo. 7s. 6d.

GALTON (F.). Art of Travel; or, Hints on the Shifts and Contrivances available in Wild Countries. Woodcuts. Post 8vo. 7s. 6d.

GEOGRAPHY. [See BUNBURY—CROKER—RICHARDSON — SMITH —STUDENTS'.]

GEOGRAPHICAL SOCIETY'S JOURNAL. (1846 to 1881.)

———————— Supplementary Papers (i), Travels and Researches in Western China. By E. COLBORNE BABER. Maps. Royal 8vo. 5s.

———————— (ii) 1. Notes on the Recent Geography of Central Asia; from Russian Sources. By E. DELMAR MORGAN.

———————— 2. Progress of Discovery on the Coasts of New Guinea. By C. B. MARKHAM. With Bibliographical Appendix, by E. C. Rye. Maps. Royal 8vo. 5s.

GEORGE (ERNEST). The Mosel; Twenty Etchings. Imperial 4to. 42s.

———————— Loire and South of France; Twenty etchings. Folio. 42s.

GERMANY (HISTORY OF). [See MARKHAM.]

GIBBON (EDWARD). History of the Decline and Fall of the Roman Empire. Edited with notes by MILMAN, GUIZOT, and Dr. WM. SMITH. Maps. 8 Vols. 8vo. 60s.

———————— The Student's Edition; an Epitome of the above work, incorporating the Researches of Recent Commentators. By Dr. WM. SMITH. Woodcuts. Post 8vo. 7s. 6d.

GIFFARD (EDWARD). Deeds of Naval Daring; or, Anecdotes of the British Navy. Fcap. 8vo. 3s. 6d.

GILBERT (JOSIAH). Landscape Art : down to the time of Claude and Salvator. With numerous Illustrations. Crown 8vo.

GILL (CAPT.). The River of Golden Sand. A Narrative of a Journey through China to Burmah. An Abridged Edition, by E. COLBORNE BABER. With MEMOIR and Introductory Essay, by Colonel H. YULE, C.B. With Portrait, Map, and Illustrations. Post 8vo. 7s. 6d.

———— (MRS.). Six Months in Ascension. An Unscientific Account of a Scientific Expedition. Map. Crown 8vo. 9s.

GLADSTONE (W. E.). Rome and the Newest Fashions in Religion. Three Tracts. 8vo. 7s. 6d.

———————— Gleanings of Past Years, 1843-78. 7 vols. Small 8vo. 2s. 6d. each. I. The Throne, the Prince Consort, the Cabinet and Constitution. II. Personal and Literary. III. Historical and Speculative. IV. Foreign. V. and VI. Ecclesiastical. VII. Miscellaneous.

GLEIG (G. R.). Campaigns of the British Army at Washington and New Orleans. Post 8vo. 2s.

———————— Story of the Battle of Waterloo. Post 8vo. 3s. 6d.

———————— Narrative of Sale's Brigade in Affghanistan. Post 8vo. 2s.

GLEIG (G. R.) Life of Lord Clive. Post 8vo. 3s. 6d.
—— Life of Sir Thomas Munro. Post 8vo. 3s. 6d.
GLYNNE (Sir Stephen). Notes on the Churches of Kent. With Preface by W. H. Gladstone, M.P. Illustrations. 8vo. 12s.
GOLDSMITH'S (Oliver) Works. Edited with Notes by Peter Cunningham. Vignettes. 4 Vols. 8vo. 30s.
GOMM (F.M. Sir Wm.). His Letters and Journals. 1799 to 1815. Edited by F. C. Carr Gomm. With Portrait. 8vo. 12s.
GORDON (Sir Alex.). Sketches of German Life, and Scenes from the War of Liberation. Post 8vo. 3s. 6d.
—————— (Lady Duff) Amber-Witch: A Trial for Witchcraft. Post 8vo. 2s.
—————— French in Algiers. 1. The Soldier of the Foreign Legion. 2. The Prisoners of Abd-el-Kadir. Post 8vo. 2s.
GRAMMARS. [See Curtius—Hall—Hutton—King Edward—Leathes—Maetzner—Matthiæ—Smith.]
GREECE (History of). [See Grote—Smith—Students'.]
GROTE'S (George) WORKS :—
HISTORY OF GREECE. From the Earliest Times to the close of the generation contemporary with the Death of Alexander the Great. *Library Edition.* Portrait, Maps, and Plans. 10 Vols. 8vo. 120s. *Cabinet Edition.* Portrait and Plans. 12 Vols. Post 8vo. 4s. each.
PLATO, and other Companions of Socrates. 3 Vols. 8vo. 45s.
ARISTOTLE. With additional Essays. 8vo. 12s.
MINOR WORKS. Portrait. 8vo. 14s.
LETTERS ON SWITZERLAND IN 1847. 6s.
PERSONAL LIFE. Portrait. 8vo. 12s.
GROTE (Mrs.). A Sketch. By Lady Eastlake. Crown 8vo. 6s.
HALL'S (T. D.) School Manual of English Grammar. With Illustrations and Practical Exercises. 12mo. 3s. 6d.
—————— Primary English Grammar for Elementary Schools. With numerous Exercises, and graduated Parsing Lessons. 16mo. 1s.
—————— Manual of English Composition. With Copious Illustrations and Practical Exercises. 12mo. 3s. 6d.
—————— Child's First Latin Book, comprising a full Practice of Nouns, Pronouns, and Adjectives, with the Active Verbs. 16mo. 2s.
HALLAM'S (Henry) WORKS :—
THE CONSTITUTIONAL HISTORY OF ENGLAND, from the Accession of Henry the Seventh to the Death of George the Second. *Library Edition,* 3 Vols. 8vo. 30s. *Cabinet Edition,* 3 Vols. Post 8vo. 12s. *Student's Edition,* Post 8vo. 7s. 6d.
HISTORY OF EUROPE DURING THE MIDDLE AGES. *Library Edition,* 3 Vols. 8vo. 30s. *Cabinet Edition,* 3 Vols. Post 8vo. 12s. *Student's Edition,* Post 8vo. 7s. 6d.
LITERARY HISTORY OF EUROPE DURING THE 15TH, 16TH, AND 17TH CENTURIES. *Library Edition,* 3 Vols. 8vo. 36s. *Cabinet Edition,* 4 Vols. Post 8vo. 16s.
—————— (Arthur) Literary Remains; in Verse and Prose. Portrait. Fcap. 8vo. 3s. 6d.
HAMILTON (Andrew). Rheinsberg: Memorials of Frederick the Great and Prince Henry of Prussia. 2 Vols. Crown 8vo. 21s.
HART'S ARMY LIST. (*Published Quarterly and Annually.*)
HATCH (W. M.). The Moral Philosophy of Aristotle, a translation of the Nichomachean Ethics, and of the Paraphrase of Andronicus, with an Introductory Analysis of each book. 8vo. 18s.

HATHERLEY (Lord). The Continuity of Scripture, as Declared by the Testimony of our Lord and of the Evangelists and Apostles. Post 8vo. 2s. 6d.

HAY (Sir J. H. Drummond). Western Barbary, its Wild Tribes and Savage Animals. Post 8vo. 2s.

HAYWARD (A.). Sketches of Eminent Statesmen and Writers. Contents: Thiers, Bismarck, Cavour, Metternich, Montalembert, Melbourne, Wellesley, Byron and Tennyson, Venice, St. Simon, Sevigné, Du Deffand, Holland House, Strawberry Hill. 2 Vols. 8vo. 28s.

——— The Art of Dining, or Gastronomy and Gastronomers. Post 8vo. 2s.

HEAD'S (Sir Francis) WORKS:—

    The Royal Engineer. Illustrations. 8vo. 12s.

    Life of Sir John Burgoyne. Post 8vo. 1s.

    Rapid Journeys across the Pampas. Post 8vo. 2s.

    Bubbles from the Brunnen. Illustrations. Post 8vo. 7s. 6d.

    Stokers and Pokers; or, the London and North Western Railway. Post 8vo. 2s.

HEBER'S (Bishop) Journals in India. 2 Vols. Post 8vo. 7s.

——— Poetical Works. Portrait. Fcap. 8vo. 3s. 6d.

——— Hymns adapted to the Church Service. 16mo. 1s. 6d.

HERODOTUS. A New English Version. Edited, with Notes and Essays, Historical, Ethnographical, and Geographical, by Canon Rawlinson, Sir H. Rawlinson and Sir J. G. Wilkinson. Maps and Woodcuts. 4 Vols. 8vo. 48s.

HERRIES (Rt. Hon. John). Memoir of his Public Life. Founded on his Letters and other Unpublished Documents. By his son, Edward Herries, C.B. 2 Vols. 8vo. 24s.

HERSCHEL'S (Caroline) Memoir and Correspondence. By Mrs. John Herschel. With Portrait. Crown 8vo. 7s. 6d.

FOREIGN HANDBOOKS.

HAND-BOOK—TRAVEL-TALK. English, French, German, and Italian. New and Revised Edition. 18mo. 3s. 6d.

——— DICTIONARY: English, French, and German. Containing all the words and idiomatic phrases likely to be required by a traveller. Bound in leather. 16mo. 6s.

——— HOLLAND AND BELGIUM. Map and Plans. Post 8vo. 6s.

——— NORTH GERMANY and THE RHINE,— The Black Forest, the Hartz, Thüringerwald, Saxon Switzerland, Rügen, the Giant Mountains, Taunus, Odenwald, Elsass, and Lothringen. Map and Plans. Post 8vo. 10s.

——— SOUTH GERMANY,— Wurtemburg, Bavaria, Austria, Styria, Salzburg, the Alps, Tyrol, Hungary, and the Danube, from Ulm to the Black Sea. Maps and Plans. Post 8vo. 10s.

——— SWITZERLAND, Alps of Savoy, and Piedmont. In Two Parts. Maps and Plans. Post 8vo. 10s.

———FRANCE, Part I. Normandy, Brittany, the French Alps, the Loire, Seine, Garonne, and Pyrenees. Maps and Plans. Post 8vo. 7s. 6d.

———FRANCE, Part II. Central France, Auvergne, the Cevennes, Burgundy, the Rhone and Saone, Provence, Nimes, Arles, Marseilles, the French Alps, Alsace, Lorraine, Champagne, &c. Maps and Plans. Post 8vo. 7s. 6d.

HAND-BOOK—MEDITERRANEAN—its Principal Islands, Cities, Seaports, Harbours, and Border Lands. For Travellers and Yachtsmen, with nearly 50 Maps and Plans. Post 8vo. 20s.

————— ALGERIA AND TUNIS. Algiers, Constantine, Oran, the Atlas Range. Maps and Plans. Post 8vo. 10s.

————— PARIS, and Environs. Maps and Plans. 3s. 6d.

————— SPAIN, Madrid, The Castiles, The Basque Provinces, Leon, The Asturias, Galicia, Estremadura, Andalusia, Ronda, Granada, Murcia, Valencia, Catalonia, Aragon, Navarre, The Balearic Islands, &c.&c. In Two Parts. Maps and Plans. Post 8vo. 20s.

————— PORTUGAL, Lisbon, Oporto, Cintra, Mafra, &c. Map and Plan. Post 8vo. 12s.

————— NORTH ITALY, Turin, Milan, Cremona, the Italian Lakes, Bergamo, Brescia, Verona, Mantua, Vicenza, Padua, Ferrara, Bologna, Ravenna, Rimini, Piacenza, Genoa, the Riviera, Venice, Parma, Modena, and Romagna. Maps and Plans. Post 8vo. 10s.

————— CENTRAL ITALY, Florence, Lucca, Tuscany, The Marshes, Umbria, &c. Maps and Plans. Post 8vo. 10s.

————— ROME and its Environs. With 50 Maps and Plans. Post 8vo. 10s.

————— SOUTH ITALY, Naples, Pompeii, Herculaneum, and Vesuvius. Maps and Plans. Post 8vo. 10s.

————— NORWAY, Christiania, Bergen, Trondhjem. The Fjelds and Fjords. Maps and Plans. Post 8vo. 9s.

————— SWEDEN, Stockholm, Upsala, Gothenburg, the Shores of the Baltic, &c. Maps and Plan. Post 8vo. 6s.

————— DENMARK, Sleswig, Holstein, Copenhagen, Jutland, Iceland. Maps and Plans. Post 8vo. 6s.

————— RUSSIA, St. Petersburg, Moscow, Poland, and Finland. Maps and Plans. Post 8vo. 18s.

————— GREECE, the Ionian Islands, Athens, the Peloponnesus, the Islands of the Ægean Sea, Albania, Thessaly, Macedonia, &c. In Two Parts. Maps, Plans, and Views. Post 8vo. 24s.

————— TURKEY IN ASIA—Constantinople, the Bosphorus, Dardanelles, Brousa, Plain of Troy, Crete, Cyprus, Smyrna, Ephesus, the Seven Churches, Coasts of the Black Sea, Armenia, Euphrates Valley, Route to India, &c. Maps and Plans. Post 8vo. 15s.

————— EGYPT, including Descriptions of the Course of the Nile through Egypt and Nubia, Alexandria, Cairo, and Thebes, the Suez Canal, the Pyramids, the Peninsula of Sinai, the Oases, the Fyoom, &c. In Two Parts. Maps and Plans. Post 8vo. 15s.

————— HOLY LAND—Syria, Palestine, Peninsula of Sinai, Edom, Syrian Deserts, Petra, Damascus; and Palmyra. Maps and Plans. Post 8vo. 20s.
     ⁎ Map of Palestine. In a case. 12s.

————— JAPAN—Being a Guide to Tokio, Kioto, Ozaka, Hakodate, Nagasaki, and other cities. The most interesting parts of the Main Island; Ascents of the Principal Mountains; Descriptions of Temples; and Historical Notes and Legends. By E. M. Satow, and Lieut. A. G. B. Hawks. With Maps and Plans. Post 8vo. 21s.

————— BOMBAY — Poonah, Beejapoor, Kolapoor, Goa, Jubulpoor, Indore, Surat, Baroda, Ahmedabad, Somnauth, Kurrachee, &c. Map and Plans. Post 8vo. 15s.

HANDBOOK—MADRAS—Trichinopoli, Madura, Tinnevelly, Tuticorin, Bangalore, Mysore, The Nilgiris, Wynaad, Ootacamund, Calicut,
Hyderabad, Ajanta, Elura Caves, &c. Maps and Plans. Post 8vo. 15s.

———————— BENGAL — Calcutta, Orissa, British Burmah,
Rangoon, Moulmein, Mandalay, Darjiling, Dacca, Patna, Benares,
N.-W. Provinces, Allahabad, Cawnpore, Lucknow, Agra, Gwalior,
Naini Tal, Delhi, &c. Maps and Plans. Post 8vo. 20s

———————— THE PANJAB—Amraoti, Indore, Ajmir, Jaypur,
Rohtak, Saharanpur, Ambala, Lodiana, Lahore, Kulu, Simla, Sialkot,
Peshawar, Rawul Pindi, Attock, Karachi, Sibi, &c. Maps. 15s.

ENGLISH HAND-BOOKS.

HAND-BOOK—ENGLAND AND WALES. An Alphabetical
Hand-Book. Condensed into One Volume for the Use of Travellers.
With a Map. Post 8vo. 10s.

———————— LONDON. Maps and Plans. 16mo. 3s. 6d.

———————— ENVIRONS OF LONDON within a circuit of 20
miles. 2 Vols. Crown 8vo. 21s.

———————— ST. PAUL'S CATHEDRAL. 20 Woodcuts. 10s. 6d.

———————— EASTERN COUNTIES, Chelmsford, Harwich, Col-
chester, Maldon, Cambridge, Ely, Newmarket, Bury St. Edmunds,
Ipswich, Woodbridge, Felixstowe, Lowestoft, Norwich, Yarmouth,
Cromer, &c. Map and Plans. Post 8vo. 12s.

———————— CATHEDRALS of Oxford, Peterborough, Norwich,
Ely, and Lincoln. With 90 Illustrations. Crown 8vo. 21s.

———————— KENT, Canterbury, Dover, Ramsgate, Sheerness,
Rochester, Chatham, Woolwich. Maps and Plans. Post 8vo. 7s. 6d.

———————— SUSSEX, Brighton, Chichester, Worthing, Hastings,
Lewes, Arundel, &c. Maps and Plans. Post 8vo. 6s.

———————— SURREY AND HANTS, Kingston, Croydon, Rei-
gate, Guildford, Dorking, Winchester, Southampton, New Forest,
Portsmouth, ISLE OF WIGHT, &c. Maps and Plans. Post 8vo. 10s.

———————— BERKS, BUCKS, AND OXON, Windsor, Eton,
Reading, Aylesbury, Uxbridge, Wycombe, Henley, Oxford, Blenheim,
the Thames, &c. Maps and Plans. Post 8vo. 9s.

———————— WILTS, DORSET, AND SOMERSET, Salisbury,
Chippenham, Weymouth, Sherborne, Wells, Bath, Bristol, Taunton,
&c. Map. Post 8vo. 12s.

———————— DEVON, Exeter, Ilfracombe, Linton, Sidmouth,
Dawlish, Teignmouth, Plymouth, Devonport, Torquay. Maps and Plans.
Post 8vo. 7s. 6d.

———————— CORNWALL, Launceston, Penzance, Falmouth,
the Lizard, Land's-End, &c. Maps. Post 8vo. 6s.

———————— CATHEDRALS of Winchester, Salisbury, Exeter,
Wells, Chichester, Rochester, Canterbury, and St. Albans. With 130
Illustrations. 2 Vols. Crown 8vo. 36s. St. Albans separately. 6s.

———————— GLOUCESTER, HEREFORD, AND WORCESTER,
Cirencester, Cheltenham, Stroud, Tewkesbury, Leominster, Ross, Mal-
vern, Kidderminster, Dudley, Bromsgrove, Evesham. Map. Post 8vo.

———————— CATHEDRALS of Bristol, Gloucester, Hereford,
Worcester, and Lichfield. With 50 Illustrations. Crown 8vo. 16s.

———————— NORTH WALES, Bangor, Carnarvon, Beaumaris,
Snowdon, Llanberis, Dolgelly, Conway, &c. Map. Post 8vo.

HAND-BOOK—SOUTH WALES, Monmouth, Llandaff, Merthyr, Vale of Neath, Pembroke, Carmarthen, Tenby, Swansea, The Wye, &c. Map. Post 8vo. 7s.

———— CATHEDRALS OF BANGOR, ST. ASAPH, Llandaff, and St. David's. With Illustrations. Post 8vo. 15s.

———— NORTHAMPTONSHIRE AND RUTLAND— Northampton, Peterborough, Towcester, Daventry, Market Harborough, Kettering, Wellingborough, Thrapston, Stamford, Uppingham, Oakham. Maps. Post 8vo. 7s. 6d.

———— DERBY, NOTTS, LEICESTER, STAFFORD, Matlock, Bakewell, Chatsworth, The Peak, Buxton, Hardwick, Dove Dale, Ashborne, Southwell, Mansfield, Retford, Burton, Belvoir, Melton Mowbray, Wolverhampton, Lichfield, Walsall, Tamworth. Map. Post 8vo. 9s.

———— SHROPSHIRE AND CHESHIRE, Shrewsbury, Ludlow, Bridgnorth, Oswestry, Chester, Crewe, Alderley, Stockport, Birkenhead. Maps and Plans. Post 8vo. 6s.

———— LANCASHIRE, Warrington, Bury, Manchester, Liverpool, Burnley, Clitheroe, Bolton, Blackburne, Wigan, Preston, Rochdale, Lancaster, Southport, Blackpool, &c. Maps & Plans. Post 8vo. 7s. 6d.

———— YORKSHIRE, Doncaster, Hull, Selby, Beverley, Scarborough, Whitby, Harrogate, Ripon, Leeds, Wakefield, Bradford, Halifax, Huddersfield, Sheffield. Map and Plans. Post 8vo. 12s.

———— CATHEDRALS of York, Ripon, Durham, Carlisle, Chester, and Manchester. With 60 Illustrations. 2 Vols. Cr. 8vo. 21s.

———— DURHAM AND NORTHUMBERLAND, Newcastle, Darlington, Stockton, Hartlepool, Shields, Berwick-on-Tweed, Morpeth, Tynemouth, Coldstream, Alnwick, &c. Map. Post 8vo. 9s.

———— WESTMORELAND AND CUMBERLAND—Map.

———— SCOTLAND, Edinburgh, Melrose, Kelso, Glasgow, Dumfries, Ayr, Stirling, Arran, The Clyde, Oban, Inverary, Loch Lomond, Loch Katrine and Trossachs, Caledonian Canal, Inverness, Perth, Dundee, Aberdeen, Braemar, Skye, Caithness, Ross, Sutherland, &c. Maps and Plans. Post 8vo. 9s.

———— IRELAND, Dublin, Belfast, the Giant's Causeway, Donegal, Galway, Wexford, Cork, Limerick, Waterford, Killarney, Bantry, Glengariff, &c. Maps and Plans. Post 8vo. 10s.

HOLLWAY (J. G.). A Month in Norway. Fcap. 8vo. 2s.

HONEY BEE. By Rev. Thomas James. Fcap. 8vo. 1s.

HOOK (Dean). Church Dictionary. 8vo. 16s.

—— (Theodore) Life. By J. G. Lockhart. Fcap. 8vo. 1s.

HOPE (A. J. Beresford). Worship in the Church of England. 8vo. 9s., or, Popular Selections from. 8vo. 2s. 6d.

——WORSHIP AND ORDER. 8vo. 9s.

HOPE-SCOTT (James), Memoir. [See Ornsby.]

HORACE; a New Edition of the Text. Edited by Dean Milman. With 100 Woodcuts. Crown 8vo. 7s. 6d.

HOSACK (John). The rise and growth of the Law of Nations : as established by general usage and by treaties, from the earliest times to the treaty of Utrecht. 8vo. 12s.

HOUGHTON'S (Lord) Monographs, Personal and Social. With Portraits. Crown 8vo. 10s. 6d.

———— POETICAL WORKS. Collected Edition. With Portrait. 2 Vols. Fcap. 8vo. 12s.

HOUSTOUN (Mrs.). Twenty Years in the Wild West of Ireland, or Life in Connaught. Post 8vo. 9s.

HOME AND COLONIAL LIBRARY. A Series of Works adapted for all circles and classes of Readers, having been selected for their acknowledged interest, and ability of the Authors. Post 8vo. Published at 2s. and 3s. 6d. each, and arranged under two distinctive heads as follows :—

CLASS A.
HISTORY, BIOGRAPHY, AND HISTORIC TALES.

1. SIEGE OF GIBRALTAR. By John Drinkwater. 2s.
2. THE AMBER-WITCH. By Lady Duff Gordon. 2s.
3. CROMWELL AND BUNYAN. By Robert Southey. 2s.
4. LIFE of Sir FRANCIS DRAKE. By John Barrow. 2s.
5. CAMPAIGNS AT WASHINGTON. By Rev. G. R. Gleig. 2s.
6. THE FRENCH IN ALGIERS. By Lady Duff Gordon. 2s.
7. THE FALL OF THE JESUITS. 2s.
8. LIVONIAN TALES. 2s.
9. LIFE OF CONDÉ. By Lord Mahon. 3s. 6d.
10. SALE'S BRIGADE. By Rev. G. R. Gleig. 2s.
11. THE SIEGES OF VIENNA. By Lord Ellesmere. 2s.
12. THE WAYSIDE CROSS. By Capt. Milman. 2s.
13. SKETCHES of GERMAN LIFE. By Sir A. Gordon. 3s. 6d.
14. THE BATTLE of WATERLOO. By Rev. G. R. Gleig. 3s. 6d.
15. AUTOBIOGRAPHY OF STEFFENS. 2s.
16. THE BRITISH POETS. By Thomas Campbell. 3s. 6d.
17. HISTORICAL ESSAYS. By Lord Mahon. 3s. 6d.
18. LIFE OF LORD CLIVE. By Rev. G. R. Gleig. 3s. 6d.
19. NORTH - WESTERN RAILWAY. By Sir F. B. Head. 2s.
20. LIFE OF MUNRO. By Rev. G. R. Gleig. 3s. 6d.

CLASS B.
VOYAGES, TRAVELS, AND ADVENTURES.

1. BIBLE IN SPAIN. By George Borrow. 3s. 6d.
2. GYPSIES of SPAIN. By George Borrow. 3s. 6d.
3 & 4. JOURNALS IN INDIA. By Bishop Heber. 2 Vols. 7s.
5. TRAVELS in the HOLY LAND. By Irby and Mangles. 2s.
6. MOROCCO AND THE MOORS. By J. Drummond Hay. 2s.
7. LETTERS FROM the BALTIC. By A Lady. 2s.
8. NEW SOUTH WALES. By Mrs. Meredith. 2s.
9. THE WEST INDIES. By M. G. Lewis. 2s.
10. SKETCHES OF PERSIA. By Sir John Malcolm. 3s. 6d.
11. MEMOIRS OF FATHER RIPA. 2s.
12 & 13. TYPEE AND OMOO. By Hermann Melville. 2 Vols. 7s.
14. MISSIONARY LIFE IN CANADA. By Rev. J. Abbott. 2s.
15. LETTERS FROM MADRAS. By A Lady. 2s.
16. HIGHLAND SPORTS. By Charles St. John. 3s. 6d.
17. PAMPAS JOURNEYS. By Sir F. B. Head. 2s.
18. GATHERINGS FROM SPAIN. By Richard Ford. 3s. 6d.
19. THE RIVER AMAZON. By W. H. Edwards. 2s.
20. MANNERS & CUSTOMS OF INDIA. By Rev. C. Acland. 2s.
21. ADVENTURES IN MEXICO. By G. F. Ruxton. 3s. 6d.
22. PORTUGAL AND GALICIA. By Lord Carnarvon. 3s. 6d.
23. BUSH LIFE IN AUSTRALIA. By Rev. H. W. Haygarth. 2s.
24. THE LIBYAN DESERT. By Bayle St. John. 2s.
25. SIERRA LEONE. By A Lady. 3s. 6d.

*** Each work may be had separately.

c

HUME (The Student's).   A History of England, from the Invasion of Julius Cæsar to the Revolution of 1688. New Edition, revised, corrected, and continued to the Treaty of Berlin, 1878. By J. S. BREWER, M.A. With 7 Coloured Maps & 70 Woodcuts. Post 8vo. 7s. 6d.
          *** Sold also in 3 parts. Price 2s. 6d. each.

HUTCHINSON (GEN.).   Dog Breaking, with Odds and Ends for those who love the Dog and the Gun. With 40 Illustrations. Crown 8vo. 7s. 6d. *** A Summary of the Rules for Gamekeepers. 1s.

HUTTON (H. E.).   Principia Græca; an Introduction to the Study of Greek. Comprehending Grammar, Delectus, and Exercise-book, with Vocabularies. Sixth Edition. 12mo. 3s. 6d.

———— (JAMES).   James and Philip van Artevelde. Two remarkable Episodes in the annals of Flanders: with a description of the state of Society in Flanders in the 14th Century. Cr. 8vo. 10s. 6d.

HYMNOLOGY, DICTIONARY OF.   [See JULIAN.]

ICELAND.   [See COLES—DUFFERIN.]

INDIA.   [See ELPHINSTONE — HAND-BOOK — SMITH—TEMPLE— MONIER WILLIAMS—LYALL.]

IRBY AND MANGLES' Travels in Egypt, Nubia, Syria, and the Holy Land. Post 8vo. 2s.

JAMES (F. L.).   The Wild Tribes of the Soudan: with an account of the route from Wady Halfah to Dongola and Berber. A new and cheaper edition with prefatory Chapter on the Soudan. - By SIR. S. BAKER. With Illustrations. Crown 8vo.

JAMESON (MRS.).   Lives of the Early Italian Painters— and the Progress of Painting in Italy—Cimabue to Bassano. With 50 Portraits. Post 8vo. 12s.

JAPAN.   [See BIRD—MOSSMAN—MOUNSEY—REED.]

JENNINGS (LOUIS J.).   Rambles among the Hills in the Peak of Derbyshire and on the South Downs. With sketches of people by the way. With 23 Illustrations. Crown 8vo. 12s.

———— Field Paths and Green Lanes : or Walks in Surrey and Sussex. Fourth and Popular Edition. With Illustrations. Crown 8vo.

JERVIS (REV. W. H.).   The Gallican Church, from the Concordat of Bologna, 1516, to the Revolution. With an Introduction. Portraits. 2 Vols. 8vo. 28s.

JESSE (EDWARD).   Gleanings in Natural History. Fcp. 8vo. 3s. 6d.

JOHNSON'S (DR. SAMUEL) Life. See Boswell.

JULIAN (REV. JOHN J.).   A Dictionary of Hymnology. A Companion to Existing Hymn Books. Setting forth the Origin and History of the Hymns contained in the Principal Hymnals, with Notices of their Authors. Post 8vo.   [In the Press.

JUNIUS' HANDWRITING Professionally investigated. Edited by the Hon. E. TWISLETON. With Facsimiles, Woodcuts, &c. 4to. £3 3s.

KING EDWARD VITH's Latin Grammar. 12mo. 3s. 6d.

———————————————— First Latin Book. 12mo. 2s. 6d.

KIRK (J. FOSTER).   History of Charles the Bold, Duke of Burgundy. Portrait. 3 Vols. 8vo. 45s.

KIRKES' Handbook of Physiology. Edited by W. MORRANT BAKER, F.R.C.S. With 400 Illustrations. Post 8vo. 14s.

KUGLER'S Handbook of Painting.—The Italian Schools. Revised and Remodelled from the most recent Researches. By LADY EASTLAKE. With 140 Illustrations. 2 Vols. Crown 8vo. 30s.

———— Handbook of Painting.—The German, Flemish, and Dutch Schools. Revised and in part re-written. By J. A. CROWE. With 60 Illustrations. 2 Vols. Crown 8vo. 24s.

LANE (E. W.). Account of the Manners and Customs of Modern Egyptians. With Illustrations. 2 Vols. Post 8vo. 12s.

LAYARD (Sir A. H.). Nineveh and its Remains: Researches and Discoveries amidst the Ruins of Assyria. With Illustrations. Post 8vo. 7s. 6d.

———— Nineveh and Babylon: Discoveries in the Ruins, with Travels in Armenia, Kurdistan, and the Desert. With Illustrations. Post 8vo. 7s. 6d.

LEATHES (Stanley). Practical Hebrew Grammar. With the Hebrew Text of Genesis i.—vi., and Psalms i.—vi. Grammatical Analysis and Vocabulary. Post 8vo. 7s. 6d.

LENNEP (Rev. H. J. Van). Missionary Travels in Asia Minor. With Illustrations of Biblical History and Archæology. Map and Woodcuts. 2 Vols. Post 8vo. 24s.

———— Modern Customs and Manners of Bible Lands in Illustration of Scripture. Maps and Illustrations. 2 Vols. 8vo. 21s.

LESLIE (C. R.). Handbook for Young Painters. Illustrations. Post 8vo. 7s. 6d.

———— Life and Works of Sir Joshua Reynolds. Portraits. 2 Vols. 8vo. 42s.

LETO (Pomponio). Eight Months at Rome during the Vatican Council. 8vo. 12s.

LETTERS From the Baltic. By A Lady. Post 8vo. 2s.

———— Madras. By A Lady. Post 8vo. 2s.

———— Sierra Leone. By A Lady. Post 8vo. 3s. 6d.

LEVI (Leone). History of British Commerce; and Economic Progress of the Nation, from 1763 to 1878. 8vo. 16s.

LEX SALICA; the Ten Texts with the Glosses and the Lex Emendata. Synoptically edited by J. H. Hessels. With Notes on the Frankish Words in the Lex Salica by H. Kern, of Leyden. 4to. 42s.

LIDDELL (Dean). Student's History of Rome, from the earliest Times to the establishment of the Empire. Woodcuts. Post 8vo. 7s. 6d.

LISPINGS from LOW LATITUDES; or, the Journal of the Hon. Impulsia Gushington. Edited by Lord Dufferin. With 24 Plates. 4to. 21s.

LIVINGSTONE (Dr.). First Expedition to Africa, 1840-56. Illustrations. Post 8vo. 7s. 6d.

———— Second Expedition to Africa, 1858-64. Illustrations. Post 8vo. 7s. 6d.

———— Last Journals in Central Africa, from 1865 to his Death. Continued by a Narrative of his last moments and sufferings. By Rev. Horace Waller. Maps and Illustrations. 2 Vols. 8vo. 15s.

———— Personal Life. By Wm. G. Blaikie, D.D. With Map and Portrait. 8vo. 6s.

LIVINGSTONIA. Journal of Adventures in Exploring Lake Nyassa, and Establishing a Missionary Settlement there. By E. D. Young, R.N. Maps. Post 8vo. 7s. 6d.

LIVONIAN TALES. By the Author of "Letters from the Baltic." Post 8vo. 2s.

LOCKHART (J. G.). Ancient Spanish Ballads. Historical and Romantic. Translated, with Notes. Illustrations. Crown 8vo. 5s.

———— Life of Theodore Hook. Fcap. 8vo. 1s.

LONDON: its History, Antiquarian and Modern. Founded on the work by the late Peter Cunningham, F S.A. A new and thoroughly revised edition. By James Thorne, F.S.A. and H. B. Wheatley. Fine library edition, on laid paper. 3 vols. Royal 8vo.

LOUDON (Mrs.). Gardening for Ladies. With Directions and Calendar of Operations for Every Month. Woodcuts. Fcap. 8vo. 3s. 6d.

c 2

LUTHER (MARTIN). The First Principles of the Reformation, or the Ninety-five Theses and Three Primary Works of Dr. Martin Luther. Translated and edited, with Introductions, by HENRY WACE, D.D., and PROF. BUCHHEIM. Portrait. 8vo. 12s.

LYALL (SIR ALFRED C.), K.C.B. Asiatic Studies; Religious and Social. 8vo. 12s.

LYELL (SIR CHARLES). Student's Elements of Geology. A new Edition, entirely revised by PROFESSOR P. M. DUNCAN, F.R.S. With 600 Illustrations. Post 8vo. 9s.
———— Life, Letters, and Journals. Edited by his sister-in-law, MRS. LYELL. With Portraits. 2 Vols. 8vo. 30s.
———— (K. M.). Geographical Handbook of Ferns. With Tables to show their Distribution. Post 8vo. 7s. 6d.

LYNDHURST (LORD). [See Martin.]   [8vo. 5s.

LYTTON (LORD). A Memoir of Julian Fane. With Portrait. Post

M°CLINTOCK (SIR L.). Narrative of the Discovery of the Fate of Sir John Franklin and his Companions in the Arctic Seas. With Illustrations. Post 8vo. 7s. 6d.

MACGREGOR (J.). Rob Roy on the Jordan, Nile, Red Sea, Gennesareth, &c. A Canoe Cruise in Palestine and Egypt and the Waters of Damascus. With 70 Illustrations. Crown 8vo. 7s. 6d.

MAETZNER'S ENGLISH GRAMMAR. A Methodical, Analytical, and Historical Treatise on the Orthography, Prosody, Inflections, and Syntax. By CLAIR J. GRECE, LL.D. 3 Vols. 8vo. 36s.

MAHON (LORD). [See STANHOPE.]

MAINE (SIR H. SUMNER). Ancient Law: its Connection with the Early History of Society, and its Relation to Modern Ideas. 8vo. 12s.
———— Village Communities in the East and West. 8vo. 12s.
———— Early History of Institutions. 8vo. 12s.
———— Dissertations on Early Law and Custom. Chiefly Selected from Lectures delivered at Oxford. 8vo. 12s.

MALCOLM (SIR JOHN). Sketches of Persia. Post 8vo. 3s. 6d.

MALLOCK (W. H.). Property and Progress : or, Facts against Fallacies. A brief Enquiry into Contemporary Social Agitation in England. Post 8vo. 6s.

MANSEL (DEAN). Letters, Lectures, and Reviews. 8vo. 12s.

MANUAL OF SCIENTIFIC ENQUIRY. For the Use of Travellers. Edited by REV. R. MAIN. Post 8vo. 3s. 6d. (Published by order of the Lords of the Admiralty.)

MARCO POLO. The Book of Ser Marco Polo, the Venetian. Concerning the Kingdoms and Marvels of the East. A new English Version. Illustrated by the light of the Oriental Writers and Modern Travels. By COL. HENRY YULE. Maps and Illustrations. 2 Vols. Medium 8vo. 63s

MARKHAM (MRS.). History of England. From the First Invasion by the Romans, continued down to 1880. Woodcuts. 12mo. 3s. 6d.
———— History of France. From the Conquest of Gaul by Julius Cæsar, continued down to 1878. Woodcuts. 12mo. 3s. 6d.
———— History of Germany. From its Invasion by Marius, continued down to the completion of Cologne Cathedral. Woodcuts. 12mo. 3s. 6d.
———— (CLEMENTS R.). A Popular Account of Peruvian Bark and its introduction into British India. With Maps. Post 8vo. 14s.

MARSH (G. P.). Student's Manual of the English Language. Edited with Additions. By DR. WM. SMITH. Post 8vo. 7s. 6d.

MARTIN (Sir Theodore). Life of Lord Lyndhurst, three times Lord Chancellor of England. From Letters and Papers in possession of his family. With Portraits. 8vo. 16s.

MASTERS in English Theology. Lectures delivered at King's College, London, in 1877, by Eminent Divines. With Introduction by Canon Barry. Post 8vo. 7s. 6d.

MATTHIÆ'S Greek Grammar. Abridged by Blomfield. Revised by E. S. Crooke. 12mo. 4s.

MAUREL'S Character, Actions, and Writings of Wellington. Fcap. 8vo. 1s. 6d.

MAYO (Lord). Sport in Abyssinia; or, the Mareb and Tackazzee. With Illustrations. Crown 8vo. 12s.

MELVILLE (Hermann). Marquesas and South Sea Islands. 2 Vols. Post 8vo. 7s.

MEREDITH (Mrs. Charles). Notes and Sketches of New South Wales. Post 8vo. 2s.

MEXICO. [See Brocklehurst.]

MICHAEL ANGELO, Sculptor, Painter, and Architect. His Life and Works. By C. Heath Wilson. With Portrait, Illustrations, and Index. 8vo. 15s.

MIDDLETON (Chas. H.) A Descriptive Catalogue of the Etched Work of Rembrandt, with Life and Introductions. With Explanatory Cuts. Medium 8vo. 31s. 6d.

MILLER (Wm.). A Dictionary of English Plant Names, with their Latin Equivalents; applied to Cultivated, Native, and Foreign Plants, Trees, and Shrubs, and including Popular Names of British, American, Australian, and other Colonial Plants. In Two Parts. Latin-English and English-Latin. Medium 8vo.

MILLINGTON (Rev. T. S.). Signs and Wonders in the Land of Ham, or the Ten Plagues of Egypt, with Ancient and Modern Illustrations. Woodcuts. Post 8vo. 7s. 6d.

MILMAN'S (Dean) WORKS:—

History of the Jews, from the earliest Period down to Modern Times. 3 Vols. Post 8vo. 12s.

Early Christianity, from the Birth of Christ to the Abolition of Paganism in the Roman Empire. 3 Vols. Post 8vo. 12s.

Latin Christianity, including that of the Popes to the Pontificate of Nicholas V. 9 Vols. Post 8vo. 36s.

Handbook to St. Paul's Cathedral. Woodcuts. Crown 8vo. 10s. 6d.

Quinti Horatii Flacci Opera. Woodcuts. Sm. 8vo. 7s. 6d.

Fall of Jerusalem. Fcap. 8vo. 1s.

———— (Capt. E. A.) Wayside Cross. Post 8vo. 2s.

———— (Bishop, D.D.,) Life. With a Selection from his Correspondence and Journals. By his Sister. Map. 8vo. 12s.

MIVART (St. George). Lessons from Nature; as manifested in Mind and Matter. 8vo. 15s.

———— The Cat. An Introduction to the Study of Backboned Animals, especially Mammals. With 200 Illustrations. Medium 8vo. 30s.

MOGGRIDGE (M. W.). Method in Almsgiving. A Handbook for Helpers. Post 8vo. 3s. 6d.

MONTEFIORE (Sir Moses). A Centennial Biography. With Selections from Letters and Journals. By Lucien Wolf. With Portrait. Crown 8vo.

MOORE (Thomas). Life and Letters of Lord Byron. Cabinet Edition. With Plates. 6 Vols. Fcap. 8vo. 18s.; Popular Edition, with Portraits. Royal 8vo, 7s. 6d.

MOTLEY (J. L.). History of the United Netherlands: from the Death of William the Silent to the Twelve Years' Truce, 1609. Portraits. 4 Vols. Post 8vo. 6s. each.

———— Life and Death of John of Barneveld. With a View of the Primary Causes and Movements of the Thirty Years' War. Illustrations. 2 Vols. Post 8vo. 12s.

MOZLEY (Canon). Treatise on the Augustinian doctrine of Predestination, with an Analysis of the Contents. Crown 8vo. 9s.

MUIRHEAD (Jas.). The Vaux-de-Vire of Maistre Jean Le Houx. With Portrait and Illustrations. 8vo. 21s.

MUNRO'S (General) Life and Letters. By Rev. G. R. Gleig. Post 8vo. 3s. 6d.

MURCHISON (Sir Roderick). Siluria; or, a History of the Oldest Rocks containing Organic Remains. Map and Plates. 8vo. 18s.

———— Memoirs. With Notices of his Contemporaries, and Rise and Progress of Palæozoic Geology. By Archibald Geikie. Portraits. 2 Vols. 8vo. 30s.

MURRAY (A. S.). A History of Greek Sculpture from the Earliest Times. With 130 Illustrations. 2 Vols. Royal 8vo. 52s. 6d.

MUSTERS' (Capt.) Patagonians; a Year's Wanderings over Untrodden Ground from the Straits of Magellan to the Rio Negro. Illustrations. Post 8vo. 7s. 6d.

NADAILLAC (Marquis de). Prehistoric America. Translated by N. D'Anvers. With Illustrations. 8vo.

NAPIER (Genl. Sir George T.). Passages in his Early Military Life written by himself. Edited by his Son, General Wm. C. E. Napier. With Portrait. Crown 8vo.

NAPIER (Sir Wm.). English Battles and Sieges of the Peninsular War. Portrait. Post 8vo. 9s.

NAPOLEON at Fontainebleau and Elba. Journals. Notes of Conversations. By Sir Neil Campbell. Portrait. 8vo. 15s.

NASMYTH (James). An Autobiography. Edited by Samuel Smiles, LL.D., with Portrait, and 70 Illustrations. Crown 8vo. 16s.

NAUTICAL ALMANAC (The). (By Authority.) 2s. 6d.

NAVY LIST. (Monthly and Quarterly.) Post 8vo.

NEW TESTAMENT. With Short Explanatory Commentary. By Archdeacon Churton, M.A., and the Bishop of St. David's. With 110 authentic Views, &c. 2 Vols. Crown 8vo. 21s. bound.

NEWTH (Samuel). First Book of Natural Philosophy; an Introduction to the Study of Statics, Dynamics, Hydrostatics, Light, Heat, and Sound, with numerous Examples. Small 8vo. 3s. 6d.

———— Elements of Mechanics, including Hydrostatics, with numerous Examples. Small 8vo. 8s. 6d.

———— Mathematical Examples. A Graduated Series of Elementary Examples in Arithmetic, Algebra, Logarithms, Trigonometry, and Mechanics. Small 8vo. 8s. 6d.

NICOLAS (Sir Harris). Historic Peerage of England. Exhibiting the Origin, Descent, and Present State of every Title of Peerage which has existed in this Country since the Conquest. By William Courthope. 8vo. 30s.

NIMROD, On the Chace—Turf—and Road. With Portrait and Plates. Crown 8vo. 5s. Or with Coloured Plates, 7s. 6d.

NORDHOFF (Chas.). Communistic Societies of the United States. With 40 Illustrations. 8vo. 15s.

NORTHCOTE'S (Sir John) Notebook in the Long Parliament. Containing Proceedings during its First Session, 1640. Edited, with a Memoir, by A. H. A. Hamilton. Crown 8vo. 9s.

ORNSBY (Prof. R.). Memoirs of J. Hope Scott, Q. C. (of Abbotsford). With Selections from his Correspondence. 2 vols. 8vo. 24s.

OTTER (R. H.). Winters Abroad : Some Information respecting Places visited by the Author on account of his Health. Intended for the Use and Guidance of Invalids. 7s. 6d.

OWEN (Lieut.-Col.). Principles and Practice of Modern Artillery, including Artillery Material, Gunnery, and Organisation and Use of Artillery in Warfare. With Illustrations. 8vo. 15s.

OXENHAM (Rev. W.). English Notes for Latin Elegiacs ; designed for early Proficients in the Art of Latin Versification, with Prefatory Rules of Composition in Elegiac Metre. 12mo. 3s. 6d.

PAGET (Lord George). The Light Cavalry Brigade in the Crimea. Map. Crown 8vo. 10s. 6d.

PALGRAVE (R. H. I.). Local Taxation of Great Britain and Ireland. 8vo. 5s.

PALLISER (Mrs.). Mottoes for Monuments, or Epitaphs selected for General Use and Study. With Illustrations. Crown 8vo. 7s. 6d.

PALMER (Professor), Life of. [See Besant.]

PARIS (Dr.) Philosophy in Sport made Science in Earnest ; or, the First Principles of Natural Philosophy inculcated by aid of the Toys and Sports of Youth. Woodcuts. Post 8vo. 7s. 6d.

PARKYNS' (Mansfield) Three Years' Residence in Abyssinia : with Travels in that Country. With Illustrations. Post 8vo. 7s. 6d.

PEEL'S (Sir Robert) Memoirs. 2 Vols. Post 8vo. 15s.

PENN (Richard). Maxims and Hints for an Angler and Chess-player. Woodcuts. Fcap. 8vo. 1s.

PERCY (John, M.D.). Metallurgy. Fuel, Wood, Peat, Coal, Charcoal, Coke, Fire-Clays. Illustrations. 8vo. 30s.

———— Lead, including part of Silver. Illustrations. 8vo. 30s:

———— Silver and Gold. Part I. Illustrations. 8vo. 30s.

PERRY (Rev. Canon). Life of St. Hugh of Avalon, Bishop of Lincoln. Post 8vo. 10s. 6d.

———— History of the English Church. See Students' Manuals.

PHILLIPS (Samuel). Literary Essays from "The Times." With Portrait. 2 Vols. Fcap. 8vo. 7s.

POLLOCK (C. E.). A book of Family Prayers. Selected from the Liturgy of the Church of England. 16mo. 3s. 6d.

POPE'S (Alexander) Works. With Introductions and Notes, by Rev. Whitwell Elwin, and W. J. Courthope. Vols. I., II., III., IV., VI., VII., VIII. With Portraits. 8vo. 10s. 6d. each.

PORTER (Rev. J. L.). Damascus, Palmyra, and Lebanon. With Travels among the Giant Cities of Bashan and the Hauran. Map and Woodcuts. Post 8vo. 7s. 6d.

PRAYER-BOOK (Beautifully Illustrated). With Notes, by Rev. Thos. James. Medium 8vo. 18s. cloth.

PRINCESS CHARLOTTE OF WALES. A Brief Memoir. With Selections from her Correspondence and other unpublished Papers. By Lady Rose Weigall. With Portrait. 8vo. 8s. 6d.

PRIVY COUNCIL JUDGMENTS in Ecclesiastical Cases relating to Doctrine and Discipline. With Historical Introduction by G. C. Brodrick and W. H. Fremantle. 8vo. 10s. 6d.

PSALMS OF DAVID. With Notes Explanatory and Critical by Dean Johnson, Canon Elliott, and Canon Cook. Medium 8vo. 10s. 6d.

PUSS IN BOOTS. With 12 Illustrations. By Otto Speckter. 16mo. 1s. 6d. Or coloured, 2s. 6d.

QUARTERLY REVIEW (The). 8vo. 6s.

RAE (Edward). Country of the Moors. A Journey from Tripoli to the Holy City of Kairwan. Map and Etchings. Crown 8vo. 12s.

RAE (EDWARD). The White Sea Peninsula. Journey to the White Sea, and the Kola Peninsula. With Map and Illustrations. Crown 8vo. 15s.

RAMBLES in the Syrian Deserts. Post 8vo. 10s. 6d.

RASSAM (HORMUZD). British Mission to Abyssinia. Illustrations. 2 Vols. 8vo. 28s.

RAWLINSON'S (CANON) Herodotus. A New English Version. Edited with Notes and Essays. Maps and Woodcuts. 4 Vols. 8vo. 48s.

———— Five Great Monarchies of Chaldæa, Assyria, Media, Babylonia, and Persia. With Maps and Illustrations. 3 Vols. 8vo. 42s.

———— (SIR HENRY) England and Russia in the East; a Series of Papers on the Condition of Central Asia. Map. 8vo. 12s.

REED (Sir E. J.) Iron-Clad Ships; their Qualities, Performances, and Cost. With Chapters on Turret Ships, Iron-Clad Rams, &c. With Illustrations. 8vo. 12s.

—— Letters from Russia in 1875. 8vo. 5s.

—— Japan: Its History, Traditions, and Religions. With Narrative of a Visit in 1879. Illustrations. 2 Vols. 8vo. 28s.

—— A Practical Treatise on Shipbuilding in Iron and Steel. Second and revised edition with Plans and Woodcuts. 8vo.

REJECTED ADDRESSES (THE). By JAMES AND HORACE SMITH. Woodcuts. Post 8vo. 3s. 6d.; or Popular Edition, Fcap. 8vo. 1s.

REMBRANDT. [See MIDDLETON.]

REVISED VERSION OF N.T. [See BECKETT—BURGON—COOK.]

REYNOLDS' (SIR JOSHUA) Life and Times. By C. R. LESLIE, R.A. and TOM TAYLOR. Portraits. 2 Vols. 8vo. 42s.

RICARDO'S (DAVID) Works. With a Notice of his Life and Writings. By J. R. M'CULLOCH. 8vo. 16s.

RIPA (FATHER). Residence at the Court of Peking. Post 8vo. 2s.

ROBERTSON (CANON). History of the Christian Church, from the Apostolic Age to the Reformation, 1517. 8 Vols. Post 8vo. 6s. each.

ROBINSON (REV. DR.). Biblical Researches in Palestine and the Adjacent Regions, 1838—52. Maps. 3 Vols. 8vo. 42s.

———— (WM.) Alpine Flowers for English Gardens. With 70 Illustrations. Crown 8vo. 7s. 6d.

———— English Flower Garden. Its Style and Position. With an Illustrated Dictionary of all the Plants used, and Directions for their Culture and Arrangement. With numerous Illustrations. Medium 8vo. 15s.

———— Sub-Tropical Garden. Illustrations. Small 8vo. 5s.

———— Parks and Gardens of Paris, considered in Relation to the Wants of other Cities and of Public and Private Gardens. With 350 Illustrations. 8vo. 18s.

———— Wild Garden; or, Our Groves and Gardens made Beautiful by the Naturalization of Hardy Exotic Plants. Being one way onwards from the Dark Ages of Flower Gardening, with Suggestions for the Regeneration of Bare Borders of the London Parks. With 90 Illustrations. 8vo. 10s. 6d.

———— Hardy Flowers. Descriptions of upwards of 1300 of the most Ornamental Species; with Directions for their Arrangement, Culture, &c. Post 8vo. 3s. 6d.

———— God's Acre Beautiful; or, the Cemeteries of the Future. With 8 Illustrations. 8vo. 7s. 6d.

ROBSON (E. R.). SCHOOL ARCHITECTURE. Remarks on the Planning, Designing, Building, and Furnishing of School-houses. Illustrations. Medium 8vo. 18s.

ROME (HISTORY OF). [See GIBBON—LIDDELL—SMITH—STUDENTS'.

ROYAL SOCIETY CATALOGUE OF SCIENTIFIC PAPERS.
8 vols. 8vo. 20s. each. Half morocco, 28s. each.

RUXTON (Geo. F.). Travels in Mexico; with Adventures among Wild
Tribes and Animals of the Prairies and Rocky Mountains. Post 8vo. 3s.6d.

ST. HUGH OF AVALON, Bishop of Lincoln; his Life by G. G.
Perry, Canon of Lincoln. Post 8vo. 10s. 6d.

ST. JOHN (Charles). Wild Sports and Natural History of the
Highlands of Scotland. Illustrated Edition. Crown 8vo. 15s. Cheap
Edition, Post 8vo. 3s. 6d.

———— (Bayle) Adventures in the Libyan Desert. Post 8vo. 2s.

SALDANHA (Duke of). [See Carnota.]

SALE'S (Sir Robert) Brigade in Affghanistan. With an Account of
the Defence of Jellalabad. By Rev. G. R. Gleig. Post 8vo. 2s.

SCEPTICISM IN GEOLOGY; and the Reasons for It. An
assemblage of facts from Nature combining to refute the theory of
"Causes now in Action." By Verifier. Woodcuts. Crown 8vo. 6s.

SCHLIEMANN (Dr. Henry). Ancient Mycenæ. With 500
Illustrations. Medium 8vo. 50s.

———— Ilios; the City and Country of the Trojans,
including all Recent Discoveries and Researches made on the Site
of Troy and the Troad. With an Autobiography. With 2000 Illustrations. Imperial 8vo. 50s.

———— Troja: Results of the Latest Researches and
Discoveries on the site of Homer's Troy, and in the Heroic Tumuli
and other sites made in 1882. With Maps, Plans, and Illustrations.
Medium 8vo. 42s.

———— The Prehistoric Palace of the Kings of Tiryns;
Its Primeval Wall Paintings and Works of Art Excavated and
Described. With Coloured Lithographs, Woodcuts, Plans, &c.
Medium 8vo.

SCHOMBERG (General). The Odyssey of Homer, rendered
into English verse. 2 vols. 8vo. 24s.

SCOTT (Sir Gilbert). The Rise and Development of Mediæval
Architecture. With 400 Illustrations. 2 Vols. Medium 8vo. 42s.

SCRUTTON (T. E.). The Laws of Copyright. An Examination
of the Principles which should Regulate Literary and Artistic Property in England and other Countries. 8vo. 10s. 6d.

SEEBOHM (Henry) Siberia in Asia. A visit to the Valley of the
Yenesay in Eastern Siberia. With Descriptions of the Natural History,
Migrations of Birds, &c. Illustrations. Crown 8vo. 14s.

SELBORNE (Lord). Notes on some Passages in the Liturgical
History of the Reformed English Church. 8vo. 6s.

SHADOWS OF A SICK ROOM. Preface by Canon Liddon.
16mo. 2s. 6d.

SHAH OF PERSIA'S Diary during his Tour through Europe in
1873. With Portrait. Crown 8vo. 12s.

SHAW (T. B.). Manual of English Literature. Post 8vo. 7s. 6d.

———— Specimens of English Literature. Selected from the
Chief Writers. Post 8vo. 7s. 6d.

———— (Robert). Visit to High Tartary, Yarkand, and Kashgar,
and Return Journey over the Karakorum Pass. With Map and
Illustrations. 8vo. 16s.

SIERRA LEONE; Described in Letters to Friends at Home. By
A Lady. Post 8vo. 3s. 6d.

SIMMONS (Capt.). Constitution and Practice of Courts-Mar-
tial. 8vo. 15s.

SMILES' (Samuel, LL.D.) WORKS:—

British Engineers; from the Earliest Period to the death of
the Stephensons. Illustrations. 5 Vols. Crown 8vo. 7s. 6d. each.

SMILES' (SAMUEL, LL.D.) WORKS:—
GEORGE STEPHENSON. Post 8vo. 2s. 6d.
JAMES NASMYTH. Portrait and Illustrations. Cr. 8vo. 16s.
SCOTCH NATURALIST (THOS. EDWARD). Illustrations. Post 8vo. 6s.
SCOTCH GEOLOGIST (ROBERT DICK). Illustrations. Cr. 8vo. 12s.
HUGUENOTS IN ENGLAND AND IRELAND. Crown 8vo. 7s. 6d.
SELF-HELP. With Illustrations of Conduct and Persever-
ance. Post 8vo. 6s.
CHARACTER. A Book of Noble Characteristics. Post 8vo. 6s.
THRIFT. A Book of Domestic Counsel. Post 8vo. 6s.
DUTY. With Illustrations of Courage, Patience, and Endurance.
Post 8vo. 6s.
INDUSTRIAL BIOGRAPHY; or, Iron Workers and Tool Makers.
Post 8vo. 6s.
BOY'S VOYAGE ROUND THE WORLD. Illustrations. Post 8vo. 6s.
MEN OF INVENTION AND INDUSTRY. Post 8vo. 6s.
SMITH (DR. GEORGE) Student's Manual of the Geography of British
India, Physical and Political. With Maps. Post 8vo. 7s. 6d.
——— Life of John Wilson, D.D. (Bombay), Missionary and
Philanthropist. Portrait. Post 8vo. 9s.
- ——— Life of Wm. Carey, D.D., 1761—1834. Shoemaker and
Missionary. Professor of Sanscrit at the College of Fort William,
Calcutta. Crown 8vo.
——— (PHILIP). History of the Ancient World, from the Creation
to the Fall of the Roman Empire, A.D. 476. 3 Vols. 8vo. 31s. 6d.
SMITH'S (DR. WM.) DICTIONARIES:—
DICTIONARY OF THE BIBLE; its Antiquities, Biography,
Geography, and Natural History. Illustrations. 3 Vols. 8vo. 105s.
CONCISE BIBLE DICTIONARY. Illustrations. 8vo. 21s.
SMALLER BIBLE DICTIONARY. Illustrations. Post 8vo. 7s. 6d.
CHRISTIAN ANTIQUITIES. Comprising the History, Insti-
tutions, and Antiquities of the Christian Church. Illustrations. 2 Vols.
Medium 8vo. 3l. 13s. 6d.
CHRISTIAN BIOGRAPHY, LITERATURE, SECTS, AND DOCTRINES;
from the Times of the Apostles to the Age of Charlemagne. Medium 8vo.
Vols. I. II. & III. 31s 6d. each. (To be completed in 4 Vols.)
GREEK AND ROMAN ANTIQUITIES. Illustrations. Medium
8vo. 28s.
GREEK AND ROMAN BIOGRAPHY AND MYTHOLOGY. Illustrations.
3 Vols. Medium 8vo. 4l. 4s.
GREEK AND ROMAN GEOGRAPHY. 2 Vols. Illustrations.
Medium 8vo. 56s.
ATLAS OF ANCIENT GEOGRAPHY—BIBLICAL AND CLASSICAL.
Folio. 6l. 6s.
CLASSICAL DICTIONARY OF MYTHOLOGY, BIOGRAPHY, AND
GEOGRAPHY. 1 Vol. With 750 Woodcuts. 8vo. 18s.
SMALLER CLASSICAL DICT. Woodcuts. Crown 8vo. 7s. 6d.
SMALLER GREEK AND ROMAN ANTIQUITIES. Woodcuts. Crown
8vo. 7s. 6d.
COMPLETE LATIN-ENGLISH DICTIONARY. With Tables of the
Roman Calendar, Measures, Weights, and Money. 8vo. 21s.
SMALLER LATIN-ENGLISH DICTIONARY. New and Revised
Edition. 12mo. 7s 6d.
COPIOUS AND CRITICAL ENGLISH-LATIN DICTIONARY. 8vo. 21s.
SMALLER ENGLISH-LATIN DICTIONARY. 12mo. 7s. 6d.

SMITH'S (DR. WM.) ENGLISH COURSE:—

SCHOOL MANUAL OF ENGLISH GRAMMAR, WITH COPIOUS EXERCISES and Appendices. Post 8vo. 3s. 6d.

PRIMARY ENGLISH GRAMMAR, for Elementary Schools, with carefully graduated parsing lessons. 16mo. 1s.

MANUAL OF ENGLISH COMPOSITION. With Copious Illustrations and Practical Exercises. 12mo. 3s. 6d.

PRIMARY HISTORY OF BRITAIN. 12mo. 2s. 6d.

SCHOOL MANUAL OF MODERN GEOGRAPHY, PHYSICAL AND Political. Post 8vo. 5s.

A SMALLER MANUAL OF MODERN GEOGRAPHY. 16mo. 2s. 6d.

SMITH'S (DR. WM.) FRENCH COURSE:—

FRENCH PRINCIPIA. Part I. A First Course, containing a Grammar, Delectus, Exercises, and Vocabularies. 12mo. 3s. 6d.

APPENDIX TO FRENCH PRINCIPIA. Part I. Containing additional Exercises, with Examination Papers. 12mo. 2s. 6d.

FRENCH PRINCIPIA. Part II. A Reading Book, containing Fables, Stories, and Anecdotes, Natural History, and Scenes from the History of France. With Grammatical Questions, Notes and copious Etymological Dictionary. 12mo. 4s. 6d.

FRENCH PRINCIPIA. Part III. Prose Composition, containing a Systematic Course of Exercises on the Syntax, with the Principal Rules of Syntax. 12mo. [In the Press.

STUDENT'S FRENCH GRAMMAR. By C. HERON-WALL. With Introduction by M. Littré. Post 8vo. 6s.

SMALLER GRAMMAR OF THE FRENCH LANGUAGE. Abridged from the above. 12mo. 3s. 6d.

SMITH'S (DR. WM.) GERMAN COURSE:—

GERMAN PRINCIPIA. Part I. A First German Course, containing a Grammar, Delectus, Exercise Book, and Vocabularies. 12mo. 3s. 6d.

GERMAN PRINCIPIA. Part II. A Reading Book; containing Fables, Stories, and Anecdotes, Natural History, and Scenes from the History of Germany. With Grammatical Questions, Notes, and Dictionary. 12mo. 3s. 6d.

PRACTICAL GERMAN GRAMMAR. Post 8vo. 3s. 6d.

SMITH'S (DR. WM.) ITALIAN COURSE:—

ITALIAN PRINCIPIA. Part I. An Italian Course, containing a Grammar, Delectus, Exercise Book, with Vocabularies, and Materials for Italian Conversation. 12mo. 3s. 6d.

ITALIAN PRINCIPIA. Part II. A First Italian Reading Book, containing Fables, Anecdotes, History, and Passages from the best Italian Authors, with Grammatical Questions, Notes, and a Copious Etymological Dictionary. 12mo. 3s. 6d.

SMITH'S (DR. WM.) LATIN COURSE:—

THE YOUNG BEGINNER'S FIRST LATIN BOOK: Containing the Rudiments of Grammar, Easy Grammatical Questions and Exercises, with Vocabularies. Being a Stepping stone to Principia Latina, Part I. for Young Children. 12mo. 2s.

THE YOUNG BEGINNER'S SECOND LATIN BOOK: Containing an easy Latin Reading Book, with an Analysis of the Sentences, Notes, and a Dictionary. Being a Stepping-stone to Principia Latina, Part II. for Young Children. 12mo. 2s.

PRINCIPIA LATINA. Part I. First Latin Course, containing a Grammar, Delectus, and Exercise Book, with Vocabularies. 12mo. 3s. 6d.
₊ In this Edition the Cases of the Nouns, Adjectives, and Pronouns are arranged both as in the ORDINARY GRAMMARS and as in the PUBLIC SCHOOL PRIMER, together with the corresponding Exercises.

SMITH'S (Dr. Wm.) LATIN COURSE—*continued.*

APPENDIX TO PRINCIPIA LATINA. Part I.; being Additional Exercises, with Examination Papers. 12mo. 2s. 6d.

PRINCIPIA LATINA. Part II. A Reading-book of Mythology, Geography, Roman Antiquities, and History. With Notes and Dictionary. 12mo. 3s. 6d.

PRINCIPIA LATINA. Part III. A Poetry Book. Hexameters and Pentameters; Eclog. Ovidianæ; Latin Prosody. 12mo. 3s. 6d.

PRINCIPIA LATINA. Part IV. Prose Composition. Rules of Syntax with Examples, Explanations of Synonyms, and Exercises on the Syntax. 12mo. 3s. 6d.

PRINCIPIA LATINA. Part V. Short Tales and Anecdotes for Translation into Latin. 12mo. 3s.

LATIN-ENGLISH VOCABULARY AND FIRST LATIN-ENGLISH DICTIONARY FOR PHÆDRUS, CORNELIUS NEPOS, AND CÆSAR. 12mo. 3s. 6d.

STUDENT'S LATIN GRAMMAR. For the Higher Forms. Post 8vo. 6s.

SMALLER LATIN GRAMMAR. 12mo. 3s. 6d.

SMITH'S (Dr. Wm.) GREEK COURSE:—

INITIA GRÆCA. Part I. A First Greek Course, containing a Grammar, Delectus, and Exercise-book. With Vocabularies. 12mo. 3s. 6d.

APPENDIX TO INITIA GRÆCA. Part I. Containing additional Exercises. With Examination Papers. Post 8vo. 2s. 6d.

INITIA GRÆCA. Part II. A Reading Book. Containing Short Tales, Anecdotes, Fables, Mythology, and Grecian History. 12mo. 3s. 6d.

INITIA GRÆCA. Part III. Prose Composition. Containing the Rules of Syntax, with copious Examples and Exercises. 12mo. 3s. 6d.

STUDENT'S GREEK GRAMMAR. For the Higher Forms. By CURTIUS. Post 8vo. 6s.

SMALLER GREEK GRAMMAR. 12mo. 3s. 6d.

GREEK ACCIDENCE. 12mo. 2s. 6d.

PLATO, Apology of Socrates, &c. With Notes. 12mo. 3s. 6d.

SMITH'S (Dr. Wm.) SMALLER HISTORIES:—

SCRIPTURE HISTORY. With Coloured Maps and Woodcuts. 16mo. 3s. 6d.

ANCIENT HISTORY. Woodcuts. 16mo. 3s. 6d.

ANCIENT GEOGRAPHY. Woodcuts. 16mo. 3s. 6d.

MODERN GEOGRAPHY. 16mo. 2s. 6d.

GREECE. With Coloured Map and Woodcuts. 16mo. 3s. 6d.

ROME. With Coloured Maps and Woodcuts. 16mo. 3s. 6d.

CLASSICAL MYTHOLOGY. Woodcuts. 16mo. 3s. 6d.

ENGLAND. With Coloured Maps and Woodcuts. 16mo. 3s. 6d.

ENGLISH LITERATURE. 16mo. 3s. 6d.

SPECIMENS OF ENGLISH LITERATURE. 16mo. 3s. 6d.

SOMERVILLE (MARY). Personal Recollections from Early Life to Old Age. Portrait. Crown 8vo. 12s.

————— Physical Geography. Portrait. Post 8vo. 9s.

————— Connexion of the Physical Sciences. Post 8vo. 9s.

————— Molecular & Microscopic Science. Illustrations. 2 Vols. Post 8vo. 21s.

SOUTH (John F.). Household Surgery ; or, Hints for Emergencies. With Woodcuts. Fcap. 8vo. 3s. 6d.

—————— Memoirs of See Felton.

SOUTHEY (Robt.). Lives of Bunyan and Cromwell. Post 8vo. 2s.

STANHOPE'S (Earl) WORKS :—

History of England from the Reign of Queen Anne to the Peace of Versailles, 1701-83. 9 vols. Post 8vo. 5s. each.

Life of William Pitt. Portraits. 3 Vols. 8vo. 36s.

Miscellanies. 2 Vols. Post 8vo. 13s.

British India, from its Origin to 1783. Post 8vo. 3s. 6d.

History of "Forty-Five." Post 8vo. 3s.

Historical and Critical Essays. Post 8vo. 3s. 6d.

The Retreat from Moscow, and other Essays. Post 8vo. 7s. 6d.

Life of Belisarius. Post 8vo. 10s. 6d.

Life of Condé. Post 8vo. 3s. 6d.

Story of Joan of Arc. Fcap. 8vo. 1s.

Addresses on Various Occasions. 16mo. 1s.

STANLEY'S (Dean) WORKS :—

Sinai and Palestine. Coloured Maps. 8vo. 12s.

Bible in the Holy Land; Extracted from the above Work. Woodcuts. Fcap. 8vo. 2s. 6d.

Eastern Church. Plans. Crown 8vo. 6s.

Jewish Church. From the Earliest Times to the Christian Era. Portrait and Maps. 3 Vols. Crown 8vo. 18s.

Church of Scotland. 8vo. 7s. 6d.

Epistles of St. Paul to the Corinthians. 8vo. 18s.

Life of Dr. Arnold. Portrait. 2 Vols. Cr. 8vo. 12s.

Canterbury. Illustrations. Crown 8vo. 6s.

Westminster Abbey. Illustrations. 8vo. 15s.

Sermons during a Tour in the East. 8vo. 9s.

—————— on Special Occasions, Preached in Westminster Abbey. 8vo. 12s.

Memoir of Edward, Catherine, and Mary Stanley. Cr. 8vo. 9s.

Christian Institutions. Essays on Ecclesiastical Subjects. 8vo. 12s. Or Crown 8vo. 6s.

Essays. Chiefly on Questions of Church and State; from 1850 to 1870. Revised Edition. Crown 8vo.

[See also Bradley.]

STEPHENS (Rev. W. R. W.). Life and Times of St. John Chrysostom. A Sketch of the Church and the Empire in the Fourth Century. Portrait. 8vo. 7s. 6d.

STRATFORD de REDCLIFFE (Lord). The Eastern Question. Being a Selection from his Writings during the last Five Years of his Life. With a Preface by Dean Stanley. With Map. 8vo. 9s

STREET (G. E.). Gothic Architecture in Spain. Illustrations. Royal 8vo. 30s.

—————— Gothic Architecture in Brick and Marble. With Notes on North of Italy. Illustrations. Royal 8vo. 26s.

STUART (Villiers). Egypt after the War. Being the Narrative of a Tour of Inspection, including Experiences amongst the Natives, with Descriptions of their Homes and Habits; to which are added Notes of the latest Archaeological Discoveries and a revised Account of the Funeral Canopy of an Egyptian Queen, With interesting additions. Coloured Illustrations and Woodcuts. Royal 8vo. 31s. 6d.

STUDENTS' MANUALS :—

OLD TESTAMENT HISTORY ; from the Creation to the Return of the Jews from Captivity. Woodcuts. Post 8vo. 7s. 6d.

NEW TESTAMENT HISTORY. With an Introduction connecting the History of the Old and New Testaments. Woodcuts. Post 8vo. 7s.6d.

EVIDENCES OF CHRISTIANITY. By H. WACE, D.D. Post 8vc.
                                                    [In the Press.

ECCLESIASTICAL HISTORY ; a History of the Christian Church from its foundation to the Reformation. By PHILIP SMITH, B.A.
PART I. A.D. 30—1003. Woodcuts. Post 8vo. 7s. 6d.
PART II.—1003—1598. Woodcuts. Post 8vo. 7s. 6d.

ENGLISH CHURCH HISTORY ; from the Planting of the Church in Great Britain to the Silencing of Convocation in the 18th Cent. By CANON PERRY. 3 Vols. Post 8vo. 7s. 6d. each.
First Period, A.D. 596—1509.
Second Period, 1509—1717.

ANCIENT HISTORY OF THE EAST ; Egypt, Assyria, Babylonia, Media, Persia, Asia Minor, and Phœnicia. By Philip Smith, B.A. Woodcuts. Post 8vo. 7s. 6d.

————— GEOGRAPHY. By Canon BEVAN, M.A. Woodcuts. Post. 8vo. 7s. 6d.

HISTORY OF GREECE ; from the Earliest Times to the Roman Conquest. By WM. SMITH, D.C.L. Woodcuts. Crown 8vo. 7s. 6d.
₊ Questions on the above Work, 12mo. 2s.

HISTORY OF ROME ; from the Earliest Times to the Establishment of the Empire. By DEAN LIDDELL. Woodcuts. Crown 8vo. 7s. 6d

GIBBON'S DECLINE AND FALL OF THE ROMAN EMPIRE. Woodcuts. Post 8vo. 7s. 6d.

HALLAM'S HISTORY OF EUROPE during the Middle Ages. Post 8vo. 7s. 6d.

HISTORY OF MODERN EUROPE, from the end of the Middle Ages to the Treaty of Berlin, 1878. Post 8vo.   [In the Press.

HALLAM'S HISTORY OF ENGLAND ; from the Accession of Henry VII. to the Death of George II. Post 8vo. 7s. 6d.

HUME'S HISTORY OF ENGLAND from the Invasion of Julius Cæsar to the Revolution in 1688. Revised, and continued to the Treaty of Berlin, 1878. By J. S. BREWER, M.A. Coloured Maps and Woodcuts. Post 8vo. 7s. 6d. Or in 3 parts, price 2s. 6d. each.
₊ Questions on the above Work, 12mo. 2s.

HISTORY OF FRANCE ; from the Earliest Times to the Fall of the Second Empire, By H. W. JERVIS. Woodcuts. Post 8vo. 7s. 6d.

ENGLISH LANGUAGE. By GEO. P. MARSH. Post 8vo. 7s. 6d.

ENGLISH LITERATURE. By T. B. SHAW, M.A. Post 8vo. 7s. 6d.

SPECIMENS OF ENGLISH LITERATURE. By T.B.SHAW. Post 8vo. 7s.6d.

MODERN GEOGRAPHY ; Mathematical, Physical and Descriptive. By Canon BEVAN, M.A. Woodcuts. Post 8vo. 7s. 6d.

GEOGRAPHY OF BRITISH INDIA. Political and Physical. By GEORGE SMITH, LL.D. Maps. Post 8vo. 7s. 6d.

MORAL PHILOSOPHY. By WM. FLEMING. Post 8vo. 7s. 6d.

SUMNER'S (BISHOP) Life and Episcopate during 40 Years. By Rev. G. H. SUMNER. Portrait. 8vo. 14s.

SWAINSON (CANON). Nicene and Apostles' Creeds ; Their Literary History ; together with some Account of "The Creed of St. Athanasius." 8vo. 16s.

SWIFT (JONATHAN). [See CRAIK—FORSTER.]

SYBEL (Von) History of Europe during the French Revolution, 1789—1795. 4 Vols. 8vo. 48s.

SYMONDS' (Rev. W.) Records of the Rocks; or Notes on the Geology of Wales, Devon, and Cornwall. Crown 8vo. 12s.

TALMUD. [See Barclay—Deutsch.]

TEMPLE (Sir Richard). India in 1880. With Maps. 8vo. 16s.

———— Men and Events of My Time in India. 8vo. 16s.

———— Oriental Experience. Essays and Addresses delivered on Various Occasions. With Maps and Woodcuts. 8vo. 16s.

THIBAUT'S (Antoine) Purity in Musical Art. With Prefatory Memoir by W. H. Gladstone, M.P. Post 8vo. 7s. 6d.

THIELMANN (Baron). Journey through the Caucasus to Tabreez, Kurdistan, down the Tigris and Euphrates to Nineveh and Palmyra. Illustrations. 2 Vols. Post 8vo. 18s.

THOMSON (Archbishop). Lincoln's Inn Sermons. 8vo. 10s. 6d.

———— Life in the Light of God's Word. Post 8vo. 5s.

———— Word, Work, & Will : Collected Essays. Crown 8vo. 9s.

THORNHILL (Mark). The Personal Adventures and Experiences of a Magistrate during the Rise, Progress, and Suppression of the Indian Mutiny. With Frontispiece and Plan. Crown 8vo.

TITIAN'S LIFE AND TIMES. With some account of his Family, from unpublished Records. By Crowe and Cavalcaselle. Illustrations. 2 Vols. 8vo. 21s.

TOCQUEVILLE'S State of Society in France before the Revolution, 1789, and on the Causes which led to that Event. 8vo. 14s.

TOMLINSON (Chas.). The Sonnet: Its Origin, Structure, and Place in Poetry. Post 8vo. 9s.

TOZER (Rev. H. F.). Highlands of Turkey, with Visits to Mounts Ida, Athos, Olympus, and Pelion. 2 Vols. Crown 8vo. 24s.

———— Lectures on the Geography of Greece. Post 8vo. 9s.

TRISTRAM (Canon). Great Sahara. Illustrations. Crown 8vo. 15s.

———— Land of Moab : Travels and Discoveries on the East Side of the Dead Sea and the Jordan. Illustrations. Crown 8vo. 15s.

TWENTY YEARS' RESIDENCE among the Greeks, Albanians, Turks, Armenians, and Bulgarians. 2 Vols. Crown 8vo. 21s.

TWINING (Rev. Thos.). Recreations and Studies of a Country Clergyman of the Last Century. Crown 8vo. 9s.

TWISS' (Horace) Life of Lord Eldon. 2 Vols. Post 8vo. 21s.

TYLOR (E. B.). Researches into the Early History of Mankind, and Development of Civilization. 3rd Edition. 8vo. 12s.

———— Primitive Culture : the Development of Mythology, Philosophy, Religion, Art, and Custom. 2 Vols. 8vo. 24s.

VATICAN COUNCIL. [See Leto.]

VIRCHOW (Professor). The Freedom of Science in the Modern State. Fcap. 8vo. 2s.

WACE (Rev. Henry), D.D. The Principal Facts in the Life of our Lord, and the Authority of the Evangelical Narratives. Post 8vo. 6s.

———— Luther's Primary Works. (See Luther).

WELLINGTON'S Despatches in India, Denmark, Portugal, Spain, the Low Countries, and France. 8 Vols. 8vo. £8 8s.

———— Supplementary Despatches, relating to India, Ireland, Denmark, Spanish America, Spain, Portugal, France, Congress of Vienna, Waterloo, and Paris. 15 Vols. 8vo. 20s. each.

———— Civil and Political Correspondence. Vols. I. to VIII. 8vo. 20s. each.

———— Speeches in Parliament. 2 Vols. 8vo. 42s.

WESTCOTT (Canon B. F.) The Gospel according to St. John, with Notes and Dissertations (Reprinted from the Speaker's Commentary). 8vo. 10s. 6d.

WHARTON (Capt. W. J. L.), R.N. Hydrographical Surveying : being a description of the means and methods employed in constructing Marine Charts. With Illustrations. 8vo. 15s.

WHEELER (G.). Choice of a Dwelling. Post 8vo. 7s. 6d.

WHITE (W. H.). Manual of Naval Architecture, for the use of Naval Officers. Shipowners, Shipbuilders, and Yachtsmen. Illustrations. 8vo. 24s.

WHYMPER (Edward). The Ascent of the Matterhorn. With 100 Illustrations. Medium 8vo. 10s. 6d.

WILBERFORCE'S (Bishop) Life of William Wilberforce. Portrait. Crown 8vo. 6s.

———— (Samuel, LL.D.), Lord Bishop of Oxford and Winchester; his Life. By Canon Ashwell, D.D., and R. G. Wilberforce. With Portraits and Woodcuts. 3 Vols. 8vo. 15s. each.

WILKINSON (Sir J. G.). Manners and Customs of the Ancient Egyptians, their Private Life, Laws, Arts, Religion, &c. A new edition. Edited by Samuel Birch, LL.D. Illustrations. 3 Vols. 8vo. 84s.

———— Popular Account of the Ancient Egyptians. With 500 Woodcuts. 2 Vols. Post 8vo. 12s.

———— (Hugh). Sunny Lands and Seas : A Cruise Round the World in the S.S. "Ceylon." India, the Straits Settlements, Manila, China, Japan, the Sandwich Islands, and California. With Illustrations. Crown 8vo. 12s.

WILLIAMS (Monier). Religious Life and Thought in India. An Account of the Religions of the Indian Peoples. Based on a Life's Study of their Literature and on personal investigations in their own country. 2 Vols. 8vo.
Part I.—Vedism, Brahmanism, and Hinduism. 18s.
Part II.—Buddhism, Jainism, Zoroastrianism, Islam, and Indian Christianity. [In preparation.

WILSON (John, D.D.). [See Smith, Geo.]

WOOD'S (Captain) Source of the Oxus. With the Geography of the Valley of the Oxus. By Col. Yule. Map. 8vo. 12s.

WORDS OF HUMAN WISDOM. Collected and Arranged by E. S. With a Preface by Canon Liddon. Fcap. 8vo. 3s. 6d.

WORDSWORTH'S (Bishop) Greece ; Pictorial, Descriptive, and Historical. With an introduction on the Characteristics of Greek Art, by Geo. Scharf. New Edition revised by the Rev. H. F. Tozer, M.A. With 400 Illustrations. Royal 8vo. 31s. 6d.

YORK (Archbishop of). Collected Essays. Contents.—Synoptic Gospels. Death of Christ. God Exists. Worth of Life. Design in Nature. Sports and Pastimes. Emotions in Preaching. Defects in Missionary Work. Limits of Philosophical Enquiry. Crown 8vo. 9s.

YULE (Colonel). Book of Marco Polo. Illustrated by the Light of Oriental Writers and Modern Travels. With Maps and 80 Plates. 2 Vols. Medium 8vo. 63s.

———— A Glossary of Peculiar Anglo-Indian Colloquial Words and Phrases, Etymological, Historical, and Geographical. By Colonel Yule and the late Arthur Burnell, Ph.D. 8vo.

———— (A. F.) A Little Light on Cretan Insurrection. Post 8vo. 2s. 6d.

BRADBURY, AGNEW, & CO., PRINTERS, WHITEFRIARS.